G000037975

REGIONAL DEVELOPMENT ON THE
NORTH ATLANTIC MARGIN

Regional Development on the North Atlantic Margin

Edited by

REGINALD BYRON
University of Wales, Swansea

JENS CHRISTIAN HANSEN
University of Bergen

TIM JENKINS
University of Wales, Aberystwyth

ASHGATE

© Reginald Byron, Jens Christian Hansen and Tim Jenkins 2004

All rights reserved. No part of this publication may be reproduced, stored in a retrieval system, or transmitted in any form or by any means, electronic, mechanical, photocopying, recording or otherwise without the prior permission of the publisher.

Reginald Byron, Jens Christian Hansen and Tim Jenkins have asserted their right under the Copyright, Designs and Patents Act, 1988, to be identified as the editors of this work.

Published by
Ashgate Publishing Limited
Gower House
Croft Road
Aldershot
Hants GU11 3HR
England

Ashgate Publishing Company
Suite 420
101 Cherry Street
Burlington, VT 05401-4405
USA

Ashgate website: http://www.ashgate.com

British Library Cataloguing in Publication Data
Regional development on the North Atlantic margin. -
    (Dynamics of marginal and critical regions) (Marginal
    regions)
    1. Regional planning - Europe, Northern 2. Regional planning
    - Europe, Northern - Case studies 3. Regional economic
    disparities 4. Tourism - Europe, Northern - Case studies
    I. Byron, Reginald II. Hansen, Jens Chr. III. Jenkins, Tim
    IV. International Geographical Union
    338.9'4

Library of Congress Cataloging-in-Publication Data
Regional development on the North Atlantic margin / edited by Reginald Byron, Jens
    Christian Hansen and Tim Jenkins.
        p. cm. -- (Marginal regions)
    Includes bibliographical references.
    ISBN 0-7546-4175-9
        1. Regional planning--North Atlantic Region. 2. Marginality, Social--North Atlantic
    Region. 3. Marginal productivity--North Atlantic Region. 4. Community
    development--North Atlantic Region. 5. Sustainable development--North Atlantic Region.
    6. North Atlantic Region--Social policy. 7. North Atlantic Region--Economic policy. I.
    Byron, Reginald. II. Hansen, Jens Christian, 1932- III. Jenkins, Tim. IV. Series.

    HT395.N615R44 2004
    307.1'4'091821--dc22
                                                            2003063538

ISBN 0 7546 4175 9

Printed and bound in Great Britain by MPG Books Ltd, Bodmin, Cornwall

Contents

PART THREE: GOVERNANCE AND DEVELOPMENT

CONCLUSION

List of Figures

List of Tables

List of Contributors

Jørgen Amdam is Professor in the Department of Commune Planning and Administration at Volda University College, Norway.

Finn Båtevik is a lecturer and researcher at Volda University College, Norway.

Paul Olav Berg is Professor at Nordland University College, Bødo, Norway.

Reginald Byron is Professor of Sociology and Anthropology at the University of Wales, Swansea, Wales.

D. Douglas Caulkins is Professor of Anthropology at Grinnell College, Grinnell, Iowa.

Jane Cherry is associated with the Department of Anthropology, Grinnell College, Grinnell, Iowa.

Jens Christian Hansen is Professor of Geography at the University of Bergen, Norway.

Christina Hanson is associated with the Department of Anthropology, Grinnell College, Grinnell, Iowa.

Dennis Holm is a researcher at the Centre for Local and Regional Development, Klaksvík, Faroe.

Tim Jenkins is Senior Research Fellow in the Welsh Institute of Rural Studies, University of Wales, Aberystwyth, Wales.

Alison McCleery is Professor in the Faculty of Arts and Social Science, Napier University, Edinburgh, Scotland.

Bjarni Mortensen is a researcher at the Centre for Local and Regional Development, Klaksvík, Faroe.

Tove Oliver is a researcher at the Welsh Institute of Rural Studies, University of Wales, Aberystwyth.

Vickie Schlegel is associated with the Department of Anthropology, Grinnell College, Grinnell, Iowa.

Peter Sjøholt is Professor of Geography in the Norwegian School of Economics and Business Administration, Bergen, Norway.

James Walsh is Professor of Geography at the National University of Ireland, Maynoot

Introduction

Marginal Communities in a Globalised Economy

REGINALD BYRON AND TIM JENKINS

In a globalised economy, marginal regions, economies, societies and communities will always exist. Despite the power of economic logic and rationality in everyday discourse, many people actively choose to live their lives in supposedly unfavourable locations, perhaps intuitively aware that the "law" of comparative advantage extends even into the most remote and disadvantaged places. Their motives vary widely and may encompass inertia, sentimentality, the feeling that life has more than an economic dimension, the wish to avoid the less-desirable trappings of modernity, and the high value placed on the quality of the natural environment and on the notion of community. Many such people are entrepreneurial and have established successful, often small-scale, businesses in their localities, although it is noteworthy that their business acumen is often tempered with considerations for the quality of their lives and with altruistic feelings towards the communities in which they live.

Nevertheless, marginal regions, economies, societies and communities have their dark side. As some of the chapters in this book will show, their problems are by no means limited to matters that can be solved by investment, education, training or other such interventions. The nature of rural social structures ensures that the circumstances prevailing in many marginal regions are, and will probably always be, unacceptable to many of those who happen to be born there, and out-migration, especially of the younger economically active population, is a factor which cannot be overlooked or avoided by development theorists, practitioners or policymakers.

However, since marginal regions and communities exist and require a sustainable future within a globalised economy, academics, practitioners and policymakers have a duty to focus on their opportunities and their strengths, and on the weaknesses and the threats these regions face in order to understand that future. The International Society for the Study of Marginal Regions has since 1972 held biannual interdisciplinary seminars which have focused on a large number of theoretical and practical issues concerning the socioeconomic development of marginal regions and communities, and which have brought together a wide range of academics, practitioners and planners. The chapters in this book are based on selected contributions to the Sixteenth International Seminar on Marginal Regions held in Norway in August 2001.

The Nature of Marginal Communities

Marginality is a multi-dimensional concept, and it is important to note that each of these dimensions has positive as well as negative aspects, especially in view of current public concerns about such issues as the quality of the natural environment, food safety, the quality of life, personal identity, and the provision of public goods. First and foremost, marginality is geographic, with all that this implies in terms of poor accessibility and an often unfavourable climate. However, many marginal regions have notable environmental assets whose cultural value is often enhanced by their marginality. Marginality is also economic, as marginal regions are usually outside the mainstream in terms of activity (especially given their typically high levels of reliance on agriculture), infrastructure and economic policy. Again, however, many of the public concerns noted above have given rise to economic opportunities (such as regional product differentiation, niche marketing and specialised tourism) which are increasingly becoming successfully exploited in many marginal regions.

The social dimension of marginality is perhaps more insidious and difficult to deal with. Many marginal regions and communities have historically experienced high levels of out-migration, and the future of young people in such regions is a continuing cause for concern. Nevertheless, the value placed on "community" in a world increasingly perceived as individualistic, harsh towards non-conformers, and materialistic makes many marginal regions singularly attractive to outsiders. Finally, for many regions, marginality is also cultural. Although now less isolated from the cultural mainstream than they once were, the relative isolation of many marginal regions and communities has left them as repositories of minority languages, cultural practices and artefacts increasingly valued by people who are concerned about homogenisation, standardisation, and the perceived decline of authenticity.

About this Book

This book is arranged into three parts. The two chapters in Part One consider the changing development discourse which has profound implications for marginal communities in a globalised economy. Part Two contains three chapters that are concerned with the marketing of marginality and history, essential if marginal communities are to realise their comparative advantages in a globalised world. Part Three focuses on governance and development, and its four chapters consider the roles of governments, planning and policy in marginal communities.

Part One: The Changing Development Discourse

Regional development has been traditionally regarded as something done to people by outside agencies rather than as something that people do for themselves. Marginal regions and communities were seen as dependent on whatever policy initiatives governments were disposed to provide. As a result, people who suffered from economic deprivation had little option but to vote with their feet, bringing about regional depopulation and further decline. More recently, against a background of further increasing human mobility, more consideration has been given to the views of those living in marginal regions as to how they would like to see their regions develop. The traditional view of regional development simply assumes that people migrate for economic reasons (jobs, housing); rarely have those who have voted with their feet actually been asked why they left, at least partly because they are no longer there to be asked, and it may be difficult to track them down. When they have been asked, their answers ought to give us pause for thought.

In Chapter 1, "The Future of Marginal Regions as Perceived by Those who are Expected to Shape It", Jens Christian Hansen takes up these themes with respect to Norway, looking at the government's current vision of the future of its marginal regions and contrasting this vision with the views of young people in those regions whose mobility is a crucial factor in their life-courses. Hansen shows that two-thirds of the women and one half of the men who lived in rural areas at the age of 15 had left before the age of 35, and makes the point that regional policy should concentrate on improving the living conditions (broadly defined) in the regions in order to create a correspondence between regional policy and the social, cultural, residential, and occupational wishes of those young people whose choices shape the future. These living conditions include not just the right kinds of housing and the right kinds of jobs, but must also include other, less easily quantifiable social and cultural satisfactions. This suggests, for example, that a focus on the major regional centres in the periphery would be the appropriate response to the aspirations of the young people who would like to return to their region of origin (but not, perhaps, to the particular locality where they grew up), as well as the wishes of many other people who would be attracted to such places.

The development discourse with regard to low income countries has been relatively well documented, as it has moved through the broad phases of growth theory, structural change theory, dependency theory, neoclassical development theory and new growth theory. In Chapter 2, "The New Development Discourse: a Farewell to Mega-Theories?", Peter Sjøholt brings out the linkages in development discourse between low income and high income countries. In a predominantly theoretical chapter, Sjøholt sees recent development thinking in terms of a shift from concentration on the means of development towards a questioning of developmental goals, and he highlights an understanding of development built less on ideological underpinnings and more on contextual principles and values. The main implication of these insights for marginal regions is that since marginality manifests itself in multiple ways, solutions to problems are only to be found contextually within regions, placing responsibility primarily on the inhabitants.

Part Two: Marketing Marginality and History

As we have already suggested, in addition to being regarded as a disadvantage, marginality may present economic opportunities in an age when increasing standardisation causes a re-evaluation of the importance of difference. In Part Two, three chapters take up this theme with particular emphasis on tourism and heritage.

In Chapter 3, "Conceptualising Integrated Tourism in Europe's Marginal Rural Regions", Tim Jenkins and Tove Oliver start from the observation that considerable unrealised rural development potential exists in improving the integrative linkages between tourism on the one hand, and local economic activities and local communities in marginal regions on the other. In a theoretical examination of such linkages, they propose the concept of "integrated tourism": tourism which is explicitly linked to, and concerned to make optimal use of, the economic, social, cultural, natural and human structures of the host locality. Their conceptualisation reflects both the cultural and economic force of integrated tourism, recognising its symbolic, ideological, aesthetic and motivational aspects, as well as analysing its commercial, instrumental and behavioural aspects. This conceptualisation of integrated tourism sets the stage for a theoretically informed research agenda which covers not only the production and consumption of tourism, but also the role of host communities, institutional structures and policy: a multi-dimensional coverage essential to the understanding of issues facing marginal regions.

In Chapter 4, "Reality and the Rural Idyll: Paradoxes of Rural Heritage and War Tourism in Normandy, France", Alison McCleery highlights the specific problem of the interiors of marginal regions and uses the example of World War II as heritage to illustrate the tensions inherent in promoting the rural idyll to tourists from urban areas. She sees war tourism in Normandy as both a "nasty necessity", given the powerful images of the Normandy landings in the popular psyche; and a lucrative additional niche market which piggybacks on, and lends added value to, Normandy's coastal and farm-based tourism industries. In Chapter 5, "The Politics of Authenticity and Identity in British Heritage Sites", Douglas Caulkins, Vickie Schlegel, Christina Hanson and Jane Cherry examine the British heritage industry and ponder the importance of the authenticity of tourists' heritage experiences, the importance of community support and goodwill for heritage sites, and (mirroring the theme addressed in Chapter 3) the need for further development of synergistic relationships among heritage sites and other local economic interests. They conclude that heritage sites need to appeal to locals as well as to visiting tourists in order to avoid a damaging factionalism which only serves to reduce the potentially beneficial impact of tourism on marginal regions.

Overall, Part Two raises questions concerning the limits to, and sustainability of, tourism and heritage industries. It would seem that many tourism and heritage enterprises have been established on weak economic foundations, and that the number of visitors may fall after the short-lived effects of novelty have worn off. Integrating tourism and heritage into local economies and societies is therefore crucial for their survival and therefore an important issue for the future of marginal regions.

Part Three: Governance and Development

The four chapters of Part Three view marginal regions from a policy perspective. Although recent development thinking places less emphasis on policy as an engine of development, the importance of governance, planning and the policy environment cannot be overlooked, whether it is seen as facilitating and enabling or as inhibiting and restrictive.

In Chapter 6, "Planning for Regional Development in a Peripheral Open Economy: the Case of Ireland", Jim Walsh illustrates the power of policy to set the context for regional development. Ireland's recent – and largely policy-driven – economic successes, which have transformed the country from being Objective 1 into being relatively high income in aggregate terms, have left the country with many marginal areas and with concerns that regional disparities could widen still further. In response, a National Spatial Strategy is being prepared which seeks to optimise local potentials and make for more balanced regional development. Walsh sees the main policy challenge as one of implementing spatial development that will lead to an improvement in the relative position of the marginal regions and simultaneously contribute to a more sustainable model of development in all dimensions: economic, social, cultural and environmental. As stressed throughout this book, such a challenge involves not only governments but all stakeholders.

In Chapter 7, "Constraints and Incentives in the Development of Northwestern Norway: Three Futures", Jørgen Amdam and Finn Båtevik see a successful future for fjord-dominated northwest Norway, where infrastructural problems are always going to be expensive to solve, in terms of increasing research, development and service activities in order to establish the best possible learning and development environment. They see the region as a "learning region" and as a "dynamic region" capable of attracting and retaining well-educated young people, provided that its communication and isolation problems can be overcome. Such a vision depends heavily on appropriate policies at central, regional and local levels.

The continuing importance of national policy, especially in the contexts of the regions and of welfare, is also emphasised in Chapter 8, "Regional Development in Norway: the Role of the State", by Paul Olav Berg. Berg particularly highlights the issues of distribution – between national, regional and local levels, between different localities, and between sectors which benefit from public investment – and suggests that minimum national quality standards (in, for example, employment, infrastructure, public service and welfare facilities) should become key components of regional policy. His emphasis on distribution has implications for investment in research and development institutions outside the main centres in order to build up knowledge and competence as competitive instruments.

The region-specific focus continues in Chapter 9, "Municipal Changes in the Faroes", by Dennis Holm and Bjarni Mortensen. By focusing on arguments concerning the numbers of municipalities and their possible amalgamation, Holm and Mortensen raise important questions regarding what "the local" ought to be and the extent to which regional and community development should be decentralised. In turn, such questions lead into wider issues concerning the nature of communities, of development, of networks, and of the balance between external policy and local initiative. The Faroese case shows that "the local" is, in most cases, a small village or hamlet, and the amalgamation debate shows a reluctance to change this system. The village satisfies most of the social needs of the elderly residents, but is too small for most of the young people growing up there and for meeting the challenges of globalisation in the fishing economy. The long-term effects of a "no change" policy may be to marginalise most of the Faroes, with the possible exception of the capital and a few regional centres.

Overall, Part Three shows the importance of the balance between regional empowerment and national policy. Both can, of course, be circumscribed, given the dependence of regions on national frameworks and sectoral policies and of nations on international pressures and circumstances. Nevertheless, interesting questions arise about the extent to which regions can help themselves and the extent to which national level interventions can be effective. The delegation of, for example, public service provision by government to local authorities may make little sense if localities do not have an adequate economic base from which to make such provision. This, in turn, raises important considerations concerning the extent of local taxation powers and the role of direct financial transfers. Whereas a decentralised regional policy may work for regions with strong resource or industrial bases, other regions may require the implementation of workable transfer systems such as regional development and structural funds. The case of non-EU Norway and EU countries such as Ireland therefore provides an instructive comparison.

In Chapter 10, a concluding essay by the editors, we comment on three issues which are suggested in one way or another in the preceding chapters, and that we regard as being of great significance for the future: the migration of young people, problematic representations of heritage and culture, and the troubled moral economy of regional development.

PART ONE:
THE CHANGING
DEVELOPMENT DISCOURSE

Chapter 1

The Future of Marginal Regions as Perceived by Those Who are Expected to Shape It

JENS CHRISTIAN HANSEN

The Background: A Brief Overview

In previous papers I have used migration data to illustrate regional imbalances in Norway (Hansen 1989, Båtevik and Hansen 1995, Hansen 1999, Hansen 2001). Net out-migration has been a persistent feature since the second half of the nineteenth century when North America was perceived as a promising alternative to subsistence farming. Later, as urbanisation progressed, people left the peripheries and moved into towns and cities. A persistently high birth rate and falling mortality rates compensated for out-migration far into the twentieth century, but after 1950 birth rates were declining and the periphery started to lose more people than it produced. The long term effect has been an ageing population.

Behind this demographic development lie processes of global and national structural change. It took the political system some time to realise that global competition weakened Norway's position as an exporter of semi-processed products based on natural resources such as minerals, timber, hydroelectricity and fish: the dominant activities of marginal regions. The postwar development of the Norwegian economy aimed at reconstructing what had been lost during the war, a relatively conservative approach. If anything, new initiatives such as the expansion of energy-consuming industries in peripheral regions made them even more dependent on natural resources.

The 1970s were years of radical restructuring of traditional industries in the Western world. In Norway, this restructuring was delayed because North Sea oil and gas gave a boost to the national economy. Oil and gas extraction and processing did not create many jobs in itself, but the mechanical and machine industries producing equipment for oil and gas industries gave new life to many communities along the west coast. More important for regional development was the income generated from oil and gas exports, much of which went into the Treasury and was spent on transport infrastructure, education, health and social services, as well as on support for traditional industries, particularly in peripheral regions. As the population redistribution process threatened the marginal areas, regional policy was directed towards them; this implied transfer of money to sparsely populated areas. The underlying objective of this regional policy was to slow down or halt the migration of young people to the larger cities. Available migration data show that this goal has not been reached, but one can always claim that the situation would have been much worse without our special brand of regional policy. A look across our common borders with Sweden and Finland gives some support to this view.

The Present: The Research Problem

In the 1990s, unemployment was very low in Norway, its marginal regions included. The paradoxical situation is that there is now a shortage of labour in peripheral Norway. Seasonal workers in agriculture and tourism come on a temporary basis from abroad: political refugees from Sri Lanka and Bosnia process our fish, Poles pick our apples and strawberries, shipyard contract workers come from Eastern Europe. There is also shortage of labour in health services – Swedish doctors and nurses from Poland and the Philippines help to run many hospitals, including those in peripheral places. Labour market authorities suggest the import of Russian contract workers on new construction sites in North Norway. Norwegians are not interested in these jobs, and workers from Finland and Sweden, who used to come in thousands to work in the oil sector, now find jobs at home. Why are Norwegians not interested in these jobs? Part of the answer lies in an expanding educational system which encourages young people to climb higher and higher, skipping vocational courses and going directly on to higher education.

This general introduction leads to the paper's main theme, which is to describe the perceptions of the future of marginal regions held by two important groups of people who through their ideas and actions will shape the future of the Norwegian periphery. One of these groups acts from above, one from below. The top-down perceptions are those of the national actors who through their political activities attempt to shape the future by defining the directions of regional policy. The bottom-up perceptions are those of young people growing up in the periphery, and who, as they progress through the educational system, individually take decisions that will result in their staying or leaving. The top-down people still think that they, through political action, can halt or slow down out-migration. The bottom-up people pursue their individual life projects, often oblivious to the ideas top-down people have about their future. Other actor groups also have convictions, such as local and regional economic actors. I leave them outside this discussion, because I think that the most serious threat to the Norwegian periphery is the top-down peoples' lack of understanding of the perceptions of young people who are about to take strategic decisions about their lives.

The Future of Marginal Regions: Perceptions of Top-down People

Top-down people think a lot. Instead of trying to penetrate the jungle of political thinking, however, I have chosen to offer a text analysis of official documents. Every fourth year, the government presents a regional policy report to parliament. The most recent report (St. meld. nr. 34 (2000-2001)) dates from April 2001. The Ministry of Municipal and Regional Affairs prepares the government's report which then goes to parliament. Its committee on municipal affairs presented its recommendations to parliament on June 6 (Innst. S. nr. 318 (2000-2001), and parliament duly discussed it on June 11 (item 19 on the agenda), five days before the end of the spring session and, as it happened, at the end of a four-year electoral period. In practice, this means that the government's report looked beyond parliament and into the electoral campaign of the parliamentary elections in early September 2001. In other words, the government told the voters what it intended to do if re-elected.

A Semantic Digression

Before identifying top-down strategies and priorities and their relevance for the young generation which will, through individual actions, shape the future geography of Norway, I shall direct your attention to the Norwegian words used to describe what regional policy is. The title of the 2001 report is *Om distrikts- og regionalpolitikken*. A literal translation into English is *About district and regional policy*. What, then, is the difference between district and region? A district, according to the *Concise Oxford Dictionary,* is either a territory marked off for special administrative purposes, or a division of a county electing its own councillors, or an area which has common characteristics. A region is, according to the same source, an area of land or division of the earth's surface, having definite boundaries or characteristics. In a comprehensive Norwegian-English dictionary, *distriktspolitikk* is translated into regional policy, whereas the word *regionalpolitikk* does not exist. The word *distrikt* in Norwegian political rhetoric is a normative expression, meaning parts of the country which are perceived as marginal or peripheral and therefore in need of political support. When the 2001 report was being prepared, under a Centrist minority government, it was seriously suggested that it should be labelled *Om distriktspolitikken*. But the Labour government got back into power in March 2000, and the title of the previous report was used. No one seemed to suggest a return to the title of the 1993 report, which was (in English) *Town and land – hand in hand: On regional development.*

What, Then, Is Norwegian Regional Policy About?

The Centrist proposal was logical. Regional policy, as defined by the Ministry of Municipal and Regional Affairs, deals mainly with peripheral areas. The main objective of regional policy is to stop or reduce out-migration in order to consolidate the settlement pattern. It follows logically that parts of Norway with population losses should be supported through spatial policy measures which by definition should not by applied in growth regions. In contrast, the main objective of regional policy in most Western European countries is to develop a spatial production system which boosts national economic growth.

In its 2001 report to parliament, the minority Labour government tried to please both periphery and centre. The distant North deserved special attention, and so did one-company towns in need of restructuring. The government also promised a special effort for sparsely populated areas far from urban settlements. But the report also made it clear that a policy of settlement and population consolidation cannot include all settlements.

Previous regional policy reports defined the municipality as a geographical arena for consolidation. Around one-half of the 435 Norwegian municipalities experienced population losses between 1990 and 2000, a prolongation of trends apparent since the 1960s. The last decade has been one of national economic growth and a generous regional policy, compared with most neighbouring countries. Table 1.1 shows that four out of five municipalities with less than 2,000 inhabitants and two-thirds of municipalities with between 2,000 and 5,000 inhabitants lost population during the 1990s. Almost one-half of municipalities with between 5,000 and 10,000 inhabitants also lost population. On the other hand, only one of ten municipalities with more than 10,000 inhabitants lost population. Most small municipalities still have out-migration and, as a long term effect, an ageing population. Is this because they are too small to attract private service enterprises and new industries?

Table 1.1 also sums up the geographical variations. Almost all municipalities in the Oslofjord region have an increasing population, and three-fourths of those in the southwest. This is where private services choose to locate, where the positive effects of the capital region are strongest, and where much of the oil industry is located (the Stavanger region). The west coast and fjords present a more complex picture. Municipalities where maritime industries are located usually have an increasing population, whereas many fjord municipalities, the location of old one-company towns, are

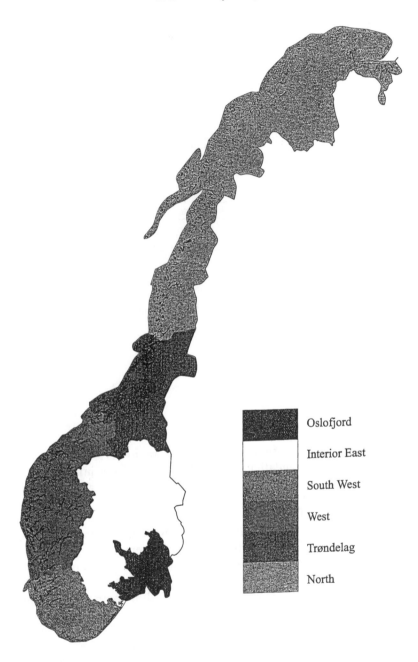

Figure 1.1 The major regions of Norway

Table 1.1 Population change 1990-2000, the municipal level

	Municipalities	M. with pop. decline	Percent
NORWAY (all municipalities)	435	228	52
Size groups (2000)			
Less than 2000 pop.	95	76	80
2001-5000 pop.	152	104	68
5000-10,000 pop.	88	40	45
More than 10,000 pop.	100	8	8
By major regions[1]			
Oslofjord[2]	69	9	13
Interior East[3]	74	53	71
South West[4]	56	15	27
West[5]	98	49	50
Trøndelag[6]	49	33	67
North[7]	89	69	78

[1] See location map (Fig. 1.1)
[2] Counties of Østfold, Akershus, Oslo and Vestfold plus Drammen economic region in Buskerud and Skien/Porsgrunn economic region in Telemark
[3] Hedmark, Oppland, Buskerud (minus Drammen), Telemark (minus Skien/Porsgrunn)
[4] Aust-Agder, Vest-Agder, Rogaland
[5] Hordaland, Sogn og Fjordane, Møre og Romsdal
[6] Sør-Trøndelag, Nord-Trøndelag
[7] Nordland, Troms, Finnmark

declining. The interior east lies behind the Oslofjord region. Here, 70 percent of the municipalities lost population during the 1990s. This inland region suffers from employment decline in primary activities (agriculture and forestry) and in manufacturing industries processing natural resources. Population densities are low, and distances between centres and their peripheries are great. This region has exported its young to the Oslofjord region, and as a result, the population is ageing. In extreme cases, old people are the main source of income, because their pensions, supplemented by money transfers from government to the municipalities they live in, generate jobs in health and social care. We are close to the kind of communities found in parts of Canada, where most people live on welfare. The farther north we get, the darker is the demographic situation. Trøndelag has many of the problems found in the east inland region, and also has its part of small, isolated fishing communities with small centres of which we find so many in North Norway, which is the "worst case" (Hansen 1999).

The 2001 regional report presented this picture clearly. The report writers in the Ministry of Regional and Municipal Affairs had access to research findings which clearly demonstrated the futility of linking the consolidation of population to the municipal level.

The New Level of Population Consolidation

In 1999, Statistics Norway (Hustoft et al. 1999) presented a new standard for economic regions. The old one, from 1966, was out-dated, reflecting that too many municipalities in Norway are too small to be functional regions (Hansen 1997). The economic region lies somewhere between the municipality and the county. NUTS 4 would be the equivalent EU term. Statistics Norway points out that the most ambitious alternative would be to make a division of Norway into functional regions, based upon data on service provision, trade and labour markets. Service and trade data are not good enough. Trade takes place across county boundaries, and no NUTS 4 region can be located in two or more NUTS 3 regions (counties). Since county boundaries in Norway were set hundred of years ago they are not functional for analysis of economic interaction data. Statistics Norway therefore had to rely upon one data source, that of commuting between municipalities. Through analysis of these data (also with shortcomings), a division of Norway into economic regions was undertaken. The result was a map of 90 regions. The procedure was to identify a municipality where commuters from neighbouring municipalities went for work. If one municipality had a commuting population to another municipality of at least 10 percent of its working population, it became part of an economic region with the in-commuting municipality as its centre. It soon became clear that there was often an exchange of commuters between two or more municipalities where at least 10 percent of the working population in one municipality commuted to the other, and vice versa. Such economic regions were defined as regions with two central municipalities with equal standing (I would call them complementary). They were looked upon as troublesome twins, difficult to classify. In reality, a region where commuters cross municipal boundaries in both (or several) directions are probably the closest we can come to a genuine economic region. But most of the economic regions in Norway are lopsided labour market regions, where most commuters go into the municipality with the biggest centre, and hardly anybody goes in the opposite direction. In such cases, the commuting data show that the regional labour market is asymmetric. When Statistics Norway started to apply the commuting principle, it soon became evident that commuting from surrounding municipalities to the regional centre in many cases was far below 10 percent. But since no municipalities by definition could remain outside an economic region, and since an economic region by definition should consist of more that one municipality, the commuting definition had to be waived in numerous cases. It would have been more correct if Statistics Norway had made a list of municipalities which did not fulfil the criteria for inclusion in an economic region.

Another tricky problem for Statistics Norway was to define the minimum size of the dominant urban settlement in the centre municipality. The definition of an urban settlement in Norway has a lower population limit of 200. Nobody would consider a settlement with 200 inhabitants as the vibrant centre of an economic region. But Statistics Norway abstained from introducing a higher minimum population limit. It agrees that a general criterion for a centre municipality should be that it ought to contain an independent (the meaning of independent is not explained) urban settlement of a certain size (Hustoft et al. 1999, p. 11), but it adds that it is difficult to give an absolute definition of "a certain size", "because an urban settlement with for instance 2,000 inhabitants relatively speaking would be small in some parts of the country and big in other parts" (my translation). One must conclude that the methodological basis of the new regional division is unsatisfactory. In addition to the quantitative criteria, unspecified qualitative criteria are used, partly as a response to objections raised in an extensive hearing of a first draft.

Let me give two examples of compromises. The island municipalities of Hitra and Frøya on the southwest coast of Trøndelag are defined as one economic region. The total population is around 8,000. The municipal centre of Hitra has 500 inhabitants, the centre of Frøya 600. Four percent of the working population of Hitra work in Frøya, and four percent of Frøya's working population commute to Hitra. The Nordfjord region consists of six municipalities. Not less than four centres are defined. They do not fulfil the commuting criteria ("but since commuting in Sogn and Fjordane county is low, we consider this criterion to be of little importance" (Hustoft et al. 1999, p. 19). Their population size lies between 1,900 and 2,500. The reason why the four centres are included is that none of them are dominant, as is the case in the Ålesund region north of Nordfjord and the Førde region south of Nordfjord. Then it is difficult to see why Nordfjord should be defined as an economic region at all.

But the new economic regions are there to be used. When comparing Table 1.2 with Table 1.1 one can easily see that the coarse-meshed 90 region division presents a more positive picture of population changes during the 1990s than the fine-meshed 435 municipalities division. Municipalities with population losses are now grouped in regions where increase in one centre municipality compensate for losses in surrounding municipalities. A good example is the Bodø economic region which consists of 11 municipalities.

Only the central municipality had an increasing population (13.2 percent), whereas the 10 surrounding municipalities experienced a decline of 9.3 percent. In the case of the Bodø economic region, there have been no noticeable positive spill-over effects from the centre to the periphery.

Table 1.2 Population change 1990-2000, economic regions

	Regions	R. with pop. decline	Percent
NORWAY (all regions)	90	38	42
Size groups (1998)			
Less than 10,000 pop.	9	8	89
10,001-20,000 pop.	27	17	63
20,001-50,000 pop.	33	13	39
50,001-100,000 pop.	11	0	0
More than 100,000 pop.	10	0	0
By major regions[1]			
Oslofjord	15	0	0
Interior East	17	9	55
South West	12	2	17
West	17	8	47
Trøndelag	12	8	67
North	17	11	65

[1] See Fig. 1.1 for location

But Table 1.2 also shows that even on the regional level, more than 40 percent of the regions had population losses in the 1990s. A majority of the less populous economic regions are losing population. In the interior east, Trøndelag and the north the majority of regions lost population. On the other hand, all regions with more than 50,000 inhabitants and all regions in the Oslofjord major region are winners, and so are most of the regions of the southwest. These variations in part reflect the dynamic regional economies of the Oslofjord and the southwest and the more stagnant regional economies of the interior east and the northern regions. But the variations are also a test of the validity of the delimitation criteria discussed above. Many of the small, peripheral economic regions are not really functional regions, but artificial constructions because all municipalities have to be ascribed to an economic region. But as long as one is aware of the shortcomings of the new regional divisions, one can take the necessary precautions to avoid the statistical traps.

This long excursion into the official statistical regional divisions would have been completely off the mark if it had not been used as a structuring element of the recent report on regional policy.

The Robust Regions

The report introduced the term *robust samfunn* as an intermediate policy arena between the municipality and the county. Literally speaking, the term means robust societies or communities. I prefer to use the term robust regions because the report emphasised that it wanted to target regions as a counterweight to increasing centralisation. By "region" the government meant an area consisting of one or more urban settlements and adjacent rural areas, bound together through commuting, functioning as one housing market, and able to offer its inhabitants a wide range of public and private services. This model was considered but rejected by Statistics Norway because the data needed were not there. But in the regional policy report it emerged again, now as a normative policy instrument. And then it became problematic. I have demonstrated above that many of the economic regions are statistical constructions, not functional regions. But the government did not seem to have seen the inherent risk of linking this spatial term to regional planning.

The political argument of civil servants and national political actors was based on the belief that it was possible to defend the existing population distribution on the economic region level. This assumption was wrong, as demonstrated in Table 1.2. Still, a wide range of policy measures were to be applied to reduce regional disparities. These measures were to be directed towards robust regions, not towards places. It was assumed that robust regions could offer their inhabitants work and services within acceptable distance from where they live, not necessarily in centres, but also in rural settings. The government did not like the term centralisation, not even on the level of economic regions. The ideal spatial configuration was to be an integrated functional region where economic growth was not concentrated in urban centres, but where there was a spill-over into more peripheral areas. A robust region ought to offer its inhabitants the best of urban life as well as the advantages of rural surroundings.

The analysis of population changes in the 1990s (Table 1.2) indicates that the conditions for a balanced urban-rural development were met in the largest economic regions in the Oslofjord and southwest major economic regions. Migration to these regions was important, the age structure favourable, the labour market for well-educated women expanding, and young people have a wide range of education and leisure opportunities.

The regional report stated that the future district and regional policy to a larger extent than previously should include the whole country (St. meld. nr. 34 (2000-2001, p. 9). But on page 7, the report emphasised that "this report will not deal with challenges and opportunities in the major urban regions". These challenges and opportunities were handed over to the report on the government's major policies for the period 2002-2005, prepared by the Ministry of Finance and published in March 2001 (St. meld. nr. 30 (2000-2001). A search in the 400-page document revealed one page (p. 224) about urban development and living conditions in the major cities. Very little was said about the economic and regional role of these urban regions within an national context. A few paragraphs reminded the reader of the need for coordinated physical planning, but the overriding message was that intra-urban social inequalities should be reduced in the major cities. In other words, the major city regions were thrown out of the report on regional policy and converted into a social problem in the long-term programme report.

In 2000, 56 percent of the national population lived in the Oslofjord region and the four major urban regions outside this region (Arendal/Kristiansand, Stavanger, Bergen and Trondheim). These regions absorbed 91 percent of the national population growth of the nineties, partly because the population of these regions was younger, partly because so much of the internal migration in Norway went to these regions, and partly because so many of the immigrants from abroad ended up here. In the 1990s, population growth in these robust regions was 10 percent, in the rest of Norway only one percent.

But these genuinely robust regions, which better than other robust regions in Norway were able to do what robust regions should do according to principles described in the regional policy report, were held to be outside regional policy. Through this ingenious twist, the regional policy report could concentrate upon the demographically stagnant districts.

The Political Handling of the Regional Policy Report

Important reports from government to parliament tend to be sent over towards the end of the parliamentary session, in the case of the regional policy report just before the Easter vacation (which is taken very seriously in Norway). The committee on municipal issues worked under serious time constraints, and produced a 36-page report where the political parties spent much more time in marketing their old and well-known views than in responding to new ideas. The committee asked parliament to vote for the following proposals:

• Parliament asks the government to contribute to the training of more positivity agents. The activities of the positivity agents' secretariat in Vega should be embedded with the municipalities and counties involved.

- Parliament asks the government in its budget for 2002 to clarify how the municipalities can be stimulated to introduce web-based education, such as electronic classrooms.

- Parliamentary Report number 34 (2001-2002) is put on record.

Parliament spent 80 minutes discussing the matter, without adding much to the debate on regional policy, and endorsed the committee's proposal. The elephant had finally given birth to a mouse.

The conclusion to be drawn from the text analysis of top-down documents is that the Ministry of Municipal and Regional Affairs did what it was expected to do. Its report gave adequate descriptions of major regional changes. The main objectives of regional policy were presented, and the need for a gender and life cycle perspective in regional development were emphasised. When it comes to policy implementations, the political canon took over, insisting on the importance of primary activities for the preservation of the existing settlement pattern. The gender and life cycle perspective, focusing on the aspirations and actions of individuals, was overshadowed by general labour market considerations.

The policy parts of the report did not really follow up the problem analysis in the first part of the report. This is a criticism not only of this report, but also of earlier regional policy reports. When political actors take over from the civil servants, a diluting process sets in. Major changes in policy are avoided, and so were changes which may be unfavourably received by specific regional interest groups. In the case of the 2001 report, things were not made easier for the civil servants because mid-way in the work on the report the minority Centrist government was replaced by a minority Labour government. Minority governments tend to avoid confrontations. So did the committee on municipal affairs when preparing its report to parliament. The different parties presented their views. There was no need to develop competing alternatives, since parliament does not take important votes when reports are presented. The important votes are taken when the budget goes through parliament late in the autumn session.

The open debate in parliament, given calendar and time constraints, inevitably became an anti-climax. It did not make newspaper headlines, and was conveniently forgotten in the hectic weeks before the summer recess.

From Top-down to Bottom-up Perceptions of Regional Policy

The general picture of changes in population distribution has been described in the first part of the paper. It can be summarised as follows: the major urban

regions are the winners. But they are not included in the government's
strategies for regional development. The marginal regions are the persistent
losers. Rural areas outside commuting hinterlands of medium-sized and small
towns also experience out-migration. Special development programmes ought
to be directed towards these marginal regions. But between the periphery and
the major centres are the robust regions. The government's idea of a robust
region is that it should offer work, housing and public and private services to
the young people growing up there. But as pointed out above, among the
economic regions of Statistics Norway, defined as regional labour markets,
many are not really regional labour market regions, but just local centres
surrounded by demographic peripheries with little contact with the centres.

The top-down people in the political system seem to believe that regional
policy measures can strengthen these robust regions, so that fewer young
people will leave, and that many of those who leave will come back. It is,
then, worthwhile investigating what really makes people stay or move. Over
the last few years, many studies have asked this question. Some of the
findings are reported and commented upon in the following paragraphs.

Mobility is the Rule

Young people, wherever they live, are very mobile. The national register of
population makes it possible to follow individuals over time (Statistisk
Sentralbyrå 1999, Sørlie 2000). Table 1.3 sums up some of the major findings
of Sørlie's general study. He follows all Norwegians born between 1960 and
1962 between the age of 15 and 35. He classifies them as either non-leavers
(still living at the age of 35 where they lived at the age of 15), return migrants
(moved out and back again between 15 and 35), leavers (not living at 35 where
they lived at 15) and newcomers (not living there at 15, but at 35). Four
categories of municipalities are used; rural municipalities without centres,
municipalities with local centres, municipalities with regional centres and
major urban regions.

The table shows that two-thirds of the women and one-half of the men who
lived in rural municipalities at the age of 15 had left before 35. The propensity
to leave is reduced the more urban the municipality, but even in the major
urban regions 40 percent of the men and 46 percent of the women are leavers.
Migration within larger urban regions often consists of short-distance moves
between municipalities within one single urban housing market.

The old idea that migration is related to work opportunities is still popular
with many politicians. If the young can find work where they grow up, they
will stay. The regional policy report to some extent echoes this view. But
when school leavers are asked about their views on the future – will they leave

or will they stay? – work is among the less important facts of life they take
into consideration. To them, future work is less important than social needs in
the near future. The transition from childhood into adolescence is also a
liberation process. They want to leave in order to experience alternatives.
Their views on the world outside the valley of their childhood are influenced
by what they read, often on the Internet, or what their older relatives and
friends who have made the move tell about life out there. Their ideas of the
good life out there are often superficial. The answers they give in
questionnaires or in written essays, or when interviewed personally, are often
glib, copycat answers. What comes into their minds is what they discuss with
friends. The point to be made is not that they do not know much of life
elsewhere, but that they know that they want to go away, perhaps not for life,
but at least for a while (Båtevik and Olsen 2000).

Table 1.3   Age cohorts aged 15 to 25, born 1960-62

	Types of municipalities							
	Rural		Local centre		Regional centre		Major urban region	
Migrant category	M	W	M	W	M	W	M	W
1. Non-leavers	35	18	42	25	43	29	42	33
2. Return Migrants	15	15	16	19	18	20	19	21
3. Leavers	50	67	42	56	39	51	39	46
4. Newcomers	18	31	25	35	35	47	57	66
Balance (1+2+4=100)	-32	-36	-17	-21	-4	-4	+18	+20

Source: Sørlie 2000, Table 3.3

Some Do Not Leave

In the good old days children went straight from school into work. They
followed the paths of their parents within a local labour market based on the
exploitation and processing of natural resources. This is now history in most
parts of Norway, but still some leave school early and find work where they
live. For them, elementary school or one or two years of vocational school is
enough. They are tired of school. Two-thirds of them are boys. The regional
policy report spends much time in pointing to job opportunities in natural
resource-based activities. But the number of jobs in these activities has been
drastically reduced, and even when available, the young people do not want
them. The boys who start work at 16 or 18 get beginners' jobs in transport,

warehouses and stores, in auto repair shops, in building and construction work, often working for relatives or other people whom they already know. When interviewed, they appreciate earning money, often spent on hobbies such as motorcycles and cars. They live at home for some years, and they keep up school friendships. They become the masters of the street, since so many of their contemporaries have left. The girls they knew may have left too, but there are new girls to get to know, two or three years younger, still at school, not saying no to an evening ride in the newly acquired second-hand Volvo station wagon. Since they have decided to stay, they talk mostly in positive terms about the place they live in. They are embedded. But some of them are not sure that they will not leave one day.

The girls who leave school early do not go into available farming and fishing jobs. They do not want them. They find temporary jobs as assistants in nursery schools, old people's homes and as shop assistants. A case study from Aurland (Hansen 2001) shows that many of these girls changed their minds after a few years of unskilled, low-paid jobs. They decided to go back to school, completing secondary school and pursuing higher education in nursing, teaching and office work. It helped if these educational opportunities were found within commuting distance. Many of these girls had found partners where they lived, and did not want to leave. The partnership becomes more important than work.

Table 1.3 shows that more men than women stay. In rural municipalities more men leave than stay (respectively 50 and 35 percent). In the other categories, the difference between leavers and non-leavers is small, but the non-leavers are never a majority of the male cohort. Only one in five women in rural municipalities are non-leavers. The proportion increases the more urbanised the municipality, but never reaches more than one-third.

Education: A Prime Mover or an Excuse for Leaving?

Studies based on the population register of Statistics Norway (Grimsrud 1999, Statistisk Sentralbyrå 1999, Sørlie 2000) show that education is a driving force. Young people from municipalities without secondary schools will have to go elsewhere if they want to continue to study after elementary school – and they want to. Many of them can commute, some have to move. In both cases, they will encounter new social environments, and begin to see the place where they grew up from an outsider's perspective. They are given a choice between places. Sooner or later, all of them must make this choice.

In a recent study, Grimsrud (2000) did in-depth interviews with 37 women who at one time in life had left or arrived in a region in interior east Norway She finds that it is fruitless to attempt to classify the migrants by motive, because the decision process leading up to migration is very complex. Education, work, partnerships, children, relatives and place-embeddedness are important elements in this decision process, but the weight of the different elements varies over time.

Over the last fifty years, an intermediary phase of life has wedged itself between childhood and work. The wedge is education, and it becomes more and more important as time goes by. Higher education means moving out for most of the young living in the so-called robust regions, so attractive to the top-down people, not only the political thinkers, but also for the members of municipal councils who have a vested interest in the locality that their own children want to leave. When students in secondary schools are asked about their immediate plans, almost all the girls and a majority of the boys believe that they are going to leave. The "official" reason is that they have to leave in order to study. Behind this reason lie other considerations.

Førlandsås (2002) has studied attitudes of young people to life in the restructured industrial town of Rjukan (the case of Rjukan is discussed in Hansen 2001 and 2002). A secondary school girl in Rjukan sums up her relationship to Rjukan: "To a 17-year-old girl this is the worst place one can live in." The place, she realises, might be attractive to her parents, to her younger sisters or brothers, or to a married cousin with two toddlers. But she is too young to go to the pub or to get a driver's licence. There are too many restrictions on her life. She often gets fed up with her friends, in particular with the boys. Always the same tiresome faces. She has definitely decided to leave, but does not exclude the possibility of coming back. Almost all the girls in Rjukan secondary school, and a majority of the boys, choose not to take vocational courses leading them into the local labour market, but instead follow the general studies curriculum. Many of them do not know what they are going to use their general studies background for, but they are convinced that by choosing general studies, they are not being tied to local jobs and can use this general education as preparation for higher education elsewhere. The higher education path leads them out of a local environment which is too small for them at this stage of their lives. Higher education is a means to an end – to get away – more than a goal in itself. One year before leaving Rjukan for higher education elsewhere, most of the pupils do not really know what kind of higher education studies they are going to follow. Quite a few of them just want to travel around the world for some months.

Will They Return?

Since so many politicians wishfully think that return migrants can give new life to ailing communities, one should look at the reality, as presented by

Sørlie (2000). Going back to Table 1.3, we find that of those who left, almost one-half returned in the best category, men to regional centres; less than one in five in the worst case, women to rural communities.

These empirical data are available for all municipalities in Norway (Statistisk Sentralbyrå 1999). Sørlie's national report was commissioned by the Ministry of Municipal and Regional Affairs, and is referred to in the 2001 regional policy report (P. 17-19). The evidence he presents must be depressing for the top-down politicians who have high hopes for the future of the Norwegian periphery. In the event, they chose to ignore these empirical findings. In her presentation, the spokeswoman for the committee on municipal affairs, a member of the Centre party, told parliament:

> We want to insist that not all those who move do so because they find very interesting opportunities or because the grass is so much greener on the other side of the fence. Questionnaire surveys in fact show that many people, not least young people, answer that they would not have moved if they could find work where they lived. In a report from 1999, more than 50 percent of those who had moved said that they definitely, or perhaps, would not have moved if they had been offered better opportunities in the place which they had left. (My translation)

One should always be careful when interpreting answers to hypothetical questions. This precaution is also valid for members of parliament.

What Makes People Return?

The general picture is relatively clear, but can be followed up with case studies which give qualitative insights into the reasons why some people return. Tinn municipality with its local centre, Rjukan, is such a case. Let us start with the quantitative background (Table 1.4). One-half of the men and 60 percent of the women born between 1949 and 1956, and who lived in Tinn at the age of 15, had left at the age of 35. This heavy out-migration took place when the chemical industry in Rjukan went into a long period of decline. For those who were born between 1960 and 1962, who lived in Tinn when they were 15, and reached the age of 35 between 1995 and 1997, the corresponding numbers showed that one-third of the men and 40 percent of the women had left. The oldest cohort left elementary school between 1965 and 1975, a period where job losses in the dominant chemical industries were considerable. By 1997, the chemical industries had closed down, but Rjukan had profited from important regional policy measures, and many new jobs in secondary and tertiary activities had been created for those in the youngest cohort. The most important difference between the 1949-56 cohort and the 1960-62 cohort is that the proportion of non-leavers increased. Local restructuring made more young people hang on, but the return rate of out-migrants was still low. Out of four who left, only one came back.

Førlandsås (2002) interviewed return migrants to Rjukan. She found that work is a necessary, but not sufficient condition for coming back. Family networks, cheap housing and good environments for bringing up small children are also important. The return migrants did not come back to escape from big cities. In the phase of life they were in (around 30-35 years old), Rjukan had become a different place from the one they left 10 to 15 years earlier. Whereas the 17-year-old youngsters today often paint Rjukan in dark colours, return migrants find many attractive features. They do not feel claustrophobic about the place. They intend to live in a more extensive social space than they did when they were 17. They are more mobile and maintain contact with people in the place where they lived previously. To them, Rjukan is not an isolated place in the middle of nowhere, but a place which together with other places constitute the spatial basis of their lives. But some of them envisage moving on. When their children grow older, they may go elsewhere. They like the work they have at present, but see few prospects of finding new and better jobs in Rjukan. They are approaching a phase in their life cycle where Rjukan once more may become too small. The point to be made is that perceptions of place and space change over time during life, and that mobility is one way of finding the right place at the right time.

Grimsrud (2000) interviewed women from interior East Norway who were living in Oslo. Some of them considered coming back. The reasons are familiar: stress in work, transport stress, expensive housing, fear of criminality. More interesting is their definition of return migration. If they move back, it is not to the municipality they left, but to small towns not too distant from the place they initially left. One of the reasons is that the most of the women want work in public and private services, not in primary activities. And these jobs are more easily found in regional centres. Another reason why they do not want to return to where their relatives live is that they are afraid of losing their own identity. They do not want to be looked upon as "the daughter of . . .", "the wife of . . ." or "the sister of . . .". They have developed their identity after they left the place of their childhood and early youth. When they come back, they do not necessarily want to join the old networks. The choice between proximity and distance is problematic. Women who left rural communities and local centres may return to the nearest regional centre. They move up the urbanisation ladder, but in their way are faithful to the region of their childhood, if not the locality.

They Thought They Would Return, But Did Not. Why?

Many young people find partners where they have chosen to pursue higher education studies. If the partners come from different places, they may chose to stay where they studied, if the job opportunities are better. If one of the partners can offer housing in his or her place of origins, the other partner may follow. One return migrant brings with him/her a newcomer. Grimsrud (1999) found that in her study area in east Norway quite a few women move into the area together with farmers' sons who have work and housing waiting for them. The women prefer jobs in public services, and appreciate living in a rural environment when the children are small. But this alternative becomes less and less important since the number of farms in Norway is being rapidly reduced.

As women become more and more educated, return migration becomes less probable. A long higher education binds them closer to the town where they studied or other large, diversified labour markets. Socially, they become gradually more and more integrated in the town where they studied. Ideas they initially had about returning home fade away.

Wiborg (1999, 2000) interviewed students at the Regional College in Bodø in North Norway about their attitudes to the place they came from and where their family still lives. She found that the women she interviewed were developing their social identities through a continuous process, and that the process also changed their identities over time. Higher education for them is a journey in time and space from one identity to another. This journey increases the distance between them and their childhood friends who stayed behind, finished their education early and formed a family with partner and children. For the educated women, in the phase of life they are in (around 25), children are seen as an obstacle to the development of their social identities. They discover, when visiting their families, that they and their childhood friends have less and less in common. They tend to look down upon these old friends, and sometimes feel that their former friends do not understand them. An alienation process sets in, which makes it more and more difficult for these educated women to return. Behind the remark "there are no jobs for us" are hidden profound personal reasons for not coming home. "Home" is family, not place.

The older the potential return migrants, the less probable is it that they will return. And what is holding them back is perhaps not the lack of adequate work when returning, but the simple fact that their continuous identity projects are more and more anchored in the place where they live now. There is not much regional policy measures can do to make them change their minds.

Are Incomers Going to Replace Those Who Left?

As already pointed out, at present there is very little unemployment in Norway, and a serious shortage of labour including in peripheral areas. The local council chairman in a very remote forest municipality in east Norway summarised the situation in his municipality: "This is a very good place to live in. The only things we are short of are work and workers". People leave such municipalities because they do not want hard physical work, in production jobs or in the social and health sector. Vacancies are not filled, or are filled by temporary immigrants or political refugees. But also in less strenuous service sector jobs there are vacancies, in particular in jobs for people with higher education. Local people who leave to educate themselves for such jobs, tend not to become return migrants. In such a situation it is important to identify the role of incomers in local labour markets. Table 1.3 shows that the number of newcomers (incomers who stay on) in all types of municipalities are higher than that of return migrants. It also shows that newcomers are more attracted by regional centres and major urban regions than local centres and rural communities. There are more women than men among the newcomers. The kinds of jobs which attract them are not the traditional local jobs of peripheral areas, but public and to some extent private service jobs which are found all over Norway. For newly educated people who want a foothold in this national labour market, it is easier to find such jobs in less central communities, because the turnover there is higher and opportunities for getting a first job better. Some of the newcomers, and especially women, come with men who are return migrants. Quite a few of the in-migrants remain newcomers only for a short period of time. They move on to the next step in their career, or because they did not like the place.

Table 1.4 shows the relation between newcomers and movers-on in Tinn. For men in the oldest cohort there were almost three movers-on for each newcomer. These men arrived when the old manufacturing industries were still in operation and needed unskilled workers, but the phasing-out had already begun. Many of them came from rural communities in the same region, and soon moved on. For each female newcomer there were two movers-on. The youngest cohort met a different labour market. The old basic industries were in their last years of existence, but new jobs were created in other manufacturing industries and in service industries. The differences between men and women were reduced, but mobility was still very marked, and the number of movers-on, especially among women, was higher than was the case for the older cohort. This must be ascribed to the fact that the new jobs available in Rjukan required skills that also could be used elsewhere. The level of education was higher in the younger cohort than in the old cohort, and higher education usually means higher mobility.

Førlandsås (2002) interviewed a few newcomers, all of whom worked in service jobs. They had previously lived in larger cities, and found life in Rjukan less stressful than where they came from. They also appreciated cheap housing and available nursery schools. They found friends easily, partly because there were so many incomers in the same situation. They did not feel isolated, because they knew that a couple of hours travel could bring them to larger towns, and – as one of them said – "Two hours to the airport and another six to the Canary Islands, that is okay with me". But they also kept an opening for moving on in their minds. It was not easy making a career in Rjukan. And when their children grew up and wanted to study – what then? For these incomers, Rjukan was a good place to live in during a specific stage of the life cycle, but perhaps not a place forever.

Table 1.4   Migrants into and from Tinn

	Cohort 1 (born 1949-56, 15 years 1964-71)		Cohort 2 (born 1960-62, 15 years 1975-77)	
Migrant category	Men	Women	Men	Women
1. Non-leavers	33	23	55	42
2. Return migrants	17	17	12	16
3. Leavers	50	60	33	42
4. Newcomers	13	23	29	21
Balance (1+2+4=100)	-37	-37	-4	-21
5. Incomers in transit	33	45	50	53

Source: Statistic Sentrabyrå 1999

Where Do We Go from Here?

The main point of this study is that human mobility is increasing, and that it is here to stay. There are many good reasons for individuals to move, and job opportunities is only one among many. A decision to move is a part of an individual's ever-changing identity project. Places are deconstructed and constructed as life goes on. Most people have the human and economic resources to change places if they want to. And many do.

In a regional policy perspective, there are losers and winners among regions. The bottom line of Table 1.3 is a balance sheet. If you add non-leavers, return migrants and newcomers, the bottom line tells you that rural areas have a negative balance of around one-third of those who lived there at the age of 15 in 1975. The negative balance persists, but less pronounced, in municipalities with local centres. When we come to regional centres, there is only a slight negative balance. The winners are the major urban regions, those – we remember – who in the government's long term plan 2002-2005 mainly were defined as areas in need of help because of the social problems, and in the regional policy report were not considered as the true objects of regional policy.

An alternative regional policy could be to improve living conditions in the regions where people want to live. That could be done in making a real effort in public housing in the major urban regions, to improve accessibility, and to improve the living conditions of the marginalised people living in these regions. Outside the major urban regions, the regional centres should be given better opportunities to receive return migrants. Then there would be correspondence between an all-inclusive regional policy and where the people who are going to shape our future want to live. One reason for presenting this alternative regional policy is that the present *distriktspolitikk*, favouring local centres and rural areas, does not seem to work well. It has been tested on almost 40 cohorts of young people, and rejected by most of them.

References

Båtevik, F. O. and J. C. Hansen. 1995. Migration and journey to work in sparsely populated areas in Norway. *Norsk geogr. Tidsskr* 49: 5-17.

Båtevik, F. O. and G. M. Olsen. 2000. *Ung i utkant: Fritidsaktivitetar og tankar om framtida blant ungdomar frå sju kommunar i Møre i Romsdal.* Arbeidsrapport nr. 100. Volda: Møreforskning Volda.

Førlandsås, B. 2002. *Er Rjukan et blivende sted? Generasjoners forhold til sted.* M.A. thesis, Department of Geography, University of Bergen.

Grimsrud, G. M. 1999. *Utdanning og flytting: En kartlegging av utdanningsnivo blant flyttere og bofaste i Nord-Gudbrandsdalen, Nord-Østerdalen og Gauldal-/Rørosområdet.* Lillehammer: Østlandsforskning.

Grimsrud, G. M. 2000. *Kvinner på flyttefot.* Lillehammer: Østlandsforskning.

Hansen, J. C. 1989. Norway: the turnaround which turned around. In A. G. Champion (ed.), *Counterurbanization: The Changing Pace and Nature of Population Deconcentration.* London: Edward Arnold.

Hansen, J. C. 1997. Municipal reform: A prerequisite for local development? In R. Byron, J. Walsh and P. Breathnach (eds.), *Sustainable Development on the North Atlantic Margin*. Aldershot: Ashgate.

Hansen, J. C. 1999. Why do young people leave fishing communities in coastal Finnmark, north Norway? In R. Byron and J. Hutson (eds.), *Local Enterprise on the North Atlantic Margin*. Aldershot: Ashgate.

Hansen, J. C. 2001. How are young people coping with local economic restructuring? In R. Byron and J. Hutson (eds.), *Community Development on the North Atlantic Margin*. Aldershot: Ashgate.

Hansen, J. C. 2002. *Ungdoms forhold til sted: Er Rjukan et blivende sted?* Geografi i Bergen 254. Bergen: Department of Geography, University of Bergen (www.nhh.no/geo/Nyesider/GIB.html).

Hustoft, A. G. et al. 1999. *Standard for økonomiske regioner: Etablering av publiseringsnivσ mellom fylke og kommune.* Rapporter 99/6. Oslo and Kongsvinger: Statistisk Sentralbyrå.

Innst. S. nr. 318 (2000-2001). *Innstilling frσ kommunalkomiteen om distrikts- og regionalpolitikken* (St.meld. nr. 34 (2000-2001). Oslo.

Statistisk Sentralbyrå. 1999. *Resultat av innenlandsk flytting gjennom første del av voksenlivet. Aktuelle befolkningstall 3/99, 4/99, 5/99.* Oslo and Kongsvinger: Statistisk Sentralbyrå.

St. meld. nr. 30 (2000-2001). *Langtidsprogrammet 2002-2005.* Oslo.

St. meld. nr. 34 (2000-2001). *Om distrikts- og regionalpolitikken.* Oslo.

Stortingets forhandlinger 11.06.01, Item 19. Oslo.

Sørlie, K. 2000. *Klassiske analyser: Flytting og utdanning belyst i livsløps- og kohortperspektiv.* Notat 2000: 121. Oslo: NIBR.

Wiborg, A. 1999. *Det er eit heilt anna liv – om unge kvinner fra distriktene i høyere utdannelse.* Bodø: Nordlandsforskning.

Wiborg, A. 2000. Høyskolestudenter fra distriktene – i spenningsfeltet mellom by og land, arbeid og tilhørighet. In M. Husmo and J. P. Johnsen (eds.), *Fra bygd og fjord til kaféliv?* Trondheim: Tapir Akademisk Forlag.

Chapter 2

The New Development Discourse: A Farewell to Mega-Theories?

PETER SJØHOLT

Introduction: Development Thinking and Development Discourse

The concept of *development* is increasingly used in most social science contexts. Mainly, it has been applied implicitly as a tacit understanding of something generally accepted and immediately understood. Far more seldom has it been treated explicitly as an epistemological problem or a contested intellectual issue. This paper is an attempt to explore some of the intricacies of the issues emanating from development thinking by pointing to the ways that the phenomenon has been treated in the literature, especially in the postwar period. Particular emphasis is put on changes taking place in development ideas and theories in current debates, linked to changes having simultaneously occurred and which are still occurring in the real world. By way of conclusion, I speculate upon some impacts of the new directions for the prospects of marginal areas.

Development thinking generally has one common denominator: it can be reduced to a concern with future conditions, structures and events. An ocean of literature already exists on this topic and very much of it represents a reduction to a few general principles. Although somewhat misinterpreted, as contended by many development researchers, among them Nederveen Pieterse (2001), the discussion is very much about development paradigms, which have shifted over time. Likewise, the literature is full of references to development ideology and development theories. To this has been added, mainly as a post-modern theorem, the concept of the *development discourse*. This is a concept originating in linguistics and literary studies, where it appeared as a method of analysing texts by careful scrutiny of language. It was transferred to the social sciences, explicitly by Foucault (1977), when he contrasted discourse with paradigm. Later it was made relevant to problematisation of development by considering it a form of storytelling or a narrative, in some cases even as myth (Crush 1996, Rist 1997). As such, it is a good instrument for seeing continuities and discontinuities. Furthermore, it implies rethinking reality through deconstruction and reconstruction (Escobar

1992).   Discourse analyses can be associated with different development trajectories or paths. Storytelling can thus imply several discourses – often conflicting ones – and may even provide a way to reconcile apparently incompatible narratives. A much quoted discursive claim is, for example, the contention that the World Bank's "stories" are always the same; although contrasted with reality, they are clearly discontinuous, particularly as far as ideas of development promotion is concerned.

Considered as a discourse, development becomes a epistemological issue, which may provide us with the conceptual tools for discussing its nature and contents and for analyses of the ways the idea has been elaborated and applied. In this way, a reflexive turn can be added to development studies: a discourse can be considered as the framework for a problematic that is to be analysed and explained.   It may be concerned with policy, and as such imply a normative orientation and valorization and reveals the importance of representation. The western variant of development discourses have, by and large, been identical with claims of the universal validity of a particular development path and, as such, have had a genuine power to constructing their own realities.

Contrasting Conventional Development Discourses

The Modernisation Project

Characteristic of the development thinking associated with the western development discourse is the understanding of development as evolution, towards ever higher values and improvement. Originally a British legacy from the late 19th century, strongly linked to the heyday of imperialism (Brohman 1996), this thinking was revived in the aftermath of the Second World War as *modernisation*. Mainly, although not exclusively, the modernisation project was an American contribution, reflecting the economic and societal structure as it developed in North America at the time and was regarded as valid in a global perspective.

When we try to deconstruct the different components inherent in this conceptualisation of development, the coherence of the many elements is striking. Modernisation is based on growth theory and includes a series of theoretical tenets from the 1940s and 1950s, such as the Harrod-Domar model of savings and investments (1948, 1957), Rodan-Rosenstein's big push theory (1943) and Nurkse's emphasis on industrialisation (1953). Typical was a broad investment push, providing for optimal return to scale. This reflects assumptions about dynamics, in stark contrast to the conventional neo-classical equilibrium economics, built on comparative advantages.   This mainly economic orientation was supplemented with and supported by an institutional approach. Its most visible manifestation was what was later known as Fordism, an integrated system of Keynesian economic principles coupled with institutional regulations and collective bargaining on the labour market. In line with this, state intervention was accepted as legitimate, giving rise to macro-economic planning systems (see Table 2.1, below). Thus the modernisation paradigm developed into a "grand theory" of mainstream development, with its own values and cultural styles. An expansive, externally induced top-down organised development regime was in this way made available to all.

Outward diffusion was one of the strongest ideas in the modernisation project. It lies beneath the duo-economic perspective (Hirshman 1982) by which developing countries are in need of particular development instruments and measures for their progress, mainly provided by more developed countries. In the industrial countries the goal was to bring to all parts of their countries the blessings of modernisation. This meant in the economic field to transfer resources from "low productive" to "high productive" sectors and regions and in the sociocultural field to induce changes, whereby more urban ways of life and lifestyles were adopted. Most industrial countries saw during this epoch the most overwhelming rural-urban exodus ever experienced.

These ideas also came to permeate regional policy and planning whose implementation was typically top-down. Although built on antecedent models from the 1930s like the American TVA (Tennessee Valley Authority) and the British industrial estates, these policies developed their own development discourse during the late 1950s and 1960s, parallel to mainstream modernisation thinking.

Applied to developing countries, increasingly designated the "Third World", the development discourse cut across the many particularities of socioeconomic, political and cultural structures, underpinned as it was by rational thinking with a clear urban bias. The impact of these attempts at homogenisation were naturally somewhat differentiated, but the results left generally much to be desired, particularly in most Third World countries. Certainly, expectations were set too high. One of the constraints was faulty institutions and a weak governance compared to the situation in the industrialised world. Instead of the rise of a benevolent state the world saw a series of examples of predatory states, where temptation of rent-seeking by the governing elite became increasingly widespread.

Simultaneously, in some countries, which were ideologically receptive, a communist-inspired development agenda was launched, originating in the then Soviet Union and later in The Peoples' Republic of China. This transfer of development ideas and praxis was aimed at rebuilding Third World societies according to and on par with a socialist model. This development thinking shared with the West many of the assumptions and features of modernisation, emphasising industrialisation and urbanisation and very often subjecting the societies which were penetrated to a new form of dependency. This was to provoke crises which became particularly grave and acute with the demise of communism in Eastern Europe on the threshold of the 1990s.

The Rise of "Dependencia"

The modernisation experiment ran its course, but ran into trouble and many of the results hoped for did not materialise. It is in this light we should see the counterpoint thinking which was launched in the late 1960s and entertained during the 1970s. Characteristic of the re-orientation was the concept of *dependencia*. Its tenets had originated in Latin America (Prebish 1950, Singer 1976). Prebish argued strongly that Third World countries were subjected to structural weakness due to the growing deterioration of the terms of trade vis-a-vis countries of the industrialised world. From the late 1960s dependency thinking was supplemented by the ideas of neo-Marxist development scholars (Frank 1969, 1981; Wallerstein 1979; Amin 1976, 1989), whose essential message was the claim that underdevelopment in the south is the logical consequence of development in the north. A new absolutist development paradigm was thus constructed: a grand theory of an exogenously induced downward spiral, impacting upon the entire Third World. This rather negative contribution to development thinking also provoked new normative development discourses of a more positive character. It lies behind the doctrine of self-reliance (Galtung 1976) and active popular participation from below (Stöhr and Taylor 1981), both favouring broader industrial development and a renewed emphasis on indigenous development paths; in its most extreme form it also argued for selective regional closure.

Inherent in dependency thinking were elements of mainstream ideology: in essence it was more economic and social than cultural. Growth was valued as a goal in itself and the driving forces behind development were structural rather than based on action. However hard its proponents sought to distance it from the mainstream, this development discourse still falls well within the mainstream tradition. The dependency theorem has been useful as an analytical tool, particularly in a Third World context, but has also contributed significantly to the regional political and planning debate in the North. Notably the Institute of Development Studies at the University of Sussex was for a long time committed to studies in dependency relations (Seers et al. 1979). This was particularly the case before the untimely death of Seers. He considered development negated if one of the three elements, poverty, unemployment and inequality had grown worse over a time period, even if per-capita income had doubled (Seers 1979). Like that of modernisation, the *dependencia* tradition had its heyday followed by decline. Only minor aspects of it lingered on in regional development and planning ideology.

The Neo-liberal Revival

In stark contrast to dependency thinking and with more scope for accounting for for agency and action, neo-liberal ideas had gained ground by about 1980. As a theoretical development, its strength lay in the mixture of neo-classical economic approaches and neo-liberal political ideas, being extremely market oriented in the economic field. In the political field the intimate market-state connections, a legacy from the modernisation project, were severed and individual rational choice was promoted. In contrast to modernisation the neo-liberal discourse prescribes a monoeconomic solution, whereby the same medicine should be applied both in the industrialised and the developing world. The structural explanation of poverty and underdevelopment is rejected. Poor countries stay poor mainly because of mismanagement. By and large the remedy implied extensive privatisation, less public control and deregulation. This leads logically to structural adjustment, indigenously promoted and administered in the industrialised world and effected by cooperation between the Bretton Woods-Washington institutions and national governments in developing countries.

When evaluating the impacts and results of these measures, it would be unjust to deny positive effects of this new development orientation. As a consequence of the renewed power given to the market, it has become fit to produce more efficiently in many parts of the world. On the other hand, conditionalities, notably applied in the developing world, have carried in their wake much social deprivation, especially in the poorest countries, as indiscriminate privatisation and the minimalist state have failed to bring the intended effects. Particularly serious has been the propensity to strip the state of its redistributive powers and capacities for policy coordination and institution-building. The collapse of the "Second World" coupled with the seemingly unchallenged hegemony of neo-liberal political regimes in most Western countries came to reinforce this picture. In the words of Fukuyama (1992), the trends on the threshold of the 1990s signified "the end of history", if "history" is understood as a competitive struggle between ideologies of political economy.

Counterpoint Discourses

The trends by the early 1990s certainly did not mean the end of development thinking, however. Commenting on the Fukuyama proposition, Tucker (1999) vehemently rejected it as "the end of imagination". Instead, Tucker strongly advocated diversity and decentredness as the most important topics on the agenda of reformulating the question of development. That there was a need for such a reformulation was evident from the fact that the 1980s had witnessed a relative dearth of development thinking apart from the liberal revival. But in the wake of this impasse, the development discourse has undergone a reorientation. On the one hand, it seems to have meant less weight has been placed on the monocultural universal and grand theories, which were supposed to be applicable to any development problem in any part of the world.

On the other hand, parallel with the neo-liberal projects ran new counterpoint development discourses. By the mid-1970s, the thesis of Alternative Development had appeared, and later ideas about Human Development contributed to the "toolkit" of the development debate. These counterpoint ideas were, in contrast to earlier thinking, incoherent when considered as theoretical edifices. At most they were attempts at generalising important development principles to serve as a critique of old solutions and as a framework of a new development discourse. The two directions had a many hallmarks in common, such as endogenous development, popular empowerment, popular participation and development on a human scale. As also shown in Table 2.1, Alternative Development particularly stresses local development, social agency, equity and cultural diversity. Human Development is preoccupied with capacity-building, and human resource development through adequate education and knowledge acquisition. The concern is primarily with social and cultural capital as opposed to physical and financial capital. Simultaneously, a new ecological awareness was born, underpinned by the Brundtland Report and several world summits, conferences and congresses, of which the Rio Conference of 1992 and the Kyoto Protocol of 1999 were the most prominent. All these fora came to underline the claim of sustainability in the widest meaning of the term as an overarching development principle.

These ideological constructions, together with others, made up a counterpoint to the global hegemonic ideas of the day by attending to the contextual dimensions of development; they had to fight formidable forces, however. They ran counter to the predominant world economic development trends, which during most of the period meant extension of global production systems, giving rise to continuous restructuring. The fierce competitive climate following in the wake of large-scale development conflicts with the main values in this alternative thinking, by putting a heavy strain on both natural and social resources.

This encouraged more extreme views of development, verging on anti-development thinking, inspired by the ideas of Amin (1990) and reiterated by

Korten (1995). This thinking, often labelled *post-development*, voices a particular critique on the present day organisation and practise of globalism. Meanwhile, new, more flexible production systems have been developed. These may presage another and more qualitative organisation of globalism. Far from reducing the multivocal development discourse to a monolithic theoretical framework, all these conflicting trends have prompted a reconsideration of parts of the development thinking, making it less dichotomic than before and thereby more open to modifications. A further elaboration of this present trend will be the subject of the remainder of the general part of the paper. First, a short summing up of the main characteristics of the development debate so far would be appropriate.

Table 2.1   Development theories and issues over time

Grand Theories

Periods	Development schools	Definitions	Development implications
1850>	Colonial economics	Management of resources	European exploitation.; selective industrialisation
1879>	Latecomers	Catch-up industrialisation	Protection of infant industries
1940>	Development economics	Growth through industrialisation	Big investment push, partly public
1940-1950>	Modernisation theory	Socio-economic political modernisation	State-led growth; macro-economic planning
1960>	Dependency theory	Autocentric; underdevelopment	Self-reliant response; national accumulation
1980>	Neo-liberalism	Economic growth through deregulation	Market-led growth; structural reform

Counterpoint Theories

1970-1980>	Alternative development	Society-led, participatory	Equitable and sustainable measures
1980>	Human development	Capacitation; new options	Social and cultural investment
1990>	Post-development	Development viewed as authoritarian	Local delinking and resistance to globalisation

Source: After Pieterse 2001

Table 2.1 is an attempt to depict contrasting currents of development thought over time. The periodisation does not mean distinctive succession of ideas and paradigms. There is considerable persistence and overlap of older ideas in later periods. Neo-liberalism, for example, is still a mighty force in the 21st century. The main impression of what crystallised during the second half of the 20th century – at any rate up to the 1990s – is articulation of mega theories and their corresponding strategies, predominantly grand schemes which were claimed to be universally valid. This uncompromising attitude made the ideas poorly fitted for implementation, given the heterogeneous sociopolitical cultural environments in which they were to be applied. The development debate was furthermore accompanied by endless, often stale dichotomous discussions on state versus market, rural as opposed to urban, import substitution versus export orientation and structural conditions versus agency as driving forces behind development. This development debate can be compared to an action-reaction sequence, oscillating between one universal absolute truth and solution and another; a dialectic, producing a series of theses and antitheses. On the other hand, real development syntheses have generally been lacking. What can now be sorted out of the seemingly chaotic development discourses are for the first time more conscious and serious attempts at synthesising, to the point of integrating apparently contrary approaches.

New Development Discourses

Changing Development Goals

There is in the development thinking of today a questioning not only of means, but question marks are explicitly being put on the goals of development, goals which in the earlier mainstream development debate were all heavily economically laden to the point of prescribing concretely particular structural development paths and of organising and sustaining production systems. A growing realisation is taking place that other factors than the pure economic ones are of importance: political culture, political institutions and history (Pieterse 2001).

To the new explicit development objectives belong the importance of living with multicultural structures and taking an interest in local knowledge and cultural practices. This stands in stark contrast to earlier monocultural approaches with put a heavy weight on generalisation and universal validity of ends and means in the development process. The reorientation also emphasises not only financial and physical capital, which were the hallmarks both of the modernisation and the neo-liberal discourses. The importance of cultivating and putting to practical use social and cultural as well as symbolic capital as advocated by Bourdieu (1977) is being put on the development agenda (see, for example, Caulkins 2001). Still another form of capital, *conceptual power* or *capital*, has been added by Neumann (2001) as a powerful tool in political discourse. To make use of social capital implies an emphasis on social relations, which are not only useful for personal interaction and consumer purposes but also as inputs in entrepreneurial activities. This is also the function of knowledge and skills which are embedded in cultural capital and of trust as inherent in symbolic capital. To make use of conceptual power means having the ability to institutionalise and activate important concepts which, in turn, impacts upon political action. This implies in reality more consideration for supply factors in the development process in contrast to the undue stress on demand, so typical of the Fordist tradition, the excessive practice of which was so heavily criticised by the proponents of the neo-liberal approach. It represents, however, a broader supply side approach than is typical of liberal capitalism. A challenging argument for an intimate relationship between culture and economic growth is given by Griffin (2000), who sees the importance of cultural diversity and cultural dynamics in the very growth process as a stimulant of innovation. Closely related to this development dimension is the new stress on capacity-building as one of the more immediate goals, paving the way among other things for people to choose among multiple options. This had been only slightly to the fore in the earlier development debate.

Developed over some time, but made more explicit in the late 1990s, is the capability approach with emphasis on human agency rather than structural factors. Mainly associated with the Nobel laureate Amartya Sen (1992, 1999), is the contention that development only has real meaning when considered as an expansion of human capabilities. Different from most welfare and development economists and certainly from the neo-liberal proponents, Sen's approach claims that emancipation from necessities which constrain human freedom and not utility is the basis of human well-being. The attainment of this well-being, which is the ultimate goal of any meaningful development, is dependent on human capabilities, which is the freedom to achieve alternative functioning combinations. Of the freedoms to be realised, Sen enumerates five as essentially instrumental: political freedom, economic faculties, social opportunities, guarantees of transparency and security of protection. Sen is a staunch proponent of democracy as a prerequisite for realising freedom. He is less explicit when it comes to ways of promoting development in the wanted direction. Later researchers have come forward with ideas of linking the capability approach more closely to social and political processes and to be concerned with relations of power, conflicts and struggles. This may be necessary in order to achieve the wanted expansion of capabilities in environments with a capability deficit. This is for instance the essence of a recent thought-provoking article by Shagmugaralnam (2001).

Simultaneously, there seems to be less controversy than before in the debate between "soft" versus "hard" supporters of growth, the former accepting growth as a prerequisite for a meaningful development and the latter admitting the necessity of reconsidering quality of growth and of acknowledging growth with redistribution as an important goal. Furthermore, the goals of Alternative Development have become less distinct from those of conventional development, as demodernisation and anti-development ideas have been abandoned by the former school (Hettne 1992). On the other side the former disciples of indiscriminate growth have incorporated softer objectives into their portfolio, as has happened with the World Bank. The revolutionary ideas of yesterday even seem, in some cases, to have become today's orthodoxy.

The sustainability debate, anchored in a consideration for the environment, has been a mighty impulse for this down-to-earth turn. Although still meeting with formidable counter-forces not only in the corporate world but also in political circles as testified by the 2001 Bonn summit, environment has become institutionalised through the notion sustainable development as a measure of economic and technological initiatives.

The convergence of different development ideas is thus increasingly tending towards a view of development as holism, whose main hallmarks are accountability, transparency, good governance, growth with a human face, participation, and eventually global reform. A new realisation has been accepted that the development discourse is in reality multiscalar, notably because the global level is increasingly being put on the development agenda. During the 1990s the world saw the most vigorous globalisation of the century. Although globalisation consists of several parallel processes that are intertwined – economic, social, and cultural – its most visible manifestation in the economic field in an extension of the power of the corporate network across the globe. Simultaneously, however, this has been accompanied in the political field by a lack of direction and regulatory institutions to set frames of reference and prevent crises. Certainly, there is inherent in the new development discourse countervailing forces to an indiscriminate individual and corporate display of power. Globalisation has brought people in different parts of the world closer together both by personal migration and other forms of interaction and by the growth of information and communication technologies.

An important aspect of globalisation is the increased power and impact of the mass media and other cultural forces. To some extent the combination of consumer mobilisation and alert mass media may become substitutes for politics as controlling and regulating institutions. "Reputation is on the stock exchange" (Matlary 2001). However, although globalisation is accepted as an irreversible fact by most development scholars, most of them as well as more and more reflecting people come out in favour of more systematic international political regulation and control systems as necessary in order to set right and sustain a balanced and sound development both on a global, regional, national and local scale. This is increasingly realised to be a strategic domain where leaving the field to corporate management alone may entail grave dangers in the long run. The establishment of new world governmental institutions is advocated by Emmerij (2000) and the quest for firmly democratically-rooted supranational institutions is reiterated by Ringen (2000). Pronk (2000), on the other hand, argues for an activation of already existing institutions. So does also Habermas (2000), who vigorously underlines the need for politics to regain the initiative lost to the corporate world primarily by activating the institutions of civil society in a global context. At the gvernmental level, he strongly advocates the development of broader unions, pointing to the EU as a beginning in a global network. Pronk also strongly warns against the dangers inherent in globalisation of annexing the whole world into a technological and economic monoculture, which in many parts of the world would mean a renewed dependency and even a cultural re-colonisation. Others, among them Suthcliffe, see globalisation as an opportunity also from a progressive point of view. A starting point in global regulation might be to fight for the right of all people "to be allowed to cross national frontiers with at least the same facility as they are now crossed by goods and money" (Suthcliffe 1999).

Several non-governmental organisations, the most well-known among these being Attac, all with an increasingly popular following, are likewise seriously preoccupied with setting new governance goals. Among these are ideas of taxing global financial accumulation, the so-called Tobin tax. Such regulatory measures and many more, would, to be realised, imply putting public institutions back into a role of management and control, so far, though, without a clear design of institutional rearrangement.

Towards a New Understanding

While a gradual reorientation is thus taking place in development thinking, development itself still seems to follow its own age-old logic. One of the threats to more balanced world socio-economic development that emerges from the new ideas sketched above is the existing unilateralism in world politics accompanied by strong military power on the one hand, and looser reins on capital on the other. The corporate world is, in addition, still more concerned with short-term financial gains than with long-term real economic development. There are, however, elements also in world economic development that may lead to a broader acceptance of and a convergence with the new development ideas over a future horizon. This ideological debate coincides with a restructuring of the production and distribution regimes towards more flexible organisation, supported by a continuous technological innovation, primarily in information technology. This fact both expands and constrains development opportunities. Primarily, however, the change has prompted a reorientation of the economic thinking towards realising that the production function is more complicated and differentiated than stated in the classical and neo-classical economic models. Knowledge has become an important factor of its own, acquired through a learning process, which is both formal and informal and where many types of knowledge are activated; there is also tacit knowledge, a form of capacity- and competence-building, which is often localised. This signifies a shift from a one-dimensional to a multi-dimensional understanding of development. Also in this respect, therefore, by eliciting traditional and indigenous knowledge, the cultural context may become crucial in understanding and promoting a development process. This is part of what we understand by indigenous modernisation, which has gained increased understanding in the emergent new development thinking. This modernisation discourse which is less universal and more contextual than the conventional modernisation ideas of fifty years ago means a revalorisation of the role of existing social and cultural capital and is valid both in the industrial and the developing world. In the Third World context increasing emphasis is put on this part of the world's role as producers of modernity, or, to be more exact and in line with the contextual approach, of different modernities (Pred and Watts 1992). Development with its costs and benefits is also seen more and more as part of a global process and a task for all parts of the world, not as in the heyday of mainstream development imperialism as something reserved for the Third World.

Development is urgently needed in the North, too. "The South is in the North and vice versa". This reorientation implies a questioning and even critique of the reigning social engineering and planning, which has resulted in the two-thirds society with a growing social exclusion (Nederveen Pieterse 2001). Nederveen Pieterse sees development promotion as a multisectoral and multiscalar project, including, as well as the state and the market as agencies of development, international and regional institutions and regimes, urban and local government and civil institutions.

The new and broader development discourse has gradually percolated into mainstream development thinking, which is still and even increasingly global in outlook as a consequence of the growing global corporate structure. There is, however, today a hiatus in the former broad agreement among the development institutions, called the Washington consensus, comprising as the main actors the Wall Street financial institutions, the IMF and the World Bank in concert. From the mid-1990s, notably, the bank has, as testified in several of its annual reports, been approaching the UN development agencies like the UNDP in its proposals of development promotion. Although critics like Wade (2001) still cast doubt on the bank's ideological "conversion", there are clear sign of the reorientation, reflected in their advocacy of a "softer" development promotion in contrast to its past reputation as a typical hardware investment institution. More attention has been paid than before to institutions and management (World Bank 1977) and to education and knowledge (World Bank 1998). This has implied a more pragmatic and positive attitude towards the state and its role in the process, which now, by and large, is seen as an enabler. This new attitude has also been voiced of late not only by advocates of official institutions but also by the research community, by proponents of Alternative Development like Friedmann (1992). In line with neo-liberals, but from a different motivation, these circles had earlier looked with suspicion upon the role of the state, often preferring NGOs as programme and project initiators and actors in the implementation process. A realisation has now grown of the limitations of civil organisations, particularly in the political field, making them less acceptable at face value. Instead, a multivocal and pluriactive understanding of development implying a synergy between state, local government, market, and civil society is gaining ground. This reorientation may open for supply-side social development, making it more stable and sustainable in the long term.

This reinterpretation means that there is in the development discourse of today fewer absolute ideological underpinnings, when disregarding some "diehard" proponents on both sides (in the neo-classical field Lal [1995], and among advocates of anti-development and post-development ideas Amin [1999] and Korten [1995]). A growing realisation has dawned that development processes are not predetermined and prestructured, but subject to human construction. As such they are less universal than is explained by the grand structural theories and to a large extent contextual in contrast to the monolithic structures which were marketed yesterday. Constructivism rather than structuralism seems to have become the new paradigm, having found a common denominator in structuration theory. We can reinterpret these currents as a farewell to the grand, unitary, universal theories, a fact which in reality means a lowering of theoretical ambition. Simultaneously, it may hopefully imply a more realistic platform of operationalisation, better adjusted to the environment in which development is going to take place than was the case with the broad generalised models. Methodologically, scenarios rather than universal models may be the answer in the structuring development discourses of the future. This reorientation may also provide a way out of the intellectual impasse which characterised so much of development thinking during the 1980s and early 1990s. However, important as this is for down to earth implementation, there is in this reorientation the danger of less holistic development approaches, a sort of pragmatism which at worst can mean an intellectual muddling through (Lindblom 1973) and can reduce the development discourse to an ideographic analysis.   Without a broader recognition of the predominant social processes, some overarching generalisation, it will be hard to formulate any common identity or community of interest, which is necessary to effect social change.

The New Development Discourse and Marginal Regions: Some Reflections

A development path following the new discourse will certainly impact upon most regional entities and definitely on marginal regions. Which will be the most preponderant consequences of a possible reorientation are, on the other hand, subject to uncertainty and what can be concluded will therefore to a large extent be speculation.

When, today, there is talk about a rural revival, as heralded among others by Ilbery (1997), this is, by and large, a city-near phenomenon, driven by an unsatisfied urban middle class in pursuit of a good life while simultaneously enjoying the fruits of city life. It is particularly, although not exclusively, an emerging Anglo-American way of life. The globalisation process up to now has, on the other hand, largely bypassed or had adverse consequences for most marginal regions of the world. It has hit the outposts of the industrial economy in sparsely populated remote areas particularly hard, such as one-company manufacturing towns and other raw material and semi-processing plants and settlements.   To be fair, some of these have succeeded in restructuring their old and partly obsolete and vulnerable economies, but the bulk of these places have failed in their restructuring efforts or have simply given up. A growing globalisation without any regulation will certainly prolong and exacerbate these trends.

If, on the other hand, some of the new ideas and the popular movements in connection with these, which have been outlined above, gain increased prominence, materialise and become implemented, there may be hope also for marginal regions to enter a more positive development path in the future. Even then, however, there are many prerequisites to be met. An important prerequisite for success is a reorientation to indigenous entrepreneurship instead of trying to promote development only by redistribution to lagging regions from the outside. To shape is more important in the long run than to share (Hansen, this volume). Consistent strategies along these endogenous lines will involve a conjunction between the new orientation on the threshold of the twenty-first century and, from a development point of view, attention to supply side economics as a complement to a predominantly demand and redistribution economy. It will, ceteris paribus, promote greater stability in the industrial structure. To the extent that external impulses are still necessary in addition to indigenous capacity-building and entrepreneurship, the conventional conception of assistance should be replaced by development cooperation through a process of mutual empowerment akin to the ideas of promotion of capabilities as voiced by Sen (1999). The assistance instruments were part and parcel of the mainstream modernisation ideas at their worst, embodied in top-down planning by moving money instead of capacity. Both these ideas and their practical implementation dominated for a disproportionately long time the development discourse for alleviation of stagnation and poverty in marginal areas both in the South and the North.

Another condition of success would be promotion of better utilisation of the non-monetary resources, particularly cultural and symbolic capital. An active use of networks can moreover serve as a good development resource (Bukve 2001). This development path has been convincingly demonstrated as a relevant device in the very region of this conference, a region which by most universal, objective standards possesses most of the criteria of a marginal region. Instead the area displays many of the characteristics of a dynamic, affluent district, where both the carving out of industrial niches, often with basis in tradition and more broadly-based economic development can be traced back to specific, close social relations, cultural identity and a particular business culture. These development resources may have a wider application for marginal areas by taking advantage of the mutual reinforcement existing in smaller, dense environments of knowledge generation and transfer, especially of tacit, not yet formalised knowledge.

Another development path is to work for a stronger emphasis on sustainability, which pertains to most forms of socioeconomic development, but primarily to the sectors of agriculture, forestry and fisheries, activities generally "over-represented" in marginal areas. The role of sustainable fisheries have been amply outlined by Grønnevet (2001). As far as agriculture is concerned, the so-called productivist paradigm which has dominated northern agriculture and frequently misinterpreted in the south, now seems to be partly succeeded by a post-productivist transition, characterised by integration of agriculture within broader rural economic and environmental objectives (Ilbery and Bowler 1997). The exaggerated belief in return to scale and hyperindustrialisation in farming has lost some of its momentum, reflected for a long time in the huge sectorwise surpluses, particularly in the EU agriculture. Industrial agriculture has also been blamed for the recent outbreaks of livestock diseases in Western Europe, a contention which is supported even in responsible political circles. The EU agricultural commissioner Fischler has had to admit that the intensive agriculture with a premium on quantity has reached an unacceptable limit. It has led to increasing concentration and, with it, centralisation. The excessive transportation of agricultural commodities has been a result. All these elements are producing adverse environmental effects. A plea for organisation on a smaller and hence more human scale (also in the context of food security) is increasingly gaining followers. This is closely linked to the notion of quality products and services promotion as a part of rural development policy (Ilbery and Kneafsey 1998, 1999). It is based on the idea of niche products, offered to a segmented market, products perceived to be unique and of high quality according to objective and subjective indicators. By giving the products a regional image, small and scattered regional supply monopolies may be created, appealing to specific consumer segments. These production niches which may include both commodities and services are mainly although not necessarily built on small-scale production, and should as such be appropriate for several marginal regions. In recent years the EU commission has developed a procedure for certification of quality agricultural products and foodstuffs with a regional origin. Still, there remains for these products a marketing problem, which is particularly acute for the small-scale individual producers in marginal areas. This was emphasized as a serious bottleneck by Jenkins and Parrot (2001). A systematic construction of marketing channels by institutional arrangements and incorporated in extra-local networks could, according to Ilbery and Kneafsey (1999), bring specialised commodities and services onto a wider market. The authors firmly believe in the potential of the quality products and services approach and cite an EU Commission-supported study, RIPPLE, from 12 European regions, as evidence of positive, outward marketing results.

Direct transactions with foreign customers in the home environment is also possible, notably in combination with tourism in a more systematic way than has been the case up to now. Environmental qualities and other tourism products also have an unrealised potential of their own. The marketing of rural places and regions still lags behind city marketing as a development instrument. It could be realised through small-scale and partly interactive tourism, as part and parcel of the idea of sustainability, increasingly being marketed as eco-tourism, a term which unfortunately more often than not is being misinterpreted and misused. But eco-tourism correctly interpreted and organised should be particularly useful for marginal regions. In its essence it presupposes small local communities to be realised. Finally, some scope exists in the environmental field for rural people in managing cultural landscapes. This is, for example, part of the reoriented agricultural policy of the EU, embodied among other measures in Agenda 2000.

It is at this point important to emphasise that what we have advocated are possibilities. Development paths along the above lines are met with a number of countervailing forces and constraints. Strong vested interests both on the supply and demand sides and in the political field will certainly still favour a highly specialised and productivistic agriculture. This type of farming will probably continue as the most common management practice. There are limits to new niches of quality production, which are also easy for newcomers to copy. Strong retail chains, increasingly international in operation, standardising their product-lines and mainly competing on price, are formidable countervailing forces in niche development. Other important problems also pertain to activities linked to globalisation and presuppose better global governance. A fundamental constraint lies in problems linked to indigenous development as such. Its prerequisites are capability, creativity and capacity-building: knowledge in the widest sense of the term. We are all painfully aware how a number of marginal areas have been drained of just these resources, many for a very long time and to the point of needing in-migration in order to accomplish a process of reactivation. This is a tricky issue. Partly, indigenous development is dependent on culture. Great differences exist in the various regions in their abilities to realise these goals as a result of different cultural attitudes and traditions. This may be one of the main obstacles in achieving niche developments where there are attitudes of suspicion and envy, endemic to the rather dense environments we are dealing with in this context and to which we as serious researchers should not close our eyes.

Finally, marginality manifests itself through a variety of forms. There is no standard marginal region but many degrees of marginality, often interspersed between and interwoven in each other. As matters stand, we would be wise to qualify our optimism. However, the chances for success are greater under the new development discourse than they were when the conventional, more universal ideologies were the leading tenets. On the other hand, realisation puts a heavy responsibility also on local people and requires in most cases far more elaborate informal and formal organisation than that which is common in most marginal regions today.

Conclusions

Development thinking has gradually become more discursive by analysing narratives and even myths, deconstructing and reconstructing them, adding reflexivity and hermeneutic interpretation to development studies. By systematizing discourses over time, we find in the aftermath of the Second World War a set of development ideas which were monolithic and claimed universal validity in the sense of being applicable at any time in any part of the world. In the form of development economics, modernisation theory, dependency theory and neo-liberalism these systems of thought have followed upon each other but also lived side by side. The essence of all these theories is a perception of development as socioeconomic growth, Eurocentric in character, although dependency thinking originated in the South and added some more indigenous qualities to the discourse. Towards the 1980s a counterpoint discourse emerged, characterised by more contextual thinking, a grassroots participatory and sustainable direction of development thought with some weight placed on sociocultural values and variables.

These cognitive development paths signify a seesawing, partly zigzaging dialectic, when seen in a historical perspective. It has been succeeded in the present development debate by a more holistic view of development. This applies to geographical scale where world systems, according to Amin and Thrift (1993), are becoming more important units, but in a dialectic with national regional and local entities. It also applies to the players in the development process, as the earlier sectorwise actors in state, market, local government and civil society have become more integrated as agents of change. This signals a rejection of the universal grand theories and their prescriptions and an adoption of more contextual principles and values, to the point though of paving the way for separate, ideographic discourses.

Marginal regions may be affected in different ways by the new development trends. Up to now globalisation has, by and large, meant negative impacts. Still, there are many constraints working against a positive development process inherent in the economic structure and cultural values of the local environments in the regions in question. Some hope has been kindled of late of a more positive development through small-scale quality commodities and services production which may give specific regions a comparative advantage by developing their own trademarks and even copyrights. Closely related to this is promotion of eco-tourism and a selective return to a small-scale and environmentally-friendly structure in agriculture, necessitated by increased concern for food security. All these are measures could favour marginal areas. However, it should be stressed that marginality manifests itself in multiple forms and solutions to the problems must be worked out contextually within each region. This puts great responsibility on the people inhabiting these regions.

References

Amin, S. 1976. *Unequal Development*. Brighton: Harvester Press.

Amin, S. 1989. *Eurocentrism*. London: Zed.

Amin, S. 1990. *Delinking: Towards a Polycentric World.* London: Zed.

Amin, S. 1999. *Spectres of Capitalism: A Critique of Current Intellectual Fashions.* London: Zed.

Amin, A. and N. Thrift. 1993. Globalisation, institutional thickness and local prospects. *Revue d'Économie régionale et urbaine* 3: 405-427.

Bourdieu. P. 1977. *Outline of a Theory of Practice.* Cambridge: Cambridge University Press.

Brohman, J. 1996. *Popular Development: Rethinking the Theory and Practice of Development.* Oxford: Blackwell.

Bukve, O. 2001. Local development networks: A comparative case study. Paper given to The Sixteenth International Seminar on Marginal Regions, Ålesund/Volda, Norway, 5-12 August.

Caulkins, D. D. 2001. Social capital and local identity as resources for development. Paper given to The Sixteenth International Seminar on Marginal Regions, Åalesund/Volda, Norway, 5-12 August.

Crush, J. 1996. *The Power of Development.* London: Routledge.

Domar, E. 1957. *Essays in the Theory of Economic Growth.* London: Oxford University Press.

Emmerij, L. 2000. World economic changes at the threshold of the twenty-first century. In J. Nederveen Pieterse (ed.), *Global Futures: Shaping Globalisation.* London: Zed.

Escobar, A. 1992. Reflections on "development": Grassroots approaches and alternative politics in the Third World. *Futures,* June: 411-436.

Friedmann, J. 1992. *Empowerment: The Politics of Alternative Development.* Oxford: Blackwell.

Foucault, M. 1977. Truth and power. In Allessandro Fontana and Pasquale Pasquino (eds.), *Microfisica del potere: interventi politici.* Torino: Einaudi. Also published in J. D. Faubion (ed.), 2001, *Power: Essential Works of Foucault 1954-1984*, Vol. 3, London: Allen Lane.

Fukuyama, F. 1992. *The End of History and the Last Man.* London: Hamilton.

Frank, A. G. 1969. *Latin America: Industrial Development or Revolution?* New York: Monthly Review Press.

Frank, A. G. 1981. *Crisis in the Third World.* New York: Holmes and Meyer.

Galtung, J. 1976. The politics of self-reliance. Conflict and Peace Research Paper 44, University of Oslo.

Griffin, K. 2000. Culture and economic growth: The state and globalisation. In J. Nederveen Pieterse (ed.), *Global Futures: Shaping Globalisation.* London: Zed.

Grønnevet, L. 2001. Threats and possibilities in modern fisheries. Paper given to The Sixteenth International Seminar on Marginal Regions, Aalesund/Volda, Norway, 5-12 August.

Habermas, J. 2000. *Den postnationella konstellationen.* Göteborg: Daidalos.

Hansen, J. C. This volume, Chapter 1.

Harrod, R. 1948. *Towards a Dynamic Economics.* London: Macmillan.

Hettne, B. 1992. New trends in development theory. The Hague: Institute of Social Studies. Unpublished paper.

Hirschman, A. 1982. The rise and decline of development economics. In Gersovitz (eds.), *The Theory of Experience of Economic Development. Essays in Honour of Sir Arthur Lewis.* London: Allen and Unwin.

Ilbery, B. (ed). 1997. *The Geography of Rural Change.* London: Longman.

Ilbery, B. and I. Bowler. 1997. From agricultural productivism to post-productivism. In B. Ilbery (ed.), *The Geography of Rural Change.* London: Longman.

Ilbery, B. and M. Kneafsey. 1998. Product and place: Promoting quality products and services in the lagging regions of the European Union. *European Urban and Regional Studies*, 5: 329-341.

Ilbery, B. and M. Kneafsey. 1999. Niche markets and speciality food products in Europe: Towards a research agenda. *Environment and Planning A*, 31: 2008-2022.

Jenkins, T. and N. Parrot. 2001. Looking to the land: Regional imagery, quality products and development strategy in marginal rural regions. In R. Byron and J. Hutson (eds.), *Community Development on The North Atlantic Margin*. Aldershot: Ashgate.

Korten, D. C. 1995. *When Corporations Rule the World*. London: Earthscan.

Lal, D. 1995. The misconceptions of development economics. In S. Corbridge (ed.), *Development Studies: A Reader*. London: Edward Arnold.

Lindblom, C. 1973. The science of muddling through. In A. Faludi (ed.), *A Reader in Planning Theory*. London: Pergamon.

Matlary, J. H. 2001. Omdømme er på børs (Reputation is on the stock exchange). *Dagens Næringsliv*, 20 July: 3.

Nederveen Pieterse, J. 2001. *Development Theory: Deconstructions. Reconstructions*. London: Sage.

Neumann, I. B. 2001. *Norge – En kritikk: begrepsmakt i Europadebatten*. Oslo: Pax.

Nurkse, R. 1953. *Problems of Capital Formation in Underdeveloped Countries*. Oxford: Blackwell.

Prebisch, R. 1950. *The Economic Development of Latin America and its Principal Problems*. New York: United Nations Department of Economic Affairs.

Pred, A. and M. J. Watts. 1992. *Reworking Modernity: Capitalisms and Symbolic Discontent*. New Brunswick, N. J.: Rutgers University Press.

Pronk, J. 2000. Globalisation: A developmental approach. In J. Nederveen Pieterse (ed.), *Global Futures: Shaping Globalisation*. London: Zed.

Ringen, S. 2002. Inn i frehetens rike. In T. Frogner et al. (eds.): *Falker: Om vitenskap og samfunn*. Oslo: Gyldendal.

Rist, G. 1997. *The History of Development: From Western Origin to Global Faith.* London: Zed.

Rodan-Rosenstein, P. 1943. Problems of industrialisation in eastern and southeastern Europe. *Economic Journal,* 52: 202-211.

Seers, D. et al. 1979. *Underdeveloped Europe: Studies in Core-periphery Relations.* Brighton: Harvester Press.

Seers, D. 1979. The new meaning of development. In D. Lehman (ed.), *Development Theory: Four Critical Studies.* London: Cass.

Sen, A. 1992. *Inequality Re-examined.* Oxford: Clarendon.

Sen, A. 1999. *Development as Freedom.* New Delhi: Oxford University Press.

Shanmugaratnam, N. 2001. On the meaning of development: An exploration of the capability approach. *Forum for Development Studies* 28, 2: 263-288.

Singer, H. W. 1978. *The Strategy of International Development: Essays in the Economics of Backwardness.* Sir Alec Cairncross and Mohinder Puri (eds.), London: Macmillan.

Stöhr, W. and D. R. F. Taylor (eds.). 1981. *Development from Above or Below? The Dialectics of Regional Planning in Developing Countries.* Chichester: Wiley.

Suthcliffe, B. 1999. The place of development in theories of imperialism and globalization. In R. Munck and D. O'Hearn (eds.), *Critical Development Theory: Contribution to a New Paradigm.* London: Zed.

Tucker, V. 1999. The myth of development: A critique of a Eurocentric discourse. In R. Munck and D. O'Hearn (eds.), *Critical Development Theory: Contributions to a New Paradigm.* London: Zed.

Wallerstein, I. 1979. *The Politics of the World Economy.* Cambridge: Cambridge University Press.

World Bank, 1997. *The State in a Changing World: World Development Report 1997.* New York: Oxford University Press.

World Bank, 1998. *Knowledge for Development: World Development Report 1998/99.* New York: Oxford University Press.

PART TWO:
MARKETING MARGINALITY
AND HISTORY

Chapter 3

Conceptualising Integrated Tourism in Europe's Marginal Rural Regions[1]

TIM JENKINS AND TOVE OLIVER

Introduction

It has often been noted that considerable unrealised rural development potential exists in more effective integrative linkages between local resources, local economic activities and tourism in marginal rural regions (MRRs). The pivotal position of tourism in this context arises because many of the products and resources of MRRs potentially have very strong connections with tourism: products such as crafts and foods, for example, can be marketed together with tourism as a form of linked exploitation of rural and regional imagery. Tourism can permeate local and regional economies in a complex manner which, on the one hand, may extend the tourism product and its value dimensions in ways which are not yet fully theorised or understood, and, on the other hand, may lead to direct income benefits to the localities concerned and to wider developmental benefits based on association, synergy and participation. This paper proposes a conceptual framework for an investigation of the nature of integrated tourism (IT). We start from the premise that tourism, and especially rural tourism, is more than an economic activity and that tourists can be involved in complex ways with their destination localities. We seek to explore the nature of IT in a way which will both stand alone as a theoretical overview and also inform the development of future research.

Tourism is an inherently ill-defined term and not an especially useful one in demarcating a distinct sphere of social practice (Rojek and Urry 1997). It is a fuzzy concept which merges and overlaps with activities such as leisure, shopping, travel, pilgrimage, hobbying, excursion, exploration and study. In investigating IT, we need to take a broad view of tourism, not least in order to encompass the multiplicity of regional traits which are inevitably encountered on a European scale. For example, in some countries and regions, visits to second homes in the countryside may be regarded as tourism, in other countries and regions, tourism may include visits to friends and relatives, while in some regions, tourism may consist largely of day visitors from nearby urban areas.

Operational definitions of tourism either in time (for example, with reference to a specified number of nights away from home) or in space (for example, with reference to specialist resorts or locations) are essentially arbitrary and analytically fruitless. Tourism's essence lies in otherness, cultural contrast and in organised dislocation from the everyday (Smith 1989 Urry 1990, Rojek and Urry 1997). Further, tourism presupposes its opposite-- eventual return to the familiarity of everyday life: this expectation of return is a pre-requisite for a worthwhile touristic experience. Tourism is one expression of the increasing importance of non-material forms of production and consumption, including the well-documented demand for rurality and its associated attributes of closeness to nature, healthy environments, tradition, heritage and authenticity. The very disadvantages of MRRs, such as extensive agriculture, distance from large population centres, and the persistence of traditional activities, cultures and ways of life, can therefore assume positive values for tourism.

Tourism, and particularly tourism in rural areas, represents a process of consumption of products and services to which real, imagined or fabricated values are attached. It is important, therefore, that tourism be seen as more than an economic activity. In addition to analysing operational data on visitor flows, financial impacts and so on, it is necessary to probe tourists" motivations in order to unpack the cultural and ideological baggage which they take with them to their destinations and to trace the "mythologies of escape" (Rojek and Urry 1997) involved. Tourism is also in many ways a "homage to territoriality" (MacCannell 1992), by tourists eager to experience otherness but, unlike other migrants, secure in the knowledge that they will shortly be reconnected with their origins. MacCannell's observation is especially pertinent to tourism in rural areas and, in discussing rural tourism, it is important to understand rurality as more than a geographical concept. In the tourism context, rurality reflects a lifestyle, a set of values and an environment desirable for its difference, relative isolation and pace of living (Long and Lane 2000), as well as for its special aesthetic qualities and even its spirituality (BlaΡek, 1995). Rural culture is a key commodity in the tourist landscape of many rural destinations (Hopkins 1998, Bonnieux and Rainelli 2000).

Tourism and its associated activities potentially offer many prospects for rural areas. They offer employment and income opportunities spread over a wide geographical range, often repeatedly utilising the same resources, and they have the potential to act as an incentive for conserving and regenerating natural and cultural assets (Greffe 1990, Patin 1997). Rural tourism goes beyond simply complementing traditional activities such as agriculture, and can act as a catalyst for a whole range of new entrepreneurial activities, partnerships and networks. Inevitably, however, there are contested opinions as to what is desirable in rural tourism development and, moreover, there is no universal agreement about the net benefits of rural tourism. In part, this reflects a shortage of theoretical research placing rural tourism in a conceptual framework (Butler and Clark 1992). As a result, tourism has only recently received serious academic attention as a mechanism for rural development (Garcia Cuesta 1996, Slee et al. 1997, Page and Getz 1997, Stríbrná 1997, Lagos 1998, Bensahel and Donsimoni 1999), and the dynamics involved in exploiting tourism as an opportunity for the revitalisation of rural communities and economies are not yet fully understood (OECD 1993). It is anticipated that some of these shortcomings can be overcome by developing the concept of integrated tourism (IT) as an aid to understanding tourism's potential for contributing to integrated rural development in MRRs.

Integrated Tourism

A brief analysis of how the term "integrated tourism" is currently understood by tourism theorists, practitioners and documentation across six European countries (Jenkins & Oliver 2001) reveals little common understanding, consensus or precision and much overlap with concepts such as "ecological tourism" (Slováčková 2000), "sustainable tourism" and "tourisme durable" (McIntyre 1997). While the concept of integration, together with analogous concepts such as partnerships, is used pervasively, it is clear that the concept is understood in a number of different ways. These include:

- *spatial integration,* as in the integration of core tourist areas with areas where tourism is less well developed;

- *human resource integration,* as in the integration of working people into the economy as a means of combating social exclusion (by education and training, for example);

- *institutional integration,* as in the integration of agencies into partnerships or other formal semi-permanent structures;

- *innovative integration,* as in the integration of new ideas and processes into the tourism "product" to achieve growth or competitive advantage;

- *economic integration,* as in the integration of other economic sectors with tourism, particularly retailing and local industries such as farming;

- *social integration,* as in the integration of tourism with other trends in the socio-economy, notably the drive for quality, and concerns for environmental (particularly landscape) protection and sustainable development;

- *policy integration,* as in the integration of tourism with broader national and regional goals for economic growth, diversification and development;

- *temporal integration,* as in the integration of the past with current economic, social and cultural needs and requirements, especially through the commodification of heritage; and

- *personal integration,* as in the integration of tourists into local communities as "guests", such that they occupy the same physical spaces, satisfy their existential and material needs in the same manner, and become embedded in the same value chains as members of the host society.

In conceptualising IT, we seek to encompass most, if not all, of these uses of the term "integration". Broadly, we define IT as:

tourism which is explicitly linked to the economic, social, cultural, natural and human structures of the localities in which it takes place.

In practical terms, it is:

tourism which has clear connections with local resources, activities, products, other production and service industries, and a participatory local community.

IT is a multi-faceted concept linking tourism into a series of domains (including those formed by tourism gatekeepers, local businesses, local resource controllers, host communities, institutions, policy and regulation) across a variety of dimensions (including the economic, social, cultural and natural) in a range of manifestations (including those represented by resources, activities, events, facilities, services and products). As a result, a wide range of potential points of integration are apparent, involving a variety of networks, integrative processes, impacts and actors. Figure 3.1 illustrates this framework for integration. Tourists are potentially associated with the business and community domains through a range of dimensions and manifestations, while institutional structures influence the whole process which in turn is underpinned by the policy and regulatory domain.

DOMAINS

Conceptual

Processes of integration	Impacts of integrated tourism	Roles of relevant actors

Tourism

Tourism gatekeepers

Resources	Activities/events	Facilities/services	Products
economic	economic	economic	economic
social	social	social	
cultural	cultural	cultural	cultural
natural		natural	natural

Businesses and resource controllers

Communities

Institutional structures

Policy and regulation

Figure 3.1   Integrated tourism: A framework for integration

In addition to taking this domain- and network-based view of IT, it is necessary to theorise IT as a logical outcome of a complex contextual environment. This includes numerous socio-economic trends in production and consumption (for example, reactions against materialism and an increasing concern for broader notions of the quality of life) and the public, actor-specific and sector-specific conventions that underpin such trends (for example, moves away from purely commercial conventions towards more ecological ones). Figure 3.2, based on conventions theory and the "four worlds of production" (Salais and Storper 1992, Storper and Salais 1997, see also Cuvelier 1998), places IT within a conventions framework. This suggests that a successful IT trajectory is towards the quadrant defined by the poles of dedicated and specialised (as opposed to generic and standardised) production, where ecological, domestic, and non-industrial, non-commercial conventions are paramount.

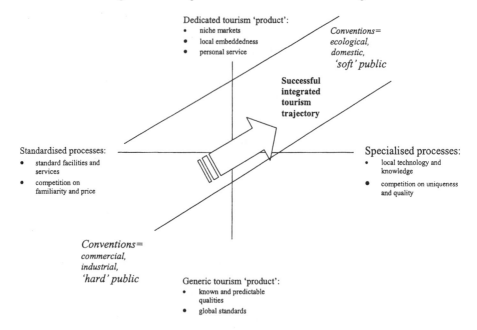

Figure 3.2   Theorising integrated tourism within a conventions framework

Source: Salais and Storper 1992, Storper and Salais 1997

Benefits and Key Features of Integrated Tourism

The theoretical benefits of IT are likely to be wide-ranging (Muñoz de Escalona 1994) and to comprise both static and dynamic benefits, benefits which can be quantified, and benefits which are best analysed qualitatively. The potential benefits can be categorised under five headings:

- *direct economic benefits:* for example, integrative linkages between tourism and local economies have considerable potential to increase the value added in, and reduce the value leakage from, rural areas, leading to improved income and employment multipliers;

- *experiential benefits:* for example, IT should provide "consumers" with a distinctively local and quality package of products and services, resulting in better experiences for both tourists and host communities;

- *conservation benefits:* for example, IT should improve the incentives for the conservation and regeneration of resources, both natural and man-made;

- *developmental benefits:* IT can become a path to rural pluriactivity and rural multifunctionality, providing valuable new opportunities for the development of MRRs which goes beyond a simple compensation for agricultural decline. IT can permit a wide range of local economic actors to benefit from the use of a locality's resources, it should stimulate positive local responses to market trends such as market segmentation, niche marketing and new product development, and it should allow for the potentially beneficial exploitation of rural and regional imagery; and

- *synergistic benefits:* IT provides an increased likelihood of co-ordinated and consistent institutional policies for rural and regional development, and it should encourage partnerships between a range of local actors who can then reap wider developmental benefits based on association, synergy and participation.

In evaluating the developmental benefits of IT, it is helpful to identify a number of its key features which we categorise under the headings of networks, scale, endogeneity, sustainability, embeddedness, complementarity and empowerment. Some of these concepts are discussed further when we develop a cultural economy approach to IT in the next main section of this chapter.

1. Networks

IT both implies and requires a focus on networks, relationships and partnerships. Networks and relationships may be historically layered, providing actors with a sense of attachment to place, or they may take newer forms, providing possibilities for new institutional structures and new types of entrepreneurial activity (Kneafsey 2001). Further, they may be vertical, involving the formation of extra-local alliances, or they may be horizontal, co-ordinating local activities and local actor relationships (Murdoch 2000a).

A major purpose of networks which implicate producers, communities and institutions within a locality is to capture an organisational rent for that locality by attracting consumers into the networks and capitalising on their willingness to pay for meanings which reflect territorial quality and thereby enhance the use-value of the locality's products and services (Pecqueur 2001).

2. Scale

IT has to be conducted at an appropriate scale with regard to local structures if integration is to be effective. Scale refers to the size and extent of tourism resources and the volume and impact of tourism activities in relation to the existing economic, social, cultural and resource base. Tourism provision can range from small-scale (for example, specialised niche market tourism and soft tourism) to large-scale (for example, low cost facilities relying on scale economies, and hard tourism).

The question of the scale of development activity within self-defined economic and cultural localities is crucial (Ray 1998, see also Daly 2000). IT needs to take account of the carrying capacity of tourism locations (Sharpley 1996): such capacity is not simply physical or ecological, but may also have social, cultural, psychological and, not least, economic dimensions.

3. Endogeneity

IT is closely associated with the concept of endogenous development and with a sense of place. Endogenous development sets development within a local (or territorial) framework and centres both on motivating development within a locality and on the relationships between a locality and its wider economic and political environments (Lowe et al. 1995). Under such forms of development, economic activity is based on place-specific resources, economic, social and cultural developments are structured to retain maximum benefits within a locality by using, and adding value to, local resources, and development is contextualised by focusing on the requirements, capacities and values of local people (Ray 2000). Endogenous development strategies include focussing on economic, environmental and cultural resources which are distinctive, and developing the products and services derived from such resources usually means a strong local participation in development which may, in turn, increase awareness of local cultural identity.

Endogenous forces (such as local entrepreneurship, specialist local knowledge and strong local partnerships) link people, innovation, products, investment and capital to place. They thus raise the profile of locality and thereby become the motivators of a form of development based on a sense of place and community involvement, which is specifically associated with local and regional resources, activities, products and actors.

4. Sustainability

Mirroring the close connection between culture and sustainability (Jenkins 2000), IT is closely linked to the notion of sustainable development, a term which in itself is normative and relative. The concept of sustainability is a useful guiding fiction which stimulates and organises discourse around a problematic issue without the rigour of a precise definition (McCool and Moisey 2001) and which, seen as a process (Aronsson 2000), stimulates the need for economic, social, institutional and structural change. Further, the concept is multi-dimensional: interpreted in its broadest sense, it has economic, socio-cultural, political, geographical and ecological aspects.

In many respects, *integrated* tourism overlaps with *sustainable* tourism. However, sustainable tourism remains a somewhat passive concept, concerned with minimising tourism's impacts rather than optimising its benefits. IT, on the other hand, is a more dynamic concept, concerned with energising local development through the creation of new partnerships and networks which link previously disparate economic, social, cultural, natural and human activities and resources.

5. *Embeddedness*

In emphasising the importance of relationships and networks, the concept of IT also recognises that networks are always embedded in particular localities. The territorial context within which network formation takes place is, therefore, crucially important. Embeddedness implies not only that resources or activities are directly linked to place (Pecqueur 2001), but also that relationships are formed within particular socio-cultural contexts in particular localities, and the unique socio-cultural characteristics and identities which are embedded in places help to shape relationships and networks (Hinrichs 2000, Murdoch 2000b).

Conceptualising IT as a developmental tool for MRRs requires an examination of its potential for embeddedness within the wider functioning economy and society. Embedded resources and activities tend to have high levels of economic, social and cultural linkage derived from attached cultural meanings: for example, embedded tourism activities may be a part of local social and recreational life. Conversely, disembedded resources and activities may result in social and cultural detachment and high levels of economic leakage from a locality. However, the picture is complicated by the fact that tourism resources normally need a degree of disembeddedness: excessive embeddedness can curtail the market reach of a local tourism product which will then remain marginal in relation to the globalised tourism sector.

6. *Complementarity*

IT recognises the importance of complementarity. Rural activities and resource use potentially involve competition by a range of stakeholders.

Tourism itself may be complementary (for example, it may take place alongside traditional agriculture on a farm where resources are available) or substitutional (for example, it may replace farming entirely, as with caravan sites on some small coastal farms). Tourism activities may also be complementary (for example, conservation-related tourism in a conservation area) or substitutional (for example, a foreign-owned all-inclusive tourist resort may conflict with conservation activities within a locality).

Complementarity among resources and activities is likely to lead to increased partnership and synergy, substitution among resources and activities is likely to lead to increased competition and conflict. It is thus essential to see tourism not as an isolated activity or sector, but to place it in a broader social context in which relationships and networking play a key role.

7. *Empowerment*

In its emphasis on place, endogeneity, embeddedness, community involvement and networks, IT is inextricably associated with empowerment. Empowerment is the manifestation of local control over resources and activities, the potential for which may be enhanced if products are tied or embedded to a particular place.

Empowerment may also be reflected in decision-making, with a high level of empowerment leading to a decision process which is inclusive and participatory and which takes into account the values and aspirations of the local actors involved in tourism resources and activities. Particular forms of endogeneity and embeddedness may result in local democratic or participatory approaches, but may also result in local oligarchies. Conversely, exogeneity and disembeddedness may result in the empowerment of actors outside the locality and hence local disempowerment.

A Culture Economy Approach to Integrated Tourism

In this section, we build upon the discussion of tourism and its integration to set out a conceptual framework which we term a *culture economy* approach to IT. The term culture economy has been coined as a general term to describe the various ways in which local or territorial identity may be used in local or regional development (Ray 2001). The term "economy" denotes the relationships between resources, production and consumption, while "culture" refers to "a set of place-specific forms that can be used to animate and define 'development'" (Ray 1999: 263). Cultures are thus viewed as sets of resources available for social and economic control, economies are partially reorganised at the geographical scale of cultures-territories (Ray 1998), and local actors determine development paths based on indigenous values, often with ethical and environmental dimensions. The culture economy, therefore, emphasises territorially-based resources, networks and partnerships, the localisation of economic control and the (re)valorisation of place by drawing upon its cultural identity.

An important element of the culture economy approach lies in the strategic commodification of resources. Local knowledge applied to local resources can be translated into products and into intellectual property (Moran, 1993), a process which often requires extra-local institutional and regulatory support, as in the case of protected denominations of origin or mechanisms such as the *appellation d'origine contrôlée* used for French wines. Such commodification involves an on-going process of symbolic (re)construction in which meanings are attached to products through, for example, their association with place imagery. In addition to the attachment of place identities to products, places themselves can also become commodified as, for example, in the so-called "commodification of the countryside" (Cloke 1993, Marsden et al. 1993). Such commodification which, at its simplest, is manifested in guidebooks and postcards, is often strongly visual, invariably idealised (for example, showing solitary walkers on green mountains in good weather), and often with an emphasis on the past.

Implicit in the culture economy approach is the need for the local to engage with the extra-local, since ultimately it is external forces which enable local activities (Ray 1998). Local identity can be used in mediating a locality's relations with extra-local forces through, for example, trading strategies which involve the selling of localities themselves or the marketing of local products to tourists or to other outsiders. Tourism, and especially rural tourism (which, almost by definition, entails interaction with people from outside a locality), is therefore a classic example of the culture economy in operation. This is particularly the case where cultural markers (such as historical and archaeological sites and landscapes, literary and art activities, music festivals and events, regional cuisines and languages) are involved (Ray 1998), which in turn are often associated with special interests, niche markets and the potential for high value-added.

Analysis of how a culture economy functions should take account of the complex interrelations between both the historically-layered networks and relationships which mediate attitudes towards commodification, knowledge and tourism in general, and the newer networks and relationships that exist within and between localities (Kneafsey 2001). Historically-layered relationships and networks provide a sense of attachment to place and a feeling of continuity to actors who are enmeshed within current social and economic relations. Newer network relations can include recently developed institutional and economic links with other places, the development of new types of entrepreneurial activity, the arrival of new inhabitants in rural areas, and the emergence of social trends such as green and heritage tourism.

It is also important to distinguish between horizontal and vertical networks. Horizontal networks often take the form of spatial strategies which attempt to co-ordinate a range of activities located within rural areas and facilitate closer relationships between locally-based producers, institutions and consumers. They include innovative product sectors, are often driven by new inhabitants with alternative lifestyle priorities (a common characteristic of rural tourism development), and are likely to be constituted through information and knowledge flows, trust-based relationships, common values and understandings, and commodities which are locally created. Sales at farmgates, workshops and through local co-operatives often provide the local market outlets for these products, many of which are enrolled into local accreditation, labelling and marketing schemes. Hence, there is often evidence of conscious efforts to fix products to place, either through the marketing outlets which are used or through the use of place-based quality assurance. Vertical networks, on the other hand, allow a locality to forge alliances with externally located consumers, suppliers, distributors, retailers and institutions. A successful culture economy is likely to be characterised by a combination of vertical and horizontal networks, and Figure 3.3 visualises an idealised trajectory for a successful culture economy which incorporates both.

To illustrate the importance of combining horizontal with vertical networks, we now return to the concept of embeddedness, mentioned above. The concept of embeddedness has been applied to short food supply-chains, whereby certain locally produced foods reach the consumer embedded with information concerning their origins and production methods. In these cases, product quality is assessed in relation to its embeddedness, not only within social relations of trust, but also within the cultural, natural and historical environment of a region: culture, nature and history are not mere backdrops to human productive activities, but are systematically and purposefully appropriated for use within them. The concept of embeddedness is equally important to tourism, in terms of the types of relationships existing between tourism providers, host communities, institutions and tourists, and also the ways in which these are inter-linked with the natural and cultural resource base of a locality.

Despite the importance of embeddedness, products also need a degree of disembeddedness from the locality if they are to be vectors of local rural development. Excessive embeddedness can curtail the market reach of products whose production will then remain small-scale, local and marginal in a globalised economy (Murdoch 2000b). Quality food chains, for example, need to perform a complex trade-off between embeddedness and disembeddedness: on the one hand, if they are too weighed down with domestic conventions, products are unlikely to travel far and will remain confined to a narrow range of consumers, on the other hand, if they are completely disembedded from a local socio-cultural and ecological system, products may carry industrial conventions that are unattractive to health-conscious or "green" consumers. Such considerations apply particularly to the tourism product: on the one hand, it needs to be differentiated and gain attraction through its embedded characteristics, on the other hand, it should also be adequately disembedded in order to make connections with spatially distant consumers.

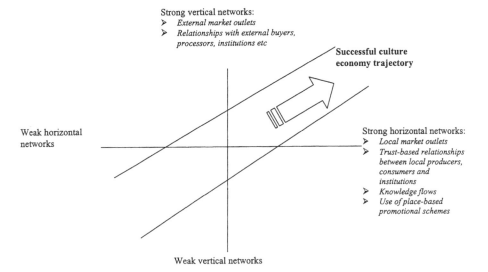

Figure 3.3   Theorising a successful cultural economy within a networks framework

Source: After Kneafsey et al. 2001

The point can be further illustrated through the distinction between *soft* and *hard* tourism. Soft tourism represents forms of tourism whereby tourists, albeit temporarily, embed themselves within a locality and adopt what Urry (1990) terms the "romantic gaze". Tourists are offered a variety of opportunities to experience locally distinct cultural activities, products and environments, and this should maximise the potential for the locality to retain value within a particular culture economy. This contrasts with hard tourism, which is typically the so-called mass tourism of package tours, perhaps adopting Urry's (1990) "collective gaze", often geographically concentrated and vertically integrated, with high levels of external capital use, and on a large enough scale to have the potential to dominate the community resources which become involved (Lane 1994). Hard tourism can be theorised as disembedded, showing low levels of horizontal integration, whereas soft tourism is typically more individual, based on a sense of place and hence involving local products and communities, associated with self-employment and hence a greater degree of self-determination, and characterised by embeddedness in a wider functioning economy, with respect for, and limited impacts on, local environments.

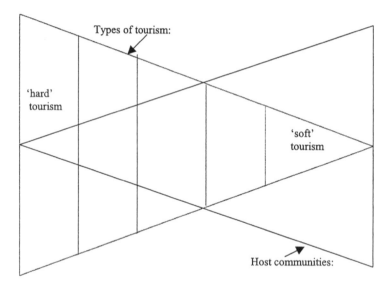

Figure 3.4   Tourism penetration and community receptivity

Source: After Smith 1989, Lane 1994, Stabler 1997

The distinction between disembedded hard tourism and embedded soft tourism is illustrated in Figure 3.4, which represents the way in which tourism and host communities interact on a continuum ranging from hard to soft. Hard tourism tends to exhibit little penetration into host communities, its links are likely to be international rather than local, and it can be predatory in that it parasitizes economic, bio-physical and socio-cultural public goods for their external benefits (Stabler 1997). Soft tourism, in contrast, is likely to exhibit deeper penetration, with good absorption possibilities and retention of control and value by host communities, and is more likely than hard tourism to meet sustainability criteria. Its economic rationale is linked to the endogenous model of rural development (van der Ploeg and Saccomandi 1995) which is based on locality, on the valorisation of local resources through small-scale and flexible capital investment and response to niche demand, and on the capacities and values of local people (cf. Ray 2000). Soft tourism is likely to generate larger income and employment multipliers per unit of tourist spending than hard tourism, although hard tourism may have larger absolute impacts on a locality because of its greater volume.

Completing the Conceptualisation of Integrated Tourism

Having theorised IT from a networks perspective, it is necessary to complete our conceptualisation by taking more explicit consideration of the motivational and behavioural aspects of IT. We term these two distinct aspects the *existential* and the *material*. To some extent, these correspond with Habermas's distinction between the symbolic and material reproductions of the lifeworld (Outhwaite 1996): under the former, there is a role for freedom and for social participation, whereas under the latter, the market economy and the administrative state are dominant. The two aspects also capture the perception that tourism itself should be defined as both "idea" (reflecting values, aspirations and aesthetic considerations) and "action" (involving specific resources, activities, facilities, services and products) in order to reconcile tourism behaviour with tourists" motivations.

Practically, too, the distinction is necessary in the IT context for a number of reasons. It broadens analysis of the tourism industry, much of which is preoccupied with logistics, marketing and profit (McIntosh and Goeldner 1986), it meets the need to better understand the nature of tourism itself, given that a lack of such understanding appears often to be a reason for its lack of integration, and, given that tourism is frequently, if vaguely, perceived to be beneficial for rural areas in need of revitalisation (Lagos 1998), it may provide a deeper understanding of a range of issues facing perceptions of, and tourism in, MRRs (Page and Getz 1997).

The material side of IT, requiring analysis of tourism's commercial, instrumental and behavioural aspects, is perhaps the simpler to deal with. Tourism as a material force is made up of an aggregate of commercial activities. This material aspect is not confined to the networks which produce the supply of tourism facilities, services and products: tourists also take account of material considerations (such as price, value for money and transport facilities) when deciding upon their entry into such networks, the nature of their touristic experience, and the location within which it is to take place.

The existential side of IT, requiring analysis of tourism's symbolic, ideological, aesthetic and motivational aspects, is analytically more problematic. Tourism has an existential framing associated with the post-modern need to escape from the mundane and everyday. It is therefore important to understand the motivations lying behind both the demand for, and the supply of, tourism. On the demand side, touristic experiences are consumed in terms of internalised meanings (such as the prior knowledge, expectations and mythologies generated within tourists' own cultures), as well as external symbolism (influenced by a range of factors, including literature and the media as well as destination marketing and the offerings found at tourist locations). However, despite being an important part of the motivation of tourists, the existential aspect is not confined to the demand for tourism: host communities also respond to existential considerations (for example, by reacting to the values of modernity and late capitalism), and actors who provide tourism services, especially those in MRRs, may also have motives which go beyond the purely commercial.

The existential aspect of IT is not only complex but also often paradoxical. While tourism can often be seen as an escape from the everyday, it can also be seen as a search for the fixed verities of tradition and familiarity in the face of an everyday life which is increasingly fluid, uncertain and unpredictable. While tourism can be allocentric and focused outwards upon the unknown other as an act of discovery, it can also be psychocentric and focussed inwards on satisfying the inner needs of the tourist for change within familiar surroundings (Plog 1974). While tourism can often be regarded as a homage to territoriality, its emphasis on movement and restlessness decomposes tourists' sense of place such that places may be reduced to temporary configurations of signs (Rojek and Urry 1997). While many forms of tourism thrive on cultural diversity (Robinson and Boniface 1999), the culture contact between host communities and tourists is often fictionalised, sometimes with the complicity of host communities, as reconstructions and valorisation of traditions lead to contrived, constructed images (Deltsou 2000, Ivars Baidal 2000, Markwick 2001) and "staged authenticity" (MacCannell 1973, Robinson and Boniface 1999). Even where the commodification of host cultures is less contrived, it is possible to distinguish weak commodification (for example, the emblematic artifacts of a museum) from strong commodification (for example, the exaggerated ethnicity of a folk festival) and the different implications that these have for host communities. The creation of heritage often leads to hyper-reality (to borrow a term from Umberto Eco) where aspects of tradition become fetishised and seemingly more authentic than the original. Tourism can encourage host communities towards a form of "positive involution" (MacCannell 1992) in which they create symbolic resources, such as historical restoration projects, which can both open up community potential and cause problems of property rights, ownership and control.

Our two-pronged approach to IT within the culture economy needs to recognise both the cultural and economic force of IT, in its symbolic and commercial dimensions. We are primarily interested in the meeting grounds (MacCannell 1992) where encounters between these two aspects of the tourism system take place and where we can analyse the dynamics of the introduction of tourism into functioning communities, cultures, societies and economies. Tourism provides a dialogic model of human interaction characterised by negotiated experiences which go well beyond simple commercialism. Tourists are semioticians (MacCannell 1992, Rojek and Urry 1997), negotiating and consuming signs as well as goods and services, and tourism is an important example of socio-economic and socio-cultural networks within which there are flows of meanings as well as of people, information, money and goods (Hannerz 1990).

Figure 3.5 illustrates our approach diagrammatically. Both the existential and the material aspects involve important and defining contextual environments within which IT takes place (see also Figure 3.2). Thus, for example, ideologies, fashion, postmodern concerns for the quality of life, and environmentalism all influence motivations, while consumerism, attitudes to leisure, and practical considerations such as economic status and travel costs all influence behaviour. The first meeting place, therefore, is that of tourism itself where these contextual environments are synthesised in decisions and actions which reflect both existential and material considerations.

Converting tourists' motivations into tourism behaviour involves a range of actors. These include the gatekeepers and the media who supply information, the host communities within which tourism-related businesses operate and where resources are controlled, and the public and private institutions which become involved both directly, such as tourist boards, and indirectly, such as other rural development institutions. These all represent further meeting places where tourism interacts with businesses which provide facilities and services, resources which characterise localities, communities which act as hosts and absorb impacts, and institutions whose activities help to define the nature of the touristic experience.

Figure 3.5 also identifies the numerous themes which lie behind existential motivations, including the imagery of the locality and the cultural constructions applied to places, resource valorisation and cultural commodification, the question of heritage and its authenticity, and the psychology of tourism in terms of its symbols, meanings and mythologies.

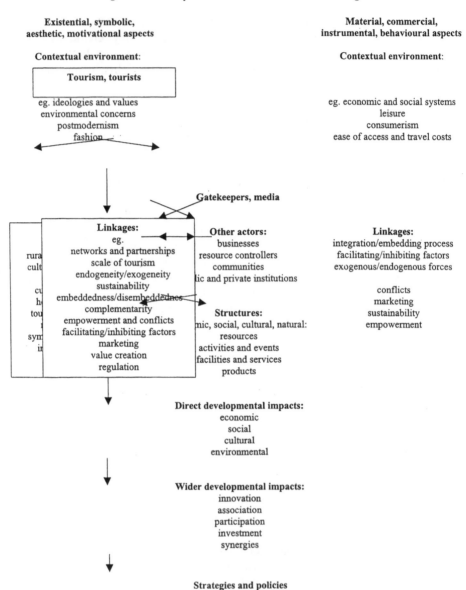

Existential, symbolic, aesthetic, motivational aspects

Material, commercial, instrumental, behavioural aspects

Contextual environment:

Contextual environment:

Tourism, tourists

eg. ideologies and values
environmental concerns
postmodernism
fashion

eg. economic and social systems
leisure
consumerism
ease of access and travel costs

Gatekeepers, media

Linkages:
eg.
networks and partnerships
scale of tourism
endogeneity/exogeneity
sustainability
embeddedness/disembeddedness
complementarity
empowerment and conflicts
facilitating/inhibiting factors
marketing
value creation
regulation

Other actors:
businesses
resource controllers
communities
public and private institutions

Linkages:
integration/embedding process
facilitating/inhibiting factors
exogenous/endogenous forces

conflicts
marketing
sustainability
empowerment

Structures:
economic, social, cultural, natural:
resources
activities and events
facilities and services
products

rural
cult
cu
h
tou
sym
in

Direct developmental impacts:
economic
social
cultural
environmental

Wider developmental impacts:
innovation
association
participation
investment
synergies

Strategies and policies

Figure 3.5   The meeting grounds of integrated tourism

Similarly, a wide range of linkages underpin the material aspects of tourism and facilitate the IT process. These include the networks involved, the issues of scale, endogeneity, sustainability, embeddedness, complementarity and empowerment, the various facilitating and constraining forces, with their value creation and power relationships, and such practical aspects such as marketing arrangements, value creation and regulatory activity.

Translating demand into effective integration requires specific structures which represent a further meeting place in which the various themes and linkages are consolidated to yield an effective tourism product. These structures include the wide range of economic, social, cultural and natural resources involved, the economic and socio-cultural activities upon which tourism impinges, and the products, facilities and other services produced for, and consumed by, tourists. IT then has various impacts, both the direct impacts on the local economy, society, culture and environment, and the wider, less direct, but no less important, developmental impacts such as the encouragement of further association and participation and the stimulation of innovation, investment and a wide range of synergies. Finally, theorising the IT process will reveal patterns and suggest hypotheses leading to strategy and policy implications of relevance to practitioners and institutions.

Conclusion

Figure 3.5, which summarises our conceptualisation of IT, sets the stage for a suggested research agenda to investigate the relevant themes, linkages, structures, actors and impacts in a number of European study regions in a theoretically-informed manner. The central column of the diagram shows the main foci of such a research agenda, whose elements lend themselves to a set of interrelated and mutually supporting research objectives.

1. Consumption Objective

As has been shown, tourism is one expression of the increasing importance of non-material forms of production and consumption, including the well-documented demand for rurality and its associated attributes of closeness to nature, tradition, heritage and authenticity. The very disadvantages of MRRs (for example, extensive agriculture, distance from large population centres, and the persistence of traditional activities, cultures and ways of life) can therefore assume positive values. Rural tourism represents a process of consumption of products and services to which real, imagined or fabricated values are attached.

MRRs are increasingly involved in this process through the construction, commodification, promotion and consumption of rural symbols. Research into IT needs to view tourists as consumers in order to reveal the critical factors necessary for a positive and holistic tourism experience, and to clarify the complex exchange relationships created when tourists buy tourism-related products and intangibles such as images, cultural property and visual amenity. This focus will highlight important linkages between local and regional resources, activities, products, communities and tourism, enable the development of classifications of rural tourists (for example, by activity or interests), and suggest opportunities for the further development of IT for regional and rural development purposes, including the development of appropriate marketing channels and community participation.

2. Production Objective

Some marginal regions have a potential competitive advantage as desirable tourist destinations since the nature of their economic, social, cultural and natural resources may be especially appropriate to the localisation of economic control and (re)valorisation of place. A focus on relevant producers of local and regional products, controllers of resources, and providers of tourism-related goods and services will reveal the nature of the entrepreneurship, partnerships, motivation, vision and skills required of local actors for the successful implementation of IT.

3. Host Community Objective

Communities are a crucial part of IT's operating environment and are largely defined by the resource and economic activity structures into which IT is linked. In addition to being hosts to visitors, communities are the guardians of local resources, form an important part of the socio-cultural environment encountered by tourists, are the beneficiaries of any regional development stimulated by IT, and bear the brunt of any undesirable changes caused by tourism. Communities also represent the arenas of conflict which may arise both between intra-community factions and between communities and tourists, and the success of IT depends to a great extent on host communities' capacity to benefit from it through willingness to participate, to commodify local identity, and to exhibit other forms of social entrepreneurship.

Communities play a significant, and increasingly recognised, role in rural development, and there is an increasing policy interest in partnership in rural areas, manifested in initiatives such as LEADER and Local Agenda 21. The extent to which communities are aware of, and involved in, IT is an important element in understanding the environment in which it operates, in evaluating its economic, social, cultural and resource impacts, and in appraising its sustainability and developmental potential.

4. Institutional Structure Objective

An important aspect of institutional structures concerns the extent to which the development of IT is agency-led and the extent to which it is driven by private enterprise responding to economic opportunities. Locally-organised collaborative tourism development involving partnerships (for example, among representative groups, producer groups and marketing groups) may be a vital ingredient in the creation of enabling institutional structures at the local level, while institutions with broader remits, particularly public-sector organisations, may provide key elements of the IT process where they are involved in marketing, information provision, and other ways of promoting the resources, activities and products of regions. In contrast, sectorally-organised institutional structures may be inappropriate for the development of small-scale integrated rural tourism.

Fulfilment of the production, community and institutional structure objectives will enable a research programme to establish the relationships, linkages, processes and critical factors among all three supply-side actors in the IT system, complementing the demand-side insights obtained from the consumption objective. Supply-side and demand-side perceptions on many issues (for example, on the potential for valorisation of local and regional resources) will be compared, and an understanding of the issues in each study region will provide a firm basis for inter-regional comparisons. In turn, this will allow the identification of strengths, weaknesses, potential opportunities and good practice as aids to the further development of IT.

5. Policy Objective

This objective brings together the results of the previous objectives in order to identify and characterise the processes through which IT is linked to the economic, social, cultural, natural and human structures of the regions in which it takes place. Such an understanding will permit an assessment of the ways in which IT's linkages with local and regional resources, activities, products and communities may be exploited more sustainably and effectively. It will also result in the specification of sustainable and transferable models of good practice, and an effective contribution to the further development of IT in Europe's MRRs.

Note

[1] This is a full version of a paper presented to ISSMR 16, Norway, August 2001. The paper is based on a collaborative programme of research funded under the EU's Quality of Life and Management of Living Resources programme (QLK5-CT-2000-01211-SPRITE) and undertaken by the Universities of Wales (Aberystwyth; co-ordinator), Caen, Patras, Ireland (Galway), Valencia, Lancaster and Coventry, together with the Institute of Landscape Ecology (Ceske Budejovice), Cemagref (Clermont Ferrand) and Teagasc (Dublin). The authors particularly acknowledge the contributions made by the other project partners to the working document (Jenkins and Oliver 2001) on which this paper is based.

References

Aronsson, L. 2000. *The Development of Sustainable Tourism.* London: Continuum.

Bensahel, L. and M. Donsimoni. 1999. *Le Tourisme, Facteur de Développement Local.* Grenoble: Presses Universitaires de Grenoble.

Blaßek, B., 1995. Spiritual dimension of the countryside today. In *What is the Countryside?* Spolek pro obnovu venkova. Ministerstvo zemedelsví CR, Pruhonice (in Czech).

Bonnieux, F. and P. Rainelli. 2000. Aménités agricoles et tourisme rural. *Revue d'Économie Régionale et Urbaine*, 5: 803-820.

Butler, R. W. and G. Clark. 1992. Tourism in rural areas: Canada and the UK. In I. R. Bowler, C. R. Bryant and M. D. Nellis (eds.), *Contemporary Rural Systems in Transition.* Wallingford: CABI.

Cloke, P. 1993. The countryside as commodity: New spaces for rural leisure. In S. Glyptis (ed.), *Leisure and the Environment.* London: Belhaven.

Cuvelier, P. 1998. *Anciennes et Nouvelles Formes de Tourisme: une Approche Socio-économique.* Paris: L'Harmattan.

Daly, H. E. 2000. *Ecological Economics and the Ecology of Economics: Essays in Criticism.* Cheltenham: Elgar.

Deltsou, E. 2000. Eco-tourism development and the designation of nature and culture: Paradigms from northern Greece. In B. Nitsiakos and C. Kasimis (eds.), *Mountainous Areas in the Balkans: Structures and Transformations.* Athens: Plethron (in Greek).

Garcia Cuesta, J. L. 1996. El turismo rural como factor diversificador de rentas en la tradiçional economía agraria. *Estudios Turísticos*, 132: 47-61.

Greffe, X. 1990. *La Valeur Économique du Patrimoine: la Demande et l'Offre de Monuments.* Paris: Anthropos.

Hannerz, U. 1990. Cosmopolitans and locals in world culture. In M. Featherstone (ed.), *Global Culture: Nationalism, Globalisation and Modernity.* London: Sage.

Hinrichs, C. 2000. Embeddedness and local food systems: Notes on two types of direct agricultural market. *Journal of Rural Studies*, 18: 295-303.

Hopkins, J. 1998. Commodifying the countryside: Marketing myths of rurality. In T. W. Butler, C. M. Hall and J. M. Jenkins (eds.), *Tourism and Recreation in Rural Areas.* Chichester: Wiley.

Ivars Baidal, J. A. 2000. Turismo y espacios rurales: Conceptos, filosofías y realidades. *Investigaciones Geográficas*, 23.

Jenkins, T. N. 2000. Putting postmodernity into practice: Endogenous development and the role of traditional cultures in the rural development of marginal regions. *Ecological Economics*, 34: 301-314.

Jenkins, T. N. and T. Oliver. 2001. *Integrated Tourism: a Conceptual Framework.* QLK5-CT-2000-01211 - SPRITE, Deliverable 1 to European Commission. Aberystwyth: Institute of Rural Studies, University of Wales.

Kneafsey, M. 2001. Rural cultural economy: Tourism and social relations. *Annals of Tourism Research*, 28: 762-783.

Kneafsey, M., B. Ilbery and T. Jenkins. 2001. Exploring the dimensions of culture economies in rural west Wales. *Sociologia Ruralis*, 41: 296-310.

Lagos, D. 1998. Tourism as a forcing factor for regional development. *Topos*, 14 (in Greek).

Lane, B. 1994. What is rural tourism? In B. Bramwell and B. Lane (eds.), *Rural Tourism and Sustainable Development*. Clevedon: Channel View.

Long, P. and B. Lane. 2000. Rural tourism development. In W. C. Gartner and D. W. Lime (eds.), *Trends in Outdoor Recreation, Leisure and Tourism*. Wallingford: CABI.

Lowe, P., J. Murdoch and N. Ward. 1995. Networks in rural development: Beyond exogenous and endogenous models. In Van der J. D. Ploeg and G. Van Dijk (eds.), *Beyond Modernization: The Impact of Endogenous Rural Development*. Assen: Van Gorcum.

MacCannell, D. 1973. Staged authenticity: On arrangements of social space in tourist settings. *American Journal of Sociology*, 79.

MacCannell, D. 1992. *Empty Meeting Grounds: The Tourist Papers*. London: Routledge.

Markwick, M. 2001. Marketing myths and the cultural commodification of Ireland. *Geography*, 86: 37-49.

Marsden, T., J. Murdoch, P. Lowe, R. Munton and A. Flynn. 1993. *Constructing the Countryside*. London: UCL Press.

McCool, S. F. and R. N. Moisey (eds.). 2001. *Tourism, Recreation and Sustainability*. Wallingford: CABI.

McIntosh, R. W. and C. R. Goeldner. 1986. *Tourism Principles, Practices and Philosophies*. New York: Wiley.

McIntyre, G. 1997. *Développement d'un Tourisme Durable: Guide à l'Intention des Planificateurs Locaux*. Madrid: World Tourism Organisation.

Moran, W. 1993. Rural space as intellectual property. *Political Geography*, 12: 263-277.

Muñoz de Escalona, F. 1994. Turismo rural integrado: una fórmula innovadora basada en un desarrollo científico. *Estudios Turǿsticos*: 5-25.

Murdoch, J. 2000a. Networks: A new paradigm of rural development? *Journal of Rural Studies*, 16: 407-419.

Murdoch, J. 2000b. Quality, nature and embeddedness: Some theoretical considerations in the context of the food sector. *Economic Geography*, 76: 107-125.

OECD. 1993. *What Future for our Countryside? A Rural Development Policy*. Paris: OECD.

Outhwaite, W. 1996. *The Habermas Reader*. Cambridge: Polity Press.

Page, S. J. and D. Getz. 1997. The business of rural tourism: International perspectives. In S. J. Page and D. Getz (eds.), *The Business of Rural Tourism*. London: International Thomson Business Press.

Patin, V. 1997. *Tourisme et Patrimoine en France et en Europe*. Paris: La Documentation Française.

Pecqueur, B. 2001. Qualité et développement territorial: l'hypothése du panier des biens et de services territorialisées. *Économie Rurale*, 261: 37-49.

Plog, S. C. 1974. Why destinations rise and fall in popularity. *The Cornell Hotel and Restaurant Administration Quarterly*, 14: 55-58.

Ray, C. 1998. Culture, intellectual property and territorial rural development. *Sociologia Ruralis*, 38: 3-20.

Ray, C. 1999. Endogenous development in the era of reflexive modernity. *Journal of Rural Studies*, 15: 257-267.

Ray, C. 2000. *Endogenous Socio-Economic Development and Trustful Relationships*. Newcastle: CRE.

Ray, C. 2001. *Culture Economies: a Perspective on Local Rural Development in Europe*. Newcastle: CRE.

Robinson, M. and P. Boniface (eds.). 1999. *Tourism and Cultural Conflicts*. Wallingford: CABI.

Rojek, C. and J. Urry. 1997. *Touring Cultures: Transformations of Travel and Theory*. London: Routledge.

Salais, R. and M. Storper. 1992. The four worlds of contemporary production. *Cambridge Journal of Economics*, 16: 169-193.

Sharpley, R. 1996. *Tourism and Leisure in the Countryside.* Huntingdon: ELM.

Slee, B., H. Farr and P. Snowdon. 1997. The economic impact of alternative types of rural tourism. *Journal of Agricultural Economics*, 48: 179-192.

Slováčková, P. 2000. Vacation smelling of manure: Ecological tourism. *Ekonom*, 44 (in Czech).

Smith, V. L. (ed.). 1989. *Hosts and Guests: the Anthropology of Tourism.* Philadelphia: University of Pennsylvania Press.

Stabler, M. J. (ed.). 1997. *Tourism and Sustainability.* Wallingford: CAB International.

Storper, M. and R. Salais. *1997. Worlds of Production: the Action Frameworks of the Economy.* Cambridge, Mass.: Harvard University Press.

Stríbrná, M. 1997. Rural tourism and enterprise. *Obec a Finance*, 2 (in Czech).

Urry, J. 1990. *The Tourist Gaze.* London: Sage.

Van der Ploeg, J. D. and V. Saccomandi. 1995. On the impact of endogenous development in agriculture. In J. D. Van der Ploeg and G. Van Dijk (eds.), *Beyond Modernization: the Impact of Endogenous Rural Development.* Assen: Van Gorcum.

Chapter 4

Reality and the Rural Idyll: Paradoxes of Rural Heritage and War Tourism in Normandy, France

ALISON McCLEERY

Context

This paper deals with heritage tourism in the semi-periphery and constitutes a development of work reported previously on farm diversification in the same area (McCleery 2001). That article sought to demonstrate how structural marginality, as much as physical peripherality, has produced various models of farm diversification in Normandy, northwest France, specifically in the department of Calvados. The purpose of the present paper is to explore further the context of that farm diversification: on the basis of first-hand observations, semi-structured interviews conducted in farm households,[1] and analysis of published data, it will examine not only the tensions inherent in promoting the rural idyll to tourists from urban areas – tensions common to the marketing of rural tourism in all marginal regions – but it will also consider an issue specific to northwest France as a peripheral area: World War II as heritage.

Introduction

Some readers may be familiar with an episode of *Fawlty Towers*, a British television comedy series, which hilariously starred and sent up Basil Fawlty as the ill-fated manager of a seaside hotel in a small town loosely based on the resort of Torquay in southwest England. A party of German tourists books in to the establishment and Basil falls over himself (literally) trying to avoid mentioning the war. Having thoroughly upset his German guests by goose-stepping around the dining room and talking in the sort of over-exaggerated German accent associated with British war films, he concedes that he did allude to it once, "but I think I got away with it!". Normandy, by contrast, can neither get away without relying upon tourism (unlike certain highly successful counties of peripheral western Norway, where the meeting which inspired this set of papers was based, and where, apparently, tourism constitutes merely the icing on the economic cake); nor can it survive without mentioning the war, which is omnipresent, given that Normandy was the scene of the famous Normandy Landings and the site of subsequent fierce ground combat between the Western Allies and the German armed forces. The conundrum for present-day providers of tourist products is how exactly to mention the Second World War sensitively and profitably in one breath, without offending any of the various parties involved, or their descendants.

Peripherality and Heritage: Some Definitions, Perceptions and Contradictions

Before proceeding to look at questions of tourism, heritage and authenticity as they affect both the presentation of rural micro-environments and societies and the presentation of the settings, artefacts and contexts of war events, it is necessary first to address the basic question of whether or not Normandy may legitimately be considered as being a marginal region. The *département* (county) of Calvados, part of the larger region of Basse-Normandie (Lower Normandy), is in fact fairly typical of western European north Atlantic rural areas. It is subject to the twin demographic phenomena of desertification and densification, the former characterising inland sections of deeper countryside, the latter manifesting itself in and around service centres and along the coastal strip. The city of Caen functions as both regional and departmental capital and is a post-1945 creation, having been destroyed in 1944 (McCleery 2001).

The defining characteristics of marginal areas have been comprehensively elaborated and refined over the years in the seminar series of the International Society for Marginal Regions and elsewhere.[2] However, recently these have been restated specifically in the context of challenges for tourism in peripheral areas, a context pertinent to the content of the present paper (Wanhill and Buhalis 1999). The authors list fourteen characteristic problems of peripheral areas, including: dependence on a primary sector economy; distance from the market place; short season; population outmigration, especially of the young and able; delivery of product through small and medium-sized (tourism) enterprises, with all the attendant problems of the family business; lack of education and training; and inward-looking societies coupled with the likelihood of adverse social and environmental impacts of tourism. On the first five of these criteria, Calvados undoubtedly qualifies, although problems associated with a lack of education and training and of an inward-looking society are more particularly associated with either more westerly (Atlantic) or more southerly (interior) parts of Basse-Normandie. On this basis, it is more correct to categorise Calvados as belonging to the semi-periphery.

Scotland and Ireland also have peripheral and semi-peripheral western Atlantic margins. Both, like western Norway and northwest France, are in the business of driving their marginal regional economies into the twenty-first century as hard as they can. Their government-agency and private-sector glossy brochures emphasise technology-driven customer focus and state-of-the-art materials and infrastructure together with human resources whose fingers are on the pulse. Yet, where heritage is concerned, the situation is precisely the obverse. McCrone (1995: 1) asserts that *heritage is a thoroughly modern concept* but there any reference to modernity ends; for what Lowenthal (1998: 1) refers to as the cult of heritage, as distinct from the practice of history, is concerned with the packaging of that history, up to and including the commodification of what Crang (1996) terms *pastness*. This is heritage ascendant, heritage rampant and increasingly heritage glut. Lowenthal (1998) leaves us in no doubt that the cult of heritage has a momentum all of its own. Accepting that there is considerable ongoing academic debate as to the origins and significance of this cult, the nature of the distinction between heritage and history, and about questions of authenticity and whose heritage to claim (Lowenthal 1998, McCrone 1995, Prentice 1993, Urry 1990, 2002), nevertheless it is submitted that commodifying the past does not really present substantial problems of an emotional or psychological nature for its producers in a metropolitan context, precisely because the contrast between the "then" and the "now" is so starkly obvious.

By contrast it does very much constitute a problem in the context of the marginal rural area, precisely because the past is so recently shrugged off, so that for some suppliers of the tourist product, living a lie may both be dishonest and feel painful. *History is layered deep within the northern archipelagos of Orkney and Shetland,* pontificates the VisitScotland (Scottish Tourist Board) website; *few places on the planet are as crammed with history as Ireland,* claims Ireland's Bord Failte (Irish Tourist Board) site; and we are enjoined by Oideas Gael – an organisation devoted to the promotion of Irish culture – to learn *our ancient ways and Celtic traditions* precisely by experiencing *the living culture of our Gaeltacht community.* While "modern" tourists may be duped, post-modern tourists must choose to act out their expected role and to savour that complicity. Attitudes to complicity on the part of the producers of cultural heritage in the rural periphery may be less straightforward and more ambivalent.

France and the Rural Idyll

One key element of rural diversification in Normandy and in France generally – which pre-dates any of the more recent post-Common Agricultural Policy manifestations of farm diversification – has been the influence of the *Gîtes de France* organisation.   Under its aegis and auspices, and underpinning its rationale, has been a deliberate philosophy of, and moral imperative to, re-educate people from French cities in the values – universally regarded as superior – of the traditional rural way of life.   It might be argued that what we have in these French back-to-nature (Ardagh 1987: 402) values is no more than a contemporary French variant of the English poet William Cowper's old adage that "God made the country, and man made the town".   Yet the rural idyll French-style perhaps runs even deeper: for not only is France singled out by Fearne (1997) as a country particularly bound by agricultural tradition, but, more than that, her family-farming agricultural economy is perceived by Hoggart (1995) to represent a key embodiment of national identity. It follows, therefore, that Gîtes de France may be pushing at an open door in promoting a week or two in the countryside for re-creation in its truest sense, i.e., the renewal of mind and body.

Yet the struggle to maintain the perception of the rural idyll entails a tension between what Hutson and Keddie (1997: 270) have referred to as the necessary mess of farming and the romantically inspired perception of farming as viewed by the tourist.   Today in Calvados as elsewhere in agriculture, mess meets hi-tech, so that the old problem of flies and smells on-farm is compounded by a new problem of massive combine harvesters blocking narrow country lanes off-farm, or gleaming stainless steel milk tankers speeding along departmental roads forcing the unwary (tourist) into the ditch in a cloud of dust.   Other scenes of contemporary rural life are acted out – fortunately – behind closed doors.   For it is not calculated to lift up the vast and scrupulously clean, free-range indoor shed of some 500 veal calves with electronic ear tags being delivered computer-controlled and monitored quantities of milk at will through a battery of distinctly non-pastoral and thoroughly un-cowlike latex teats.   Rural life does not simply have to be tidy, it also has to be traditional: as Hoggart (1995: 100) has noted, "a (rather ill-defined) traditional rural way of life is [seen to be] superior both to urban and to contemporary rural life".   If the tourist gaze should stray, possible ambivalence and tension on the part of rural suppliers of tourism products is inevitably paralleled with disappointment and disillusionment on the part of more naïve consumers.

For the rural tourist in Calvados, this may be only one of several frustrations.   After a day or two exploring the farm and its surroundings, things bucolic may begin to pall.   The clean fine sand of the Channel coast beckons – not only are the beaches tidal but they are also routinely combed in season for litter and excess seaweed by the local commune authorities – at least for those within reasonable driving distance of the littoral.   Having parked the people-carrier by a tank or gun emplacement, and glimpsed the ubiquitous map of Omaha, Gold, Sword and Juno beaches on the back wall of the ice-cream kiosk en route to the sand, holidaymakers may find that what started off as spits of rain has turned into the sort of steady drizzle which waters the lush pastures which bequeathed to Normandy its dairy industry. With no breaks evident in a uniformly overcast sky, it is logical to opt for an indoor heritage attraction. Certainly there are a few non-war related museums in Calvados, such as the hot air balloon museum inland at Balleroy and the seafront aquarium at Courseulles, and there is also a wealth of abbey and cathedral churches. But with all the tanks, Commonwealth War Graves Commission cemeteries, landing beach maps and other wartime memorabilia, curiosity about World War II is inevitably aroused, even or perhaps especially if its significance was not previously appreciated. The various war museums are also both heavily advertised and easy to spot.

War Tourism

Wartime events and sites represent important tourist attractions, drawing visitors to a diversity of locations, including the World War II landing beaches of Normandy. In this connection, two points of significance should be noted, namely: the study of the relationship between war and tourism is emerging as an incipient area of specialised tourism research (Weaver 2000); and wartime events and sites pose a series of challenges with regard to presentation and interpretation (Henderson 2000). Weaver – whose pronouncement above may owe something to the notion of the self-fulfilling prophecy – has proposed for the purposes of tourism analysis and explanation a war-distorted destination life-cycle model.

Developed from Butler's (1980) S-curve sequence representing the conventional non-war-distorted tourist resort life-cycle dynamics more usually applicable to holiday destinations, the war-distorted model exhibits demand deficit in its early phases (Butler 1980, Weaver 2000). In plain language, what this means is that after about thirty years of a tourism vacuum, you may expect to see the progressive conversion of battle sites into attractions, and the return of veterans as visitors. This results in a demand surplus, with the so-called war dividend (Weaver 2000: 151) continuing for an indefinite period into the future. Weaver has refined his model to incorporate very specific life-cycle stages, as follows: pre-war; war; post-war A; and post-war B, with the post-war A stage being disaggregable into a number of discrete phases. Applying the model to Normandy, it is apparent that the battlefields of this particular former theatre of war have reached the late development and commemoration plateau phase of the post-war A stage, a point which will be elaborated upon later. As Henderson (2000) notes, it is because of the sensitivity of the subject matter that wartime tourist "attractions", i.e. events and sites, pose particular challenges with regard to presentation and interpretation. Unlike with ordinary tourist attractions, there is not, or at least not in the same way, the reinforcement of education through entertainment – a now well-known and well-exploited concept with its own ugly neologism of "edutainment". There may also be, as in the Normandy case, the problem of some of those affected still being alive. That having been said, there can be no doubt that the same entertainment value, which drives some rather macabre voyeurs to gather at air crashes, ferry sinkings and motorway pile-ups, may also motivate what Seaton (1999) calls thanatourism – "dark" tourism, characterised as travel to a location wholly, or partially, motivated by the desire for actual or symbolic encounters with death.

While not suggesting that any more than a minority of Normandy's tourists belong in this somewhat politically incorrect category, it cannot be denied – as Valene Smith (1996: 248) has proposed – that "the memorabilia of warfare and allied products . . . probably constitutes the largest category of tourist attractions in the world". Year 2000 visitor numbers for World War II sites in Calvados (CDT, n.d.) do not contradict this statement: rather they confirm the view of a senior Vietnamese tourist professional that war tourism is big business (Henderson 2000). And if we come to accept reluctantly that war tourism, like the poor, is always with us – and commercial interests alone will determine that this is so – then it is incumbent upon us to ensure that offence to participants and their progeny is minimised. It is also essential to ensure that the matter of heritage dissonance – a term coined by Tunbridge and Ashworth (1996) to describe the bringing of different sets of values, attitudes and experiences to war sites by different parties – is carefully handled. In other words, rarely is there a single truth.

Case Study

This is well illustrated in the case of a children's drawing book, *Ma Promenade en Normandie: le Calvados / My Trip to Calvados, Normandy,* widely available during summer 2001 in Calvados bookshops and newspaper kiosks (Hervieu-Bothelin et al. 2000). The landing beaches page does not actually mention the phrase "*les plages du débarquement*" once but does have several lines in French suggesting that the Germans were distinctly naughty to occupy France, that fortunately France was liberated as a result of soldiers from allied countries such as [sic] the U.S., England [sic] and Canada landing on the coast of Normandy to set our country and the whole of Europe free (this author's translation of "*des soldats venus des pays alliès comme les Etats-Unis, l'Angleterre, le Canada, etc . . . on débarqué sur la côte normande pour délivrer notre pays et l'Europe toute entiére*) and that now the Germans have seen the error of their ways and so the French have made up with them. The one-line equivalent text in English, meanwhile, is strictly limited to the facts (place, date, event) conveyed with a faint hint of heroism on the part of the (unspecified) allied troops but only in as much as it was their duty towards the rest of Europe. (*On Normandy beaches, on june [sic] 6th 1944, the allied troops landed to free continental Europe*). Despite rising numbers of German visitors, there is no German version, which of itself speaks volumes. Explaining to young children exactly why their fellow countrymen felt unable to stay at home and mind their own business is bound to be tricky.

Until recently the huge Mémorial war museum in the regional capital of Caen gently but firmly discouraged younger visitors, with suitable overt warnings to parents as to the length of the visit and the inappropriateness of some of the displays and interpretations for those of tender years while offering well-resourced crèche facilities for different age groups. A less explicit covert message being conveyed may have been either that bored and disruptive children would disturb the ambiance of respectful solemnity for the fallen and might spoil the experience for other visitors, perhaps most especially those French visitors whose childhood was directly affected by the events portrayed and members of whose families were involved in resistance activities. At any rate, the "spin" being adopted to justify such an enormous investment in keeping war live is that informing people about the war as it affected Normandy, and now modern war more generally, is designed to ensure that it never happens again, and, therefore, may be vindicated on that basis. In reality, the management's motivations may be less pure from a financial perspective and those of the clientele from a psychological perspective. At the very least, both are more complex than the advertising blurbs would have us believe. (While nobody – and certainly nobody in a public position – quite points the finger at the Germans and says "We"ll never forgive you", unsurprisingly German is a less popular choice and less widely available than Spanish as a second foreign language in schools in these parts, something which one farm household interviewee was especially concerned that I should understand.)

To establish the precise degree of sensitivity of museum managements and publishing houses to heritage dissonance would require a specific and rigorous study of, for example, publicity materials, interpretive displays, publishers' lists and institutional goals within the framework of prevailing political, social and economic contexts; nevertheless it does appear that certain key interpretations identified here match reasonably well three of Smith's (1998) war tourism type sub-classifications, namely: for the French, reliving the past; for Anglophones, belonging to a heroic past; and for Germans, reminding existing generations of the horrors of war.

The Normandy Landings 50 Years Later

First-time visitors to Normandy in high season often arrive with certain pre-conceptions. Associating the beaches there only with the sorts of images portrayed in Steven Spielberg's 1998 blockbuster film *Saving Private Ryan*, they are more than likely to enquire in hushed tones as to whether it is possible actually to get down on to the sand and, once there, whether it is appropriate to allow their children play. As they will discover, the French – who traditionally are more faithful for a variety of reasons to home-grown seaside resorts than are the British (Ardagh 1987) – have long since discarded their sensibilities about the wartime associations of the landings beaches. The same reasons which made it possible for serried ranks of soldiers to pour out of landing craft – long stretches of shallow water over gently inclining sands – also make the beaches perfect for more conventional and prosaic summertime seaside activities.

At Arromanches, the tide washes in and out over the remains of the famous artificial harbour which was arguably the lynchpin of the entire operation to recapture occupied France for the Allies. There are notices warning swimmers and sailors of the dangers of climbing on the decaying concrete icebergs, but that apart, the thousands of tourists disporting themselves on the sands of the Bay of Normandy might be anywhere. The other detritus of war, such as blockhouses, gun emplacements, monuments to the fallen and repainted tanks have all become part of the scenery, incorporated into the everyday and used unselfconsciously as informal public space. It does not take a genius to work out that it is as a wet weather activity for many of these same thousands of holidaymakers that the World War II museums come into their own. And if rain does succeed in driving holidaymakers off the beach, whether to a modest museum above the breakwater as at Arromanches or St Laurent, or to a massive museum inland as at Bayeux or Caen, they will find that when they are moved to tears or filled with revulsion, dazed with shock or swollen with pride, not only are they not alone in experiencing these emotions, but neither are they experiencing these emotions alone.

Rather they constitute part of a massive and carefully engineered people-processing operation, which underpins the livelihoods of the proprietors of the thousands of small and medium-sized enterprises in the service sector, which spend upon tourists as their principal customers. Excluding the Basilica at Lisieux – famous for its connection with St Theresa, the possessor of miraculous powers of healing and prophecy, and with an estimated 900,000 visitors in 2000 – out of twenty *sites et musées de l'espace historique de la Bataille de Normandie* (sites and museums of the historic theatre of the Normandy Campaign) eleven exceeded the maximum numbers for any castle or other historic monument, four of these by a factor of ten. Of other sites and museums and what French endearingly labels *distractions* (zoos, aquaria, theme parks, gardens and a bungee-jumping venue) only the world-famous Bayeux tapestry (with some 400,000 visitors) and the Carmelite Foundation at Lisieux also associated with St Theresa (with some 300,000 visitors) can begin to compete with the top three war attractions: the United States Military Cemetery at Omaha Beach (1.4 million), the Mémorial museum at Caen (0.4 million) and the underground bunkers at the Pointe du Hoc cliff-top site of Colonel Rudder's U.S. assault (an estimated 0.5 million) (CDT, n.d.: 7-10).

Deconstructing War Tourism in Normandy

Prentice (1993) has produced a useful disaggregated definition of heritage as a production, and as a benefit – something presented and something felt. Exactly how war tourism in Normandy is experienced by its range of visitors constitutes the subject matter of a study yet to be carried out. It is not therefore possible, as yet, to assess how far the experiences of visitors match the expectations and objectives of the deliverers of the tourist product offered for consumption. However, it is certainly possible to emphasise that as far as war tourism is concerned, the claims of history, profitability, authenticity and integrity are not coincident. Especially where "hot" interpretation[3] is concerned, it is preferable that the producers of this particular brand of cultural heritage are not the same people as the producers of the rural idyll, whose childhood was utterly changed by the war and its aftermath. The latter know only too well where their house guests go and what they do in wet weather, and they acknowledge the importance of these tourist draws to their own livelihoods.

Yet thinking about it too much produces at the very least mixed feelings, if not a guilty conscience or even frankly painful memories. For example, one bed and breakfast proprietor revealed to me her relief at the Year 2000 eclipse of the sun, approved by her as a much more appropriate and wholesome tourist draw, which was able to swell her bookings without any psychological or emotional misgivings. Another farmer and guest house proprietor acknowledged his good fortune in being well located for the landing beaches but steered the conversation deftly and firmly towards a discussion of the Romano-Norman arch which forms the entrance to what was once an abbey farm – a topic which clearly constituted a more distant and therefore palatable historical ware to ply to visitors along with his *pommeau* and his cider. Be that as it may, World War II tourism is undoubtedly here to stay in Normandy. In fact, Weaver (2000) suggests that, because World War II is still a relatively recent event, it is not even possible as yet to identify a terminal point to the war-distorted destination life-cycle curve as far as Normandy is concerned.

He also hypothesises that the war dividend there will be even more robust and long-term than that experienced in those destinations associated with long-past wars. The reason for this is because Normandy acts as a geographical focal point for a much more all-encompassing event.

Certainly, the legacy of the 50th anniversary events – which included *inter alia* former president Clinton's official visit to Omaha Beach and the subsequent release of *Saving Private Ryan* – appears to be that the "commemoration plateau" phase of the post-war A stage of the Weaver model, which Normandy reached some years ago, is likely to extend indefinitely, at least in the medium term. Due to the *Saving Private Ryan* effect, visits to the U.S. Rangers Assault site and memorial at Pointe du Hoc peaked at an estimated 0.9 million in 1999, before falling back by 400,000 the following year to the same level as in 1998. The corresponding blip for the American Cemetery above Omaha Beach was much less pronounced, with an estimated increase of 200,000 followed by a smaller decrease of 100,000 to 1.4 million (CDT, n.d.: 8), roughly coincident with the erecting of a notice on the promenade indicating the "Dog Green" and "Dog White" sections of the wartime beach.[4] Especially as the film was actually shot on location in another north Atlantic marginal region, on the beaches of the Irish Gaeltacht, there is a certain dissonant incongruity in unexceptional holiday activities of paddling, picnicking, sunbathing, flying kites and playing *boules* being stared at by North American and other tourists, including many from the Far East, who spill out of the chartered coaches doing the World War II landing beaches circuit of the artificial harbour, Omaha beach and Pointe du Hoc. For, arguably, the selfsame beach packed with holidaymakers, fifty years on, is no more Omaha beach than the one in the film.

The irony is that the rather solemn 1994 acts of commemoration were intended to achieve some kind of closure, on the basis that this was the last major anniversary at which a significant numbers of war veterans would be present. Yet what appears to have happened is that rather than signifying the end of an era, these events have instead constituted the official handover of the war in Normandy from one set of owners to the next: from the politicians to the people. History has become heritage, and that change signals that there is now nothing disrespectful or irreverent about cashing in that war legacy. Perhaps that is why the Caen Memorial has now sought to reposition itself. In the words of its English language website:

> Far from concentrating solely on commemoration, the Memorial . . . presents the stakes involved in the Second World War, and the course and significance of the war. Broadening the perspective, the Memorial covers the second half of the century, and shows how the end of World War II did not signal the end for violence, of all types of violence.

While still describing itself as *un musée pour la paix* (a museum for peace) the museum is now also styling itself as a place for thinking about 20th century history and it has recently created not only a new interpretation area promoting *des mondes pour la paix* – comprising conceptualisations of peace drawn from different world religions and cultures – but also an additional thematic zone devoted to the Cold War. Complete with an actual Russian MiG fighter, the attraction to small boys in particular is magnetic, and even if such an artefact does not glorify war, it does appear to lend to it a frisson of excitement. Perhaps the additional of the this new niche market represents insurance in the face of even a suspicion of declining general interest (a drop of 5,750 visitors or 1.4 percent between 1999 and 2000), In fact today the main website, far from discouraging younger visitors, is distinctly child-friendly, with various options for different age groups from eight years upwards, as well as advice for their teachers. And if some children should whoop or giggle inappropriately too near Battle of Normandy displays, then it is no more than the price to be paid for the greater good of civic education for peace. In other words, the Mémorial has moved on from the geographically specific effects of the Second World War in Normandy and the need respectfully to honour the dead, to any twentieth century war anywhere and for anyone, just as long as lip service is paid to the supposed peace dividend.

Yet, as a cash cow to be milked in this less than robust semi-peripheral economy, what is in truth a war dividend may fail to prove any more reliable than Normandy's real and rather troubled dairy sector. Tourism, and especially international tourism, is fickle, with demand notoriously elastic in response to external events. Ironically, while economic and social possibilities of a shrinking world may bring destinations such as Normandy to the attention of international tourists, political factors inherent to that same globalised world – such as the terrorist attack on the United States of 11 September 2001 – can also act as a powerful, unpredictable constraint.

Discussion

War tourism in Normandy constitutes a nasty necessity, an additional weapon in the armoury of a semi-peripheral economy that is over-dependent on the primary sector. In Basse-Normandie in particular, which is further away from France's metropolitan core, and with family-style resorts which are altogether less chic than more up-market resorts such as Deauville and Trouville further east on the Côte Fleurie, war tourism provides a lucrative additional niche market attracting visitors from the U.K. (and particularly England), and increasingly the U.S. and also Germany, as well as Belgium and the Netherlands. It also provides a ready-made foul-weather complement to fair-weather beach activities for family holidaymakers, both of which types of activity are themselves essential to give added value to potentially rather boring week or two-week long stays down on the farm.

Today's less naïve and much more politically and environmentally aware tourist is not taken in by superficial rurality and can spare Monsieur le fermier and Madame la fermiére the indignity of pretending they are country hicks. But only if a blind eye is turned to promiscuity – that is, in terms of allegiance to tourist attractions – so that it is possible for visitors to sneak away surreptitiously for a bit of "hot" interpretation, to find out how it felt to stumble terrified up the beach in a heavy, clinging uniform, hell-bent on "knocking Jerry for six". For they do not necessarily want to go over the gory, guilty details with their hosts. But, importantly, nor do they want to go inland to the Suisse Normande, where promoting the rural idyll is much less like living a lie, but where, unfortunately, there is neither beach nor war museum in sight. The hills of the Suisse Normande are not like the mountains of Switzerland at all and the sea is just too far away.

Conclusion

Just as in northwest Norway, the Highlands of Scotland, the west of Ireland, and the maritime provinces of Canada, so in northwest France: the real problem lies with the North Atlantic rural interior. In the case of the semi-peripheral region of Basse-Normandie, World War II lends added value to an existing tourist product along the economically well-developed Calvados coastal strip. As war events move from belonging to a painful history to being part and parcel of a diverse cultural heritage, difficult issues, whether for the producer or the consumer, gradually recede. Increasingly, distanced in time as it now is, World War II at local level in Calvados may be counted as asset without deficit. Yet this raises two important regional economic development questions: what can now substitute for the absence of a similar war legacy in the rest of Lower Normandy – in the rural interior to the south, in the Atlantic department of Manche next door, or in neighbouring Brittany even further to the west, an uncompromisingly peripheral Atlantic region? And how can vulnerable peripheral tourist destinations more generally protect themselves against the unpredictability of demand associated with political uncertainty in a globalising world?

Notes

[1] For full details of the conduct of the semi-structured interviews with members of farm households, see McCleery (2001).

[2] See, for example, Byron and Hutson (2001) passim, as well as previous volumes of collected papers from the seminar series of the International Society for the Study of Marginal Regions. However, it is both relevant and significant that Peter Sjøholt, a longstanding and highly respected member of the ISSMR, during the course of the 16th International Seminar on Marginal Regions, stated categorically in Ålesund, western Norway, that there is no such thing as the definitive marginal region.

[3] "Hot" interpretation is described by Uzell (1989) and is intended to shock and to move, providing a type of catharsis, so that the visitor is both challenged and changed as a result of the experience.

[4] While there is no reason to doubt the directional trend of these estimated visitor numbers, nevertheless it should be noted that when actual visitor number counting at the U.S. Cemetery became possible in 2001 with a revamp of entry procedures, the absolute volume of admissions was in fact found to be in excess of two million. (Additional unpublished statistics for 1998 and 2001 courtesy of CDT via e-mail).

References

Ardagh, J. 1987. *France Today*. London: Penguin.

Bord Failte. <www.ireland.ie/usefulfacts/artsandculture.asp>.

Butler, R. W. 1980. The concept of a tourist area cycle of evolution: implications for management of resources. *Canadian Geographer*, 24: 5-12.

Caen Memorial. <www.memorial-caen.fr/> (main site, bilingual); <www.memorial.fr/indexgb.shtml> (subsidiary site, English-language).

Comité Départemental du Tourisme du Calvados (CDT). n.d. *Données Statistiques 2000*. Caen: CDT.

Crang, M. 1996. Magic kingdom or a quixotic quest for authenticity? *Annals of Tourism Research*, 23: 415-431.

Fearne, A. 1997. The History and development of the CAP, 1945-1990. In C. Ritson and D. R. Harvey (eds.), *The CAP*. Second edition. Wallingford and New York: CABI Publishing.

Henderson, J. C. 2000. War as a tourist attraction: The case of Vietnam. *International Journal of Tourism Research*, 2: 269-280.

Hervieu-Bothelin, E. et al. 2000. *Ma Promenade en Normandie: le Calvados/ My Trip to Calvados, Normandy*. Condé-sur-Noireau: Loisirs de Campagne.

Hoggart, K., H. Buller and R. Black. 1995. *Rural Europe: Identity and Change*. London: Arnold.

Hutson, J. and D. Keddie. 1997. Tourism and alternative employment among farm families in less-favoured agricultural regions of Wales. In R. Byron, J. Walsh and P. Breathnach (eds.). *Sustainable Development on the North Atlantic Margin*. Aldershot: Ashgate.

Lowenthal, D. 1998. *Heritage Crusade and the Spoils of History*. Cambridge: Cambridge University Press.

McCleery, A. 2001. Strategic marginalisation and coping mechanisms: farm households in north west France. In R. Byron and J. Hutson (eds.). *Community Development on the North Atlantic Margin*. Aldershot: Ashgate.

McCrone, D., A. Morris and R. Kiely. 1995. *Scotland the Brand: The Making of Scottish Heritage*. Edinburgh: Edinburgh University Press.

Oideas Gael. <www.oideas-gael.com/tours/itinerary.html>.

Prentice, R. C. 1993. *Tourism and Heritage Attractions*. London: Routledge.

Seaton, A. V. 1999. War and thanatourism: Waterloo 1815-1914. *Annals of Tourism Research*, 26: 130-158.

Smith, V. L. 1996. War and its tourist attractions. In A. Pizam and Y. Mansfeld (eds.). *Tourism, Crime and International Security Issues*. Chichester: Wiley.

Smith, V. L. 1998. War and tourism: An American ethnography. *Annals of Tourism Research*, 25: 202-227.

Tunbridge, J. E. and G. J. Ashworth. 1996. *Dissonant Heritage.* Chichester: Wiley.

Urry, J. 1990 (2002). *The Tourist Gaze: Leisure and Travel in Contemporary Societies.* Second edition, 2002. London: Sage.

Uzzell, D. L. 1989. *Heritage Interpretation, Vol. 1.* London and New York: Belhaven Press.

VisitScotland. <www.visitscotland.com/guide/index.htm>.

Wanhill, S. and Buhalis, D. 1999. Introduction: Challenges for tourism in peripheral areas. *International Journal of Tourism Research*, 1: 295-297.

Weaver, D. B. 2000. The exploratory war-distorted destination life-cycle. *International Journal of Tourism Research*, 2: 151-161.

Chapter 5

The Politics of Authenticity and Identity in British Heritage Sites

D. DOUGLAS CAULKINS, VICKIE SCHLEGEL,
CHRISTINA HANSON, AND JANE CHERRY

Our American cousins are here to enjoy history, Tommy. Not to live it.
John Brady, *A Carra King*, p. 17

In the globalised economy of the post-imperial, post-industrial period, the United Kingdom has increasingly exploited a resource more plentiful than coal and iron: its eventful past. In Hewison's (1987) memorable phrase, Britain has developed a heritage industry that has become increasingly important for creating a global tourism industry as a replacement for the declining British manufacturing sector. The rest of the North Atlantic fringe is also finding that much of their potential for competition in a global economy is tied to heritage tourism. For heritage tourism, the so-called authenticity of experiences at heritage sites is often an important issue (Chambers 2000, MacCannell 1976, Boissevain 1996, Cohen 1988, Urry 1990). Do tourists wish to gaze on real artifacts from the past or be immersed in experiences that theatrically represent some aspects of the past? Or, on the other hand, are tourists satisfied with any kind of representations of a world or a period that contrasts with their own lives? The answer is probably yes to all three questions, although perhaps for different tourists and at different times. Not all tourism is heritage tourism, focusing on an interpretation of historical events, places, or cultural traditions. Tourists may come for sun and sand, mountain climbing, boating, skiing, birding, and other outdoor pursuits that draw on a location's natural qualities, but we regard this as a different kind of tourism, also found in many marginal regions, but one that we will not address here. Similarly, we are not concerned here with entertainment tourism, in which tourists may be attracted to gambling, stage shows, rides, spectacles, and other forms of entertainment. While these categories are not absolute, we consider them sufficiently useful to locate the phenomena that we wish to discuss. We will argue for a reassessment of the role authenticity in heritage tourism, particularly at a time of declining numbers tourists have electing to visit the UK.

The Crisis in UK Tourism

Not all is well in the tourism industry in the UK and not all of the problems can be traced to the outbreak of foot and mouth disease in the spring of 2001. Take the case of Scotland. Writing in *The Scotsman* (June 26, 2001), Bill Jamieson asks about what has gone wrong with tourism in Scotland. Under a headline "Time for a rethink as tourism crisis grows", he notes the decline in tourism in the UK for the fifth straight year. Jamieson asserts that there is "little in Scotland that is not affected", including

> Food, and drink sales, catering, hotels, restaurants, pubs, clothes and giftware retailing, pubs, clothes and giftware retailing, arts events attendance, taxis, buses and trains and services in the broadest sense: tourism brings in (or did) L2.5 billion of income. It accounts (or did) for 8 per cent of all jobs, and a large number of Scotland's 230,000 small businesses. When tourism is hit, much else suffers. (Jamieson 2001: 12)

Jamieson argues that the downturn in tourism from Europe is traceable to the strength of the pound against the Euro and this is not likely to change in the near term. His suggestion for coping with the threat of a long-term decline in tourism is a radical reassessment of Scotland's tourism strategy, to target a more upscale market and high-income tourists looking for lifestyle holiday choices, including hotel retreats and healthcare facilities. In addition, Jamieson argues for more international sports events and "also arts, academic, and special interest events and conferencing". Not surprisingly, Jamieson is more persuasive in his characterisation of the nature of the problem than he is about the proposed solution.

Jamieson's warning to the Scottish tourist industry provides an occasion for a more detailed consideration of some of the issues involved in Britain's heritage industry, and the prospects for appealing to an upscale, educated, and affluent customer. We turn our attention to the issue of authenticity, a concept that is often assumed to be the key to heritage tourism. MacCannell (1989) suggests that tourism is an attempt to escape from inauthentic every-day existences into a nostalgic world, usually pre-capitalist, of authentic goods and experiences.

Adapted and Intentional Heritage Sites

In this paper we examine the politics of authenticity and identity in case studies of heritage sites in England, Wales, and Scotland. By "heritage sites" we mean locations and organisations that that have developed information and experiences concerning an historical site, period, or theme to educate, enlighten, inspire, and entertain tourists and natives. Heritage sites normally charge an entrance or membership fee; some are managed by charities and others are run as for-profit ventures. Some adapt an existing structure or location (such as the Callanish Stones in the Western Isles, or the Bannockburn battlefield near Stirling, Scotland). Others, such as Canterbury Tales in Canterbury, or Celtica in Machynlleth, Wales, are intentionally developed to offer an interpretation of a literary text or the culture of a particular historical population. Both of the latter were designed by John Sunderland, an entrepreneur who specialises in creating theatrical heritage sites that rely on audiovisual media for their effect. These heritage sites are postmodernist in their attempt to draw a wider audience by emphasising "the spectacular, the popular, the pleasurable and the immediately accessible" (Featherstone 1991: 96-97). Intentional sites do not necessarily feature, as part of their exhibition, any historical artifacts that have a direct connection with the events or periods that they intend to interpret. Thus, neither Canterbury Tales nor Celtica are museums that house authentic artifacts; their authenticity resides in their effort to create an intellectual and emotional understanding of and empathy for the period and events that they depict. This distinction between intentional and adapted heritage sites is a matter of degree, since all sites are constructed but they may build on different components. We prefer this dichotomy to the authentic/inauthentic distinction suggested by Urry (1990: 83) since all heritage sites attempt to convey authenticity.[1] Our distinction between intentional and adapted sites, in contrast, draws attention to the foundations for the site's claim to authenticity.

We show how the reception, popularity, and the uses of heritage sites by different audiences are tied to the politics, both global and local, of authenticity and identity. We argue that the politics of authenticity and national, regional, or ethnic identity are closely connected. To assert authenticity of an artifact, performance, or interpretation is to make a claim about its importance as a way of viewing the past that might be contested by others. National or ethnic identity is often predicated on these claims for the authenticity of a particular interpretation of the past. Of course, these politics are fluid, responding to media events, cultural and political trends, and changes in the globalised economy. Finally, these politics are never just about the past, but about situating and interpreting the present and future as well.

Comparing Intentional and Adapted Heritage Sites

In contrast to some of the critical and theoretical studies of heritage sites (Urry 1996, Hewison 1989, MacCannell 1976) or case studies (Boissevain 1966,

Macdonald 1996, Macdonald and Fyfe, 1996), our approach is broadly comparative, drawing on participant observation and interviews with staff members at a sample of both intentional and adapted heritage sites in England, Wales, and Scotland, as shown in Table 5.1.

Table 5.1   Intentional and adapted heritage sites

Location	International Site	Adapted Site
Canterbury, England	Canterbury Tales	
York, England		York Minster
York, England	Jorvik, Viking Village	
Machynlleth, Wales	Celtica	
Stirling, Scotland	Wallace Monument	
Stirling, Scotland		Bannockburn Battle Ground
Stirling, Scotland	Stirling Highland Games	
Crieff, Scotland		Glenturret Distillery

Canterbury Tales, Jorvik, Celtica, and the Wallace Monument all offer interpretations of a way of life inscribed in a text (Canterbury Tales), an archaeological site (Jorvik), an empathetic story of a marginalized population (Celtica), or in historical records of a martyr for national independence (Wallace Monument). The first three sites were conceived by John Sunderland and a team of heritage designers in the 1980s and 1990s, while the Wallace Monument, a product of Victorian romanticism, was constructed by public subscription in the 19th century.

The Stirling Highland Games is not a heritage site, but an annual heritage event. It began more than 30 years ago as a summer fun fair, a carnival with a few main events. Later, the elements of typical highland games, including heavy athletic events, bagpipe band competitions, and highland dancing, were added. These highland events take place on the periphery or corners of the grounds, with the main programme directly in front of the grandstand. These main events may include parachute teams, motorcycle team demonstrations, falconry, terrier races, and other crowd-pleasing events. All of the grandstand events are highly accessible to tourists and others and require little cultural knowledge or background as do many of the highland events. The novice may not know what to look for in highland dancing or in the other competitions, but everyone can appreciate the efforts of parachutists to land closest to the prize bottle of whisky that marks the target in the middle of the field before the grandstand. Thus, the Stirling Highland Games combine two kinds of heritage events, the "fun day out" carnival and the events of the typical highland games. In the local context, the latter is an "appropriated" tradition rather than an "invented" tradition (Hobsbawm and Ranger, 1983). In terms of historical depth, the "fun day out" is more authentic local heritage than the second, a reversal of the usual assumption. In addition, it is more accessible to the global tourist, although the romantic tourist may be attracted to the so-called traditional events. The combination seems was selected to interest the local residents as well as address a variety of tourist "gazes", to use Urry's (1990) word.

The Wallace Monument is a fanciful Victorian tower built from locally quarried stone on Abbey Craig, overlooking the site of the Battle of Stirling Bridge, where William Wallace defeated an English army in 1297. Braveheart, the highly romantic 1966 academy-award winning film starring Mel Gibson, sparked interest in Wallace's life and death, bringing a flood of visitors as a consequence of the popularity of the film internationally. In contrast, York Minster, one of the most spectacular medieval cathedrals in England, has attracted thousands of tourists and visitors annually over the centuries.

The last two sites are Scottish. Bannockburn monument overlooks the field where the Scots, lead by Robert the Bruce, defeated the English army in 1314 and established their independence. A small visitors' centre, cafe, and gift shop are housed near the parking lot. Glenturret Distillery, near Crieff, Scotland, has transformed itself from a small business, employing three persons in the manufacture of single malt whisky, into a heritage site that continues production. Having visited this distillery a number of times over more than a decade, the senior author has observed this transformation from a distillery that gives tours into a heritage site that makes whisky.

We devote special attention to Glenturret since it represents a special type of the adapted site. Recall that Robert Hewison (1987) complains that British manufacturing industries have collapsed and have been replaced by heritage industries that produce only nostalgia. Glenturret is an exception to this trend since it continues to manufacture its original product as well as heritage values. The relationship between the two types of production is reciprocal, since the heritage site tourists, like the senior author, become consumers of the primary product. In contrast, Bannockburn, another adapted site, has no direct continuity in its original product, with one exception, since the struggles for Scottish independence have been transferred to other fields, particularly with the devolution of a number of powers from Westminster to the new Scottish parliament in Edinburgh. The one exception is the annual meeting of the Scottish Nationalist Party on the Bannockburn grounds on the anniversary of the battle, June 23-24. This annual meeting has been going on since before the acquisition of the site by the National Trust for Scotland, who otherwise do not permit party-political uses of the site.

Success in an Adapted Site

A closer look at the transformation of Glenturret into a producer of both whisky and heritage values will enable us to envision a strategy for avoiding the substitution of nostalgia for products that so troubles Hewison.[2] Glenturret combined the following dozen components that constitute a blueprint for a successful adapted heritage site. No single component, except perhaps the first, seems essential for the success of an adapted site, but the more components, the better the prospects for success. Table 5.2 shows the components, each illustrated with an example from Glenturret. The point, of course, of extracting these components is to suggest a trajectory for the development of other adapted heritage sites from current industrial or craft firms within the UK or other marginal regions to enhance both the tourist interest and the marketing of the primary products.[3]

The twelve components can be glossed as (1) establishing identity, (2) creating an icon, (3) making a claim of authenticity, (4) establishing a narrative, (5) articulating the narrative in some medium, (6) reinforcing the narrative in another medium, (7) offering themed goods, (8) prolonging visits with meal opportunities, (9) offering further information to those interested, (10) differentiating the site from some negative group or idea, (11) enhancing the opportunity for hands-on experience, and (12) creating or allowing a media tie-in.

Let us consider each of these points briefly. While most peripheral regions will find it easier to claim the identity of industrial or craft sites on the basis of antiquity, rather than large size, it may be possible to claim the "largest remaining" or "once the largest" example of an industry. Creating an icon may be unproblematic: a founder, skilled employee, an imaginary being, or, in the case of Glenturret, distillery cat. Towser, of course, was a record-making mouser, but was otherwise normal in its feline habit of not reliably putting in an appearance for guided tours of the distillery. Now that Towser has passed on, a bronze statue of this noble cat stands at the entrance to the visitation

Table 5.2   Twelve components of adapted heritage sites

COMPONENTS	EXAMPLE FROM GLENTURRET
1. Be a superlative example (the oldest, the largest, the best, the last, the only) of that type of site or at least a "typical" example of that kind of site	1. Oldest distillery of single malt whiskey in Scotland
2. Adopt an icon or character to represent the site or industry.	2. Towser, the cat, the Guiness Book of Records champion mouser (28,000 + mice)
3. Claim authenticity: evidence of an historic product, process, event, or a representation thereof.	3. Traditional distilling process for manufacturing of single malt whiskey
4.Narratized the site with (single or multiple) morals, consequences, lessons, or outcomes.	4. Tour guide: We honor the traditional distilling methods to obtain the best product
5.Articulate the narrative in audiovisual displays, exhibits, and or demonstrations.	5. "The Water of Life" audiovisual presentation; exhibition of traditional crafts associated with distilling.
6. Reinforce the narrative using symbols in a different medium than the audio-visual presentation.	6. Tour guide shows the tartan of the distillery: Green for the surrounding woods, blue for the water, gold for the

	whiskey, and black for the illegal still before the beginning of the legal operation..
7. Make themed souvenirs of the tour available for purchase.	7. Souvenirs range from bottles of whiskey to "Towser" pens.
8. Prolong the visit and offer meals or snacks.	8. Range of meal possibilities from snacks and bar to full-service Smuggler's Room and conference facilities.
9 Make further information available for those who have a greater interest; the lore or history of the site should be thought to be rich, even if the tourist does not want to pursue it.	9. Books about the industry on sale in the gift shop.
10. Draw attention to conflict between the locals and some other dominant, class, region or level of government.	10. Depicting skirmishes with tax agents of the English Crown during the illegal period, 1717-1774.
11. Enhance the opportunity for hands-on experience.	11. Whiskey tasting at end of tour.
12. Create a media tie-in, with the site serving as a backdrop or setting for a film or TV program.	12. Distillery used as set for a feature film.

centre where it cannot be missed. The claim of authenticity of the product or process could be modified by showing "the way we used to do it" in contrast to current production methods. The greater the distinction between those two, however, the more fragile the claim for authenticity. Formulating a narrative or story is a major task, although not necessarily difficult, but needs to be undertaken with the other points in mind. A story that can be articulated in audiovisual terms is most appropriate, given the increasing emphasis on the visual in postmodernism (Urry 1990: 138-140). From a semiotic perspective, the more that the narrative or story can be reinforced in other media, the more rich and memorable it will be. Themed goods have always had this function, whether it is a shirt or cap with the company logo or a Towser pen. Most heritage sites have found that their cafes, tearooms, or restaurants not only prolong the time at the site, and hence the possibility of selling more themed goods, but are important sources of revenue themselves. Unlike sites that intend to dispense pure entertainment, heritage sites need to convey the richness of the information and experience on offer, with a clear indication of how the visitor might gain additional information on the topic, whether that involves purchasing a book or pamphlet, coming back next month when there will be a new exhibit, and/or by visiting another heritage site. The site may also wish to note or emphasise – there is a continuum of possibilities – an opposition to some cultural force, group, or agency. Noting the conflict between Glenturret's 18th century founders and the king's taxmen is harmless enough, while giving dramatic impact to the narrative. Finally, any hands-on, participatory activity or media tie-in is likely to engage postmodern tourists. Becoming a set for an episode of a TV serial or feature film, particularly given the global distribution of English-language entertainment, is a heritage site publicist's dream.

Politics of Authenticity

> Culture and history and heritage, they're all very hot issues now. We're responsible for a lot more than digging up an oul pot and putting it in a glass case for a busload of schoolchildren to gawk at now. The way histories are handled and researched and presented is all very contentious.
>
> John Brady, *A Carra King*, p. 109

While a number of theorists (Featherstone 1991: 102, Metcalf 2001: 166, Urry 1990: 11) argue that no heritage site is truly authentic, and some argue that tourists are interested only in the appearance of authenticity (Zarkia 1996), our experience suggests that the issue of authenticity, nevertheless, constitutes an important contested ground for tourists, critics, and interpreters and managers of heritage sites. For example, Urry contrasts the traditional museum, where authenticity is a property of real artifacts, with new-style heritage centres (intentional heritage centres in our terminology), including Celtica, Jorvik, and Canterbury Tales.

> The new-style heritage centres, such as Jorvik Viking Centre in York or the Pilgrim's Way in Canterbury, are competitors with existing museums and challenge given notions of authenticity. In such centres there is a curious mixing of the museum and the theatre. Everything is meant to be authentic, even down to the smells, but nothing actually is authentic. These centres are the products of a York-based company Heritage Projects, whose work is perhaps the most challenging to existing museums who will be forced to adapt even further. (Urry 1990, 132)

The newly-renovated exhibit at Jorvik Viking Village, which was closed for renovation when we did our fieldwork, is taking pains to revise errors in the previous interpretation. Many of these revisions involve technical issues that would not be of noticed by most visitors, but a passion for accuracy in small things helps to convince that the main experience, too, is genuine.

Celtica, which is an intentional heritage site also designed by heritage entrepreneur John Sunderland, features an audio-visual programme as its main attraction. Because Sunderland wanted to help project his audience back into an oral, story-telling culture, rather than print culture, so the entire exhibit is "told" through earphones by a narrator and mannequins representing Celtic village characters: the bard, the warrior, the druid, the blacksmith, the wife, and so on. There are no written texts for the visitors to read. In its characterisations of the Celtic peoples, past and present, narration in Celtica is essentialist and fails to reveal the source of its authority. For example, when the programme identifies innovativeness as one of the notable characteristics of the Celts, the observer wonders whether the intention is to suggest that the Celts were more innovative than other populations. However, the goal of this section of the exhibition is to provide an aesthetic and emotional experience, to help the viewer to empathise with the Celts, who have been romantically cast as history's martyrs and have great nostalgic appeal for many contemporary individuals who may be alienated from contemporary consumer capitalism. The visitor can supplement these interpretations by examining the extensive written documentation in the Interpretive Centre and in the web-based Historium that cites extensively from standard scholarly sources. We found, however, that the development of the web-based interpretation had not been revised to take account of more recent scholarship, including some that questions the continuity of a "Celtic" culture into the present (e.g. James 1999) nor, perhaps understandably, does it mention that there is much historical evidence to suggest that the idea of Celticness, and what we now take to be its attributes, are largely mythical: the products of nineteenth-century European nation-building and the Victorian romantic imagination (e.g. Chapman 1992).

Canterbury Tales, like Celtica, is an intentional site whose sense of authenticity lies in characterising the historical period through the tour of an exhibit and an audio narration of only four of the tales in Chaucer's work. Intentional sites, unlike traditional or static museums, tend to have set programmes, so that each visitor sees the whole audiovisual presentation. The visitor witnesses a theatre performance, not a museum exhibition. In static museum displays, of course, the visitor is usually free to spend as much or as little time with each exhibit as he or she wishes. The theatre agenda of the intentional site puts a heavy burden on the audiovisual technology, which needs to be upgraded every five years or so in order to avoid appearing dated. Obsolete or non-functional technology tends to underscore the artificiality of the intentional heritage site, threatening the aura of authenticity that the designers intend to create. Authenticity appears least contentious in the case of the York Minster. The heritage aspects of this structure are carried out side by side with its continuous functioning over the centuries as a religious centre. In that sense, the Minster is not representing a particular period in time. It belongs to a continuous stream of lived history, and is both contemporaneous as well as medieval.

Perhaps the greatest battle for authenticity related to our sites has been fought over *Braveheart*, Mel Gibson's academy-award winning film about the life and death of Scottish patriot William Wallace. The film, which premiered in Stirling, Scotland, had an enormous impact on regional tourism, especially the Wallace Monument. After the film opened in the United States, according to the manager of the site, Americans swarmed to the monument, often coming directly from the Glasgow airport. Formerly a sleepy little Victorian national romantic edifice, the Wallace Monument was overwhelmed with pilgrims to this shrine of Scottish heroism and resistance. A new shop, pavilion, and expanded coach and car park were constructed to cope with more than 160,000 visitors a year. The debate about *Braveheart* centred on its historical inaccuracies and the fact that it was filmed mainly in Ireland, both of which were grounds for rejecting its authenticity by Scottish middle class intellectuals. "Just a bunch of Irish men in skirts" was one contemptuous comment by a Glasgow University student.[4] Scottish nationalists and many working class people, however, tended to be less offended by the historical inaccuracies and more persuaded of the authenticity of the portrayal of the injustices suffered by the common people at the hands of the English and the Scottish nobles.

In 1996 the Monument gift shop implicitly participated in this debate by selling videotapes of the film as well as erudite brochures that detailed the inaccuracies of the film. In a 1999 survey of 100 diverse respondents in the Stirling region ("Braveheart Country"), virtually everyone had seen the film and had a strong opinion, pro or con.[5] By the year 2001, people had tired of the controversy and the Wallace Monument gift shop no longer stocked videotapes of the film or copies of the critical brochures. In 2001, however, the critics of *Braveheart* launched a guerrilla campaign, rather than a frontal assault, in the name of authenticity.   The management of the Wallace Monument contracted with retired Army weapons specialists to create a display of weapons from the Wallace era and to lecture about their use. Previously, a much-restored two-handed long sword allegedly belonging to Wallace had been the only weapon on display at the monument. Mel Gibson used a replica of this weapon in the film. The lectures by the weapons specialists obliquely attack Gibson's interpretation of the way that the two-handed sword could be used in battle. For good measure they also attack the interpretation of the equestrian statue of Robert the Bruce at near-by Bannockburn. Brace's horse could not possibly have gone to battle in the fetlock-length, skirt-like cloth protection depicted in the sculpture. The point is that heritage sites such as the Wallace Monument offer almost endless possibilities for the thrust and counterthrust of the politics of authenticity. From the perspective of the visitor, the development of revisionist interpretations at Jorvik or the Wallace Monument can be an important incentive for a return visit to the site. Given the emergence of our popular game-show culture where we are rewarded for knowing things, preferably things that others don't know, the visitor can be pleased to learn new interpretations, large and small, significant and insignificant.   The accumulation of this kind of cultural capital (Bourdieu 1984) may be seen as part of postmodern class competition in consumption of symbolic goods (Urry 1990: 111). Heritage sites, it appears, never are completed or finished, but must be open to new interpretations, as well as new technology, in order to attract a new or repeat clientele and to contribute to the contestation or affirmation of identity.

Politics of Identity

People are coming to Ireland for a lot more than forty shades of green now. They want to see nature, yes, but they want to see a place and a people full of history too, people on the periphery of the continent. I'm not sure that we know what we're sitting on here.

John Brady, *A Carra King*, pp. 120-121

The politics of identity deal with the manipulation of heritage so that it influences interpretations of national or ethnic identity. It emerges most clearly in the National Curriculum for schools in the England, Wales, and Scotland. To pick one example, the curriculum for England and Wales previously focused on the Roman invasion rather than indigenous populations of the time. Now, as Mytum (1999: 189) has noted, the new syllabus has been important in increasing the interest and attention of schools and teachers to indigenous Iron Age ways of life, including forts such as Castell Henllys in Pembrokeshire, Wales. Instruction linked to site visits can focus on the topics of tribes, hill forts and chieftains, on farming and daily life, or on Celtic religion.

Before the 1960s, English and British history – not Scottish history – were taught most extensively in Scottish schools. Because the Wars of Independence between Scotland and England are now an important part of the curriculum, school groups often visit such heritage sites as the Wallace Monument. School parties heavily book in June at Bannockburn, the battle site where Robert the Bruce defeated the English in 1314. Similarly, many school parties visit Celtica, in Wales, to enrich the teaching about the ancient Celts of Wales and elsewhere. Many heritage sites have education officers, animateurs, or re-enactment specialists to put on special programmes for school parties. Sites may send teachers a packet of information and study guides when they book a visit. At Bannockburn, for example, schoolchildren often arrive, pencils in hand, ready to fill in the information in their study guides. One example is a "Wanted" poster that invites the imaginative pupil to draw a picture of outlaw William Wallace and fill in the following information: name, description, crime, issued by. The pupils who provide this information often have an ironic interpretation of Wallace's crime; while Wallace may have been guilty of killing the sheriff of Lanark and disobeying King Edward I, Wallace had good reason to do so!

British educators sometimes complain about the selectivity of the national curriculum. The heritage sites that benefit from the current focus of the curriculum could be out of favour after the next revision. For the foreseeable future, however, some sites such as the Wallace Monument and Bannockburn should enjoy continued popularity. Bannockburn receives more school visits than any other National Trust for Scotland site. The Wallace Monument, owned by Stirling District Council, also helps provide revenue to supplement the costs of supporting other less-visited heritage attractions.

Canterbury Tales hosts many French school parties. Strategically located on the rail line to the continent, Canterbury, and the heritage site, are part of the defence of English language and literature within the EU. While the designers of the attraction may not have had French tourists and the politics of the EU in mind, Canterbury Tales is an important representation of Englishness for visitors from the continent. The UK has been a reluctant partner in the European Community in many ways, and the celebration of English language and literature can be considered one form of resistance to European dominance. Chaucer was not himself nationalistic (Pearsall 1999: 90-93), but that does not prevent others from using his works in a different way in the current generation. Globally, of course, Anglo-American culture has been notoriously hegemonic.

Connecting the Politics of Authenticity and Identity

In the case of both Scotland and Wales we have stateless nations embedded within a larger state. As McCrone, Morris, and Kiely (1995) note, the heritage sites in Scotland have the potential of conferring (and confirming) identity for local residents. Heritage sites are not just for foreign tourists, but also for local residents. In post-devolutionary Wales and Scotland, heritage has assumed greater importance in confirming the identity of these nations that have been granted more powers by central government. During the buildup to devolution and the establishment of a separate Parliament for Scotland and a separate Assembly for Wales, the promotion and interpretation of heritage sites has tended to emphasise the distinctness of the national cultures in contrast to English or British heritage. After all, if the heritage of Scotland and Wales fit neatly into a grand narrative English or British history, devolution would be much less defensible. John Urry (1996: 61) made a similar point more generally, suggesting that "The key then for the post-modern cultural performer is to offer strategies of resistance and to emphasize traces of non-dominant cultures which fit awkwardly with nationally dominant cultures". Concretely, this means that in periods when the identity of non-dominant cultures – such as Wales and Scotland – is contested, the examination and interpretation of heritage is likely to be connected with the examination and interpretation of identity. In the wake of devolution in Scotland, one young Scot was overheard to say in awe and reverence at the view from the top of the Wallace Monument, "I've lived here for more than 18 years but this is the first time that I have been to up here". The lad's tone of chagrin suggested that he regretted his delay. Each person is likely to have a partly idiosyncratic, partly shared interpretation of the experience of a heritage site that influences their understanding of their national identity.

In the construction of Welsh and Scottish heritage sites, a bit of anti-English sentiment (but not too much), may be good for business. Too much anti-English sentiment might be thought to drive away English tourists. For example, locals speculate that the withdrawal of the Welsh Tourist Board and Welsh Development Agency from sponsorship of the development of Celtica may have resulted from the allegedly anti-English tone of the script. The end of the audiovisual programme shows a local Welsh choir dramatically singing a protest song that translates as "We (the Welsh) are still here". Written in the 1980s, the song is a forceful condemnation of Thatcherite policies and cultural politics. An ethical issue arises concerning this point, which we have raised earlier in discussing transformation of adapted sites. While we would discourage any attempt to inflame intergroup enmity as a means of increasing the popularity or notoriety of a site, we would encourage attempts to create greater empathy on the part of tourists for the circumstances of marginal or disadvantaged populations.

The Stirling Highland Games also incorporates a bit of anti-English sentiment in at least one of the featured presentations in front of the grandstand. In 1999, one of a growing number of Scottish battle re-enactment groups used assorted weapons of the 12th and 13th centuries to stage several (unnamed) battles in which the Scots decimated the English. The games are held on a field less than a few hundred yards from the site of the Battle of Stirling Bridge, Wallace's great victory in 1297, so we would expect as much. In the final battle re-enactment, however, the cowardly English ambushed and killed all of the Scottish men, only to be dispatched by vengeful Scottish women. The crowd, which included many tourists, loved it.

The linkages between authenticity and identity within Scotland or Wales are not necessarily winning combinations when it comes to generating local customers for heritage sites. Early in our fieldwork at one site, Marie, one of the young waiters in the cafe, asked me what we were doing. "Studying heritage sites, like this one", I began. She wrinkled her nose in disgust and said "Don't you find that dead boring?" Our conversation convinced me that she was not interested in anything resembling "Tartanry", (McCrone et al. 1995), the highly romanticized, constructed "tradition" of Scotland that is so dear to the hearts of many older Scottish-Americans and Scottish-Canadians who come to Scotland in search of the nostalgic remnants of the pre-diasporic culture. For Marie, intentional heritage sites, with their dramatic audiovisual presentations might be more entertaining, but she might not be sufficiently motivated to go through the door of such an establishment. Heritage, for this young working-class person, is for the affluent who can afford to indulge in the consumption of symbols irrelevant to her life. Coming from the opposite direction, other consultants have told us that they had no interest in the intentional heritage site in their town since it really had nothing authentic, in comparison with the local museum. It was too focused, they thought, on entertainment and insufficiently attentive to substance. In addition, the site was created and managed by people from outside the community. Clearly, there are multiple modes for experiencing heritage sites, by locals, by other tourists from the same nation, by international tourists of the same heritage, and by other international tourists.

Conclusion

Let us return to the problem articulated by Bill Jamieson (2001) concerning the decline in UK tourism and Scottish tourism in particular. Remember that Jamieson recommends developing a new focus for tourism, on "arts, academic, and special interest events and conferencing" aimed at attracting the affluent visitor from abroad. While it seems wise to seek an additional clientele that is less sensitive to economic downturns, we are convinced that the upscaling of the tourist industry in the UK should not be done at the cost of marginalising and alienating the local population. We have seen how fragile community support and goodwill can be for heritage sites. Perhaps relationships with the local community should be higher on the agenda of heritage sites in order to encourage synergistic relationships within the local economy. In Machynlleth, Wales, a visit to Celtica is sometimes followed by a visit to the Alternative Technology Centre, or visa versa. A synergistic relationship could develop if visitors were also encouraged to visit the Owen Glendower Parliament building museum as well as the local art gallery. Visitors might also get in a round of golf at the local club and keep in contact with friends using the local cybercafe. In Stirling, which has a high density of heritage sites, the tourist board has encouraged this kind of synergy, with discounts for attending multiple sites. Stirling is envisioning an additional tourist focus that resonates with Jamieson's recommendations. They want to develop a greater reputation for the arts, theatre, and culture. Their "Stirling Festival" during the summer before the Edinburgh Festival is both well-timed and well-situated to help build that reputation. Glasgow, which has reinvented itself as a city of culture, escaping its earlier image as a decaying industrial slum, also provides a model. Because our study, thus far, has confirmed what Urry (1996: 54) hypothesised as the multivocality and multiplicity of uses of heritage sites, we would be reluctant to suggest that agencies pursue strategies that marginalise existing heritage sites. The appropriate strategy, we suggest, should be to increase the synergy among heritage sites and other economic interests. Where there is a potential for turning a business or industry into a heritage site, that possibility should be pursued, using the checklist of components described earlier. Sites need to speak to locals as well as foreign tourists. Any community or region with a portfolio of heritage sites, some intentional and some adapted, should be able to pursue a synergistic strategy that will attract a broad range of visitors, provide that they avoid the kind of factionalism that is all too common is developing regions.

Acknowledgements

The authors are grateful for the support by the Grinnell College Mentored Advanced Project programme, administered by Associate Dean Paula Smith. The Grinnell College Committee for the Support of Faculty Scholarship, chaired by Dean James Swartz, also provided generous funding for this research. Finally, we are most grateful to the staff and management of the heritage sites that we sampled. Without their patience and helpfulness this study could not have been completed. We, not they, however, are responsible for the interpretations offered here.

Notes

[1] Featherstone (1991: 102) asserts that, "Post-tourists have no time for authenticity and revel in the constructed simulational nature of contemporary tourism, which they know is only a game". We are unconvinced by this homogenising, totalising, deterministic interpretation since it fits so poorly with our ethnographic experience. Rather than uniformity, we find great diversity in tourists' degree of attention to issues of authenticity. We agree with Metcalf (2001: 166) that anthropologists "now begin with a presumption of invention, and are automatically skeptical of any claim of authenticity". For that reason we prefer to avoid Urry's proposed dichotomy of authentic/ inauthentic in order to examine the processes or foundations for the claims for authenticity. In this paper, in short, we attempt to problematise that which Featherstone and Urry have, in different ways, made unproblematic. In addition to authentic/inauthentic, Urry (1990: 83) also draws our attention to the classificatory dichotomies of historical/modern and romantic/collective. Different taxonomies are useful for different purposes, of course.

[2] Urry (1990: 111) criticises Hewison's assumption that "certain meanings, such as nostalgia for times past, are unambiguously transferred to the visitor". We agree and are careful to argue for the plasticity and multiplicity of meanings at heritage sites. These meanings may change rapidly in response to current events and media events.

[3] Participants in the 2001 Seminar on Marginal Regions in Alesund and Volda, Norway might, for example wish to consult the list to consider the possibilities for turning Ekorness Furniture into a heritage site. The participants toured the factory in Sykkylven, Norway. The first component is easy: Ekorness is the largest furniture manufacturer in Norway. It would also need to develop an icon, a clear organisational story, and so on. This story

might be narratised by a video that describes the furniture-making tradition of the region, along with the small factory system, emphasising the relations among peripherality, sparse population, the geographical challenges of the fjord environment, and Sunnmore innovation.   One could imagine constructing a success story of a firm in a peripheral region that, against all odds, triumphs in a global market place, while retaining a social and environmentally responsible approach to production of high-quality goods. The target, of course, would be the kind of up-scale tourists that Bill Jamieson wanted to target for Scotland.

[4]   We are indebted to Amy Kucera for this quotation.

[5]   The research team that collected these data in the summer of 1999 included Anna Painter, Assistant Project Director, and Brooke Heaton, Elizabeth Neerland, Laurelin Muir, Lara Ratzlaff, Sarah Silberman, Kristina Valada-Viars. The research was supported by Grinnell College under an experimental Mentored Advanced Projects Program administered by Associate Dean Paula Smith.

References

Boissevain, Jeremy. 1996. *Coping with Tourists: European Reactions to Mass Tourism.* Providence: Berghahn.

Bourdieu, Pierre. 1984. *Distinction.* London: Routledge and Kegan Paul.

Chambers, Erve. 2000. *Native Tours: The Anthropology of Travel and Tourism.* Prospect Heights, Illinois: Waveland Press.

Chapman, Malcolm. 1992. *The Celts: The Construction of a Myth.* London: Macmillan.

Featherstone, Mike. 1991. *Consumer Culture and Postmodernism.* London: Sage.

Hewison, Robert. 1987. *The Heritage Industry: Britain in a Climate of Decline.* London: Meuthen.

Hobsbawn, E. J. and Terence Ranger (eds.). 1983. *The Invention of Tradition.* Cambridge: Cambridge University Press.

James, Simon. 1999. *The Atlantic Celts: Ancient Peoples or Modern Invention?* London: British Museum Press.

Jamieson, Bill. 2001. Time for a rethink as tourism crisis grows. *The Scotsman*, 26 June 2001.

Macdonald, Sharon. 1996. A people's story: Heritage, identity, and authenticity. In C. Rojek and J. Urry (eds.), *Touring Cultures*. London: Routledge.

MacCannell, Dean. 1976. *The Tourist: A New Theory of the Leisure Class.* London: Macmillan.

Macdonald, Sharon and Gordon Fyfe (eds.). 1996. *Theorizing Museums: Representing Identity and Diversity in a Changing World.* Oxford: Blackwell.

McCrone, D., A. Morris and R. Kiely. 1995. *Scotland – the Brand.* Edinburgh: Edinburgh University Press.

Metcalf, Peter. 2001. Global "disjuncture" and the "sites" of anthropology. *Cultural Anthropology*, 16 (2): 165-185.

Mytum, Harold. 1999. Pembrokeshire's pasts. Natives, invaders and Welsh archaeology: The Castell Henllys experience. In Peter G. Stone and Philippe G. Planel (eds.), *The Constructed Past: Experimental Archaeology, Education, and the Public.* London: Routledge.

Pearsall, Derek. 1999. Chaucer and Englishness. *Proceedings of the British Academy*, 101: 77-99.

Urry, John. 1990. *The Tourist Gaze.* London: Sage.

Urry, John. 1996. How societies remember the past. In Sharon Macdonald, Sharon and Gordon Fyfe (eds.), *Theorizing Museums: Representing Identity and Diversity in a Changing World.* Oxford: Blackwell.

Zarkia, Cornelia. 1996. Philoxenia: receiving tourists – but not Guests – on a Greek island. In Jeremy Boissevain (ed.), *Coping with Tourists: European Reactions to Mass Tourism.* Providence: Berghahn.

PART THREE:
GOVERNANCE
AND DEVELOPMENT

Chapter 6

Planning for Regional Development in a Peripheral Open Economy: The Case of Ireland

JAMES WALSH

In 1991 at the Eleventh International Seminar on Marginal Regions in Lillehammer I presented two papers in which I treated all of Ireland as a marginal region in the context of the European and global economies. The first paper on demographic and labour market adjustments highlighted the extent of emigration, and the emergence of many symptoms of marginalisation in the capital city region thereby adding a new dimension to the regional problem in Ireland. The second paper analysed the adjustments taking place within a productivist model of agriculture that was very strongly supported by the CAP. Anticipating reform of the CAP the paper pointed to the very significant challenges that would arise in many rural areas where already the majority of farmers were marginalised. Both papers concluded rather pessimistically with calls for a new approach to development and for greater attention to the local and regional impacts of centrally devised and administered sectoral policies (Walsh 1993a, b).

Ten years later the situation in Ireland is very different. Ireland can no longer claim to be one of the poorer regions of Europe. Per capita GDP levels increased from about 70 percent of the EU average to the second highest in the EU in 2000. Annual economic growth rates in excess of 7 percent were experienced from the mid 1990s reaching a peak of over 11 percent in 2000. Net emigration has been replaced by relatively high levels of net in-migration including large numbers of return migrants and also many others from diverse ethnic backgrounds. The unemployment rate declined from about 17 percent to under 4 percent with evidence of shortages of workers in most sectors.

The extraordinary turn-around since the early 1990s is the result of many interrelated factors that have been described in detail by others, for overviews see Bradley et al. 1997, Barry 1999, Walsh 2000. The Irish "success story" has attracted widespread international attention and has been applauded by many including the OECD which now regards Ireland as a model for many other developing regions and countries. The transformation that has occurred is all the more extraordinary given the openness of the economy. After Luxembourg, Ireland is the second most open economy among the OECD members.

The economic growth of the last decade has improved the relative position of Ireland vis-a-vis other more developed parts of Europe when measured according to standard economic indices. Equally within Ireland the vast majority of people are enjoying a higher standard of living (recent surveys confirm that fewer are living in poverty) and some positive impacts of change have been experienced throughout most regions (Nolan et al. 2000). However, while there have been improvements in absolute terms there has been an increase in relative levels of inequality between and within regions, and also between different categories of households. Using a variety of indices it has been shown that outcomes from rapid development in the 1990s were uneven: see for example Boyle et al. (1998/99), Duffy et al. (1999) and Walsh (2000) on the regional trends in output and employment; O'Leary (2001) on trends in living standards, and Commins and McDonagh (2000) for the impacts on rural areas.

The focus in this chapter is on the regional or spatial aspects of development in Ireland. There is substantial evidence that the economic growth rates and the associated labour market and demographic trends have varied between and within regions. In response the government has prepared a National Spatial Strategy that will seek to provide a framework for achieving balanced regional development. The next section will outline briefly the background to the formulation of the strategy that will be followed by a discussion of the processes involved in its preparation. The final sections will address some of the key concepts underlying the strategy before setting out the principal proposals.

The current enthusiasm in Ireland for strategic spatial planning owes much to the completion of the European Spatial Development Perspective (ESDP) in 1999 and its endorsement by the member states of the European Union (Faludi and Wasterhout 2002). The EU initiative was followed in 2000 by the Council of Europe in its publication, *Guiding Principles for Sustainable Spatial Development of the European Continent* (CEMAT 2000). The ESDP process and outline proposals have generated much debate (see for example Richardson 2000, Richardson and Jensen 2000, Kunzmann 1998, Jensen and Jorgensen 2000, Eser and Konstadakopulos 2000, Copus 2001, Albrechts 2001). There is already widespread evidence of a return to strategic spatial planning within many member states – for example in the U.K., a strategy has already been prepared for Northern Ireland and the process is under way in Scotland and Wales (Department for Regional Development 2001, Department of Transport, Local Government and the Regions 2001).

The Context for the National Spatial Strategy

The need for a spatial strategy emerged in response to the uneven regional spread of development over the past decade, and also in response to changes occurring within a number of policy areas, both in Ireland and the EU. The exceptionally rapid growth since the early 1990s took place against a background of serious infrastructural deficits arising from very limited capital investment in the 1980s. A major driver of the new economy has been foreign direct investment in selected manufacturing sectors and in internationally traded services which has resulted in a major shift in investment, employment and population towards Dublin and the other cities. The total population increased by 250,000 from 1990 and the number at work by about 500,000 (almost 50 percent). Additional numbers at work, higher incomes and an abundance of loan finance resulted in an increase of 50 percent in the number of cars on the roads leading to enormous problems of congestion especially in and around Dublin. The concentration of employment also contributed to a sharp rise in demand for housing which lead to spiralling house prices and also a rapid growth of new residential developments in towns, villages and the open countryside (Horner 2002). This in turn has resulted in increased volumes of long distance commuting, mostly by private car.

The pressures are not confined to the major urban areas. The general rise in affluence has resulted in increased demand for second homes and holiday accommodation, especially in coastal areas. There has been a proliferation of new house building in many rural areas, giving rise to concerns about the sustainability of this type of settlement in the future. At the same time there are some rural areas, largely remote inland areas, where there appears to have relatively little new activity. At the same time there are some rural areas, largely remote inland areas, where there appears to have been relatively little new activity. Furthermore many of the previously strong farming areas are undergoing structural changes associated with the transition to post-productivist agriculture and experiencing decline in population and employment (McHugh and Walsh 2000).

The trends just outlined have emerged from a period during which the economic growth rates were much higher than anticipated by anybody and for which there was no overall spatial framework nor were there appropriate administrative structures to ensure co-ordination and integration and policies and actions. Serious concerns about the emerging spatial patterns of development were articulated in relation to a number of policy areas. These can be summarised very briefly.

From the mid 1990s a number of reports were produced by the principal agencies responsible for promoting enterprises in the manufacturing, food processing and international services sectors. A recurrent theme was the need for a coherent regional policy. For example, *Enterprise 2010,* published in January 2000 by the agency with responsibility for enterprise planning, makes a very strong case for a spatial strategy that will ensure, inter alia, "co-ordinated provision of access, communication and utilities infrastructure and serviced land at an appropriate scale for towns of different size" and "a good regional spread of educational and training facilities".

Sustainable Development: A Strategy for Ireland prepared by the Department of the Environment and published by the Government in 1997 was a landmark report. Effectively a new concept of development was proposed which affirms the centrality of the environment in the process of development. The overall aim of the strategy is "to ensure that economy and society in Ireland can develop to their full potential within a well protected environment, without compromising the quality of that environment, and with responsibility towards present and future generations and the wider international community" (p. 25). Chapter 14 of the strategy emphasises the function of the physical planning system to achieve integration on a territorial basis. The strategy also envisages planning authorities taking a more strategic view of settlement patterns, development needs and major infrastructural services, and the need to link the statutory five-yearly review of the development plan with a coherent longer-term rolling plan.

The legal planning framework for promoting sustainable development is articulated in the Planning and Development Act, 2000, which adopts sustainable development as a guiding principle, thereby extending the concept of development that underpinned much of the previous legislation. The general thrust of the act is towards a comprehensive and integrated approach to spatial planning extending from the local authority level (counties and cities in Ireland) through the regional to the national level so that the overall objective of balanced and sustainable development can be achieved in a manner that is compatible with the emerging supranational perspective represented by the European Spatial Development Perspective published by the European Commission in 1999 (for a comprehensive overview of the preparation of the ESDP see Faludi and Wasterhout 2002).

In parallel with the initiatives emanating from the Department of the Environment other departments and fora were dealing with policy issues where the need for a spatial development strategy was also identified. Following the publication of a number of reports on rural development the Department of Agriculture and Food published in August 1999 a white paper on rural development, *Ensuring the Future – A Strategy for Rural Development in Ireland.* Among its many proposals there is a commitment that the objectives for rural development need to be approached within a framework for spatial development that will take account of the relationships between rural and urban areas and also of the diverse functional role of towns and villages for those residing in the countryside.

In advance of preparing the National Development Plan for the period 2000-2006, which would form the basis for negotiating EU structural funds, the Department of Finance commissioned a study from the Economic and Social Research Institute (ESRI) on the priorities for investment over the period to 2006. Significantly, while the ESRI report is mainly an investment strategy it contains a lengthy analysis of regional trends leading to recommendations that a national spatial strategy is needed to provide a framework for a massive investment programme proposed over the medium to long term.

Contemporaneously with the preparation of the ESRI report and on-going work on the National Development Plan by the Department of Finance, the National Economic and Social Council (NESC) was engaged in the preparation of an outline strategy for development over the next decade. It sets out a new vision for Irish society that has many components including the objective of "sustainable and balanced development between regions and between urban and rural areas". The report places considerable emphasis on a comprehensive programme of infrastructural investment that will encompass economic, social and environmental dimensions. The Council report concludes with a strong recommendation for a National Spatial Development Strategy.

One of the consequences of the rapid economic growth of the early 1990s was that all of Ireland is no longer eligible for Objective One status in relation to EU structural funds (eligibility is based on a per capita GDP less than 75 percent of the EU average). During the course of preparing the National Development Plan, the government negotiated with the EU for the division of Ireland into two NUTS 11 level regions in order retain Objective 1 status for the poorer Border, Midland and West (BMW) regions. The remainder of the country is designated as an Objective One in transition region and will cease to receive structural funds after 2006.

The *National Development Plan 2000-2006* (NDP) published in November 1999 has four core objectives: continuing sustainable national economic and employment growth, consolidating and improving Ireland's international competitiveness, fostering balanced regional development, and promoting social inclusion.

This is the first of the three national development plans since 1989 to accord such prominence to the objective of balanced regional development. The government's objective for regional policy in the NDP is "to achieve more balanced regional development in order to reduce the disparities between and within the two regions and to develop the potential of both to contribute to the greatest possible extent to the continuing prosperity of the country. Policy to secure such development must be advanced in parallel with policies to ensure that this development is sustainable with full regard to the quality of life, social cohesion, and conservation of the environment and the natural and cultural heritage" (paragraph 3.19, p. 43).

The plan is by far the most ambitious ever, involving a projected gross investment programme costing just over 50 billion euro, almost two and half times the scale of investment projected under the previous plan for 1994-1999. The plan is being implemented through four inter-regional operational programmes and two regional programmes. The regional programmes account for approximately 12 percent of the total planned investment. In total, per capita expenditure in the Border Midland West region will be about 38 percent higher than in the other region and the region's share of total investment is set to increase from approximately 30 percent under the 1994-99 programmes to 33 percent. When this shift is combined with the overall enlargement of the investment programme it will lead to almost a trebling of the level of per capita investment in the BMW region. In addition to the investment programme, the regional aid guidelines (covering grant aid to productive enterprises) permit significantly higher levels of incentives in the BMW region.

Such an enormous increase in the scale of investment will undoubtedly have profound impacts on the economy, society and the environment and especially on the landscape. The introduction of regional programmes with significant budgets to be administered by regional assemblies and the introduction of a more differentiated schedule of permissible levels of regional support through financial instruments makes it all the more important to have an overall spatial framework to guide investment decisions and to facilitate co-ordination and integration across programmes.

The National Development Plan includes a commitment from the government to prepare a strategy for spatial development in order to achieve the regional policy objectives within the guiding principles of maintaining economic competitiveness and sustainable development. The proposed framework is intended to provide a blueprint for spatial development over a twenty-year horizon. Two outcomes are expected from the National Spatial Strategy (NSS). The first is that it will "identify broad spatial development patterns for areas and set down indicative policies in relation to the location of industrial development, residential development, services, rural development, tourism and heritage". Secondly, it will "develop and present a dynamic conception of the Irish urban system, together with links to rural areas, which recognises inter alia and utilises their economic and social interdependence". As a result it is envisaged the NSS will provide the basis for longer term co-ordination and co-operation in policy formulation and decision-making on major investment in infrastructure, including public and private transport infrastructure.

Preparation of the National Spatial Strategy

Preparation of the National Spatial Strategy commenced in Spring 2000. A Spatial Planning Unit was established within the Department of the Environment and Local Government. In Spring 2000 it produced a scoping report that set out the objectives and methodology for preparing the strategy (Department of Environment and Local Government 2000a). The objectives involved some modification of those in the National Development Plan with more explicit reference to quality of life, and the natural and cultural heritage. Specifically the objectives are:

- continuing national economic and employment growth

- continuing improvement in Ireland's international competitiveness

- fostering balanced regional development

- improving the quality of life for all sections of society and

- maintaining and enhancing the quality and diversity of the natural environment and cultural heritage.

These will enable future patterns of development to be set within a context that will accord with the Government's overall aims on sustainable development which have been defined in a manner that encompasses

- environmental sustainability: living within the capacity of natural environmental systems;

- economic sustainability: ensuring continued prosperity and employment opportunities; and

- social sustainability: ensuring greater opportunities to participate in economic success in a way that adds to personal well-being and quality of life.

Preparation of the strategy was guided by two parallel and complementary methodological processes. The first was an extensive research programme undertaken by staff of the Spatial Planning Unit and external consultants. The second was an extensive programme of consultation. The latter involved mechanisms for consultation across government departments and also engaging many of the state agencies, presentations to the cabinet, and also to national fora that include representatives of all the social partners as well as the third sector.   In addition a number of roadshows were organised throughout the country. The SPU was also guided by an interdepartmental steering committee and by an expert advisory group that included representation from Northern Ireland, the UK, and the EU.

Before proceeding to consider some of the outcomes form the research programme it is useful to summarise the key issues that arose from the public consultations. They can be grouped according to a number of themes as follows:

1. Quality of Life

This was an overriding concern for many people as they perceived that there had been a deterioration.

2. Transport

Present systems of public transport were regarded as insufficient for the growing numbers of users. There was a widespread perception of poor accessibility and availability of public transport in rural areas. The inadequate condition of many sections of the national roads was also a concern.

3. Employment Prospects

There had been job losses, particularly outside the main cities, and the range of employment options in rural areas was limited. Large companies were reluctant to locate outside of Dublin due to poor infrastructure, and the unavailability of skilled staff.

4. Declining Populations in Rural Areas

This was linked to poor job prospects, lack of public transport and absence of recreational facilities for young people. Long distance commuting from rural areas was considered to be leading to a fragmentation of rural communities.

5. Access to Health/Education Facilities

Good access is required to hospitals and universities via private or public transport.

6. Fitting the NSS in with other Plans and Programme

Will the NSS fit in with county and city development plans and other strategic plans?

7. Scope of the NSS

Less developed areas may not be given as much priority as areas that are better developed economically. On the other hand, there is a need to avoid becoming diverted from sustaining present growth in areas that are doing well.

The research programme involved over twenty separate studies covering issues related to urban and rural areas, linkages to Europe, transportation and IT infrastructures, access to education, and provision of social infrastructure. In addition regional population projections were prepared up to 2020. Here it is possible to refer to only some of the most salient findings. Before doing so it is necessary to note that the research had to be undertaken within a very limited timeframe and by relatively small numbers of researchers. For micro-level spatial analysis census data are a vital resource but unfortunately the most recent population census was taken in 1996 (a new census was taken in 2002 but none of the results were available during the preparation of the NSS) Given the enormity of the changes that have occurred since then it is inevitable that the extent of some of the key spatial adjustments have been underestimated.

A comprehensive analysis of the structure of rural areas was undertaken in order to identify the diversity of socio-economic conditions and adjustment patterns throughout the state. About 40 percent of the total population resides in rural areas. There were major differences between urban and rural areas in the changes in population and employment between 1991-96. The rural population increased by 0.4 percent compared with an increase of 4.4 percent in urban areas. The total number of employed persons increased by 4 percent in rural areas compared to an increase of 16 percent in urban areas.

Within the rural areas there were very pronounced differences in adjustment. A rural typology was constructed from a dataset of 30 census-based indicators measured for over 2700 districts. It shows that there are six area types: two traditionally strong rural area types, two weak areas types, and two types of areas where there are significant urban impacts. The latter category consists of, on the one hand, peri-urban areas on the fringe of urban centres and on the other hand, remote areas that are mostly coastal and subject to changes related to tourism and other forms of consumption that emanate mainly from the larger urban centres. A striking but perhaps not surprising feature of the typology map is that the area boundaries do not always coincide with the administrative map and the likelihood is that the boundaries are unstable over time (McHugh and Walsh 2000).

Research on the urban system revealed the increasing dominance of the capital city within the Irish urban system but also its pivotal role in linking Ireland to the international space economy and also to the sources of cultural, social and political change. The research identified a number of urban sub-systems including regional capitals, county towns, potential duo-centric and polycentric clusters and also extensive areas where the settlement pattern is particularly weak. An important conclusion from this research is that apart from Dublin none of the other cities is likely to be large enough to become a significantly competitive location for economic development in the context of the European urban system. An analysis of urban functions revealed a lack of correspondence between population rank and functional rank in many cases leading to a trichotomous categorisation. The first consists of a number of strategically located towns that have functional roles in excess of what their population size might suggest. A second grouping represents mainly dormitory towns with large numbers of commuters that have relatively restricted functional bases. The third category are those towns where there is a broad level of correspondence between population and functional ranks (Department of the Environment and Local Government 2000b).

Linking with the rural analysis the urban research noted many urban centres in previously strong rural areas that are now in decline. There was a striking difference in the performance of towns with populations either above or below 5,000 persons. The majority of towns with more than 5,000 population are growing and are the most likely locations for new manufacturing or service enterprises. Over half of the towns and villages with populations <1,500 and 40 percent of those between 1,500-3,000 declined in population between 1991-96. When the uneven distribution of large urban centres is combined with the relative remoteness of many rural areas a map of (in)accessibility scores was produced which illustrates the very significant challenge in relation to access to markets that has to be overcome by residents of extensive areas in the northwest and also in parts of the southwest. The analysis of recent trends in the location of new enterprises established a significant negative relationship between remoteness and employment change.

Research on transportation pointed to the lack of coordination between investment in roads and rail services. The roads investment programme planned under the NDP is likely to seriously erode the competitiveness of rail for long distance movements, even though the resultant movement patterns will be less environmentally sustainable. The analysis of the IT infrastructure provision revealed the existence of a major digital divide with the weaker rural areas particularly disadvantaged. While it is technically feasible to roll out the fibre optic cables across and within the regions and to establish connections through multiple mechanisms the main challenge lies in the fact that most of this activity is being driven by the private sector which is most likely to concentrate its investments in areas of high population density where service demand is likely to be high.

The lack of investment in electricity generation and also in the transmission network in the 1980s coupled with an enormous increase in demand to support a more energy intensive burgeoning economy has resulted in serious bottlenecks. These are particularly serious in extensive parts of the west and northwest and are now a major constraint in relation to future industrial and service sector development.

The bulk of the research has analysed the contemporary socio-economic situation in so far as it is possible to do so given the data limitations referred to earlier. Preliminary results from the 2002 Census of Ireland confirm that there has been a very rapid increase since 1996 (more than eight percent) with net in-migration exceeding natural increase. The distribution of the population growth highlights in particular the attraction of urban centres, the very significant spillover from Dublin to parts of the Midland and Southeast regions, and also the continued dynamism of selected rural areas especially at scenically attractive locations (CSO 2002).

On the basis of the most reasonable set of assumptions for population projections it is anticipated that the total population could increase by about 900,000 (approximately 25 percent) between 1996 and 2021. In the absence of a spatial strategy it is expected that up to 80 percent of the increase will occur in the greater Dublin area. They also suggest outside of the Dublin region the next highest levels of population growth are likely to be around Limerick and Galway cities. The prospects for the Midlands and the Southeast are least encouraging (CSO 2001).

Key Concepts in the National Spatial Strategy

A number of key concepts emerged in the preparation of the national spatial strategy (DOELG 2001). A central objective is to facilitate the promotion of balanced regional development (BRD), while at the same time maintaining the competitiveness of the economy, improving the quality of life of all persons, and ensuring that the development model is sustainable. After much analysis it was concluded that an approach based on measures to ensure equity in distributions across regions is unrealistic and unlikely to succeed. Rather, an approach that seeks to optimise the utilisation of the specific and unique potential within definable areas is more realistic and more likely to succeed. The manner in which the concept of BRD was defined and interpreted was a crucial issue in the formulation and ultimately in the acceptability of the strategy. The indications from the consultation process are that there is widespread support for a "potential-" rather than a "redistribution-based" approach to BRD.

The types of economic activity in an area, the nature of its urban and rural areas, its people, skills and resources, all comprise potential for economic and social progress and development. Potential might be defined, therefore, as the capacity which an area possesses for development arising from its endowment of natural resources, population, labour, economic and social capital and location relative to markets (DOELG 2001). Different areas have differing types and levels of potential. The NSS explores how the level of potential that an area is capable of sustaining can be strengthened and built upon.

Critical mass is an important concept in optimising local and regional potential. It has been defined as the size, concentration and characteristics of populations that enable a range of services and facilities to be supported and which, in turn, can attract and support higher levels of economic activity. This in turn tends to enlarge the population and so further supports a strengthening of services and facilities. The transformation that has occurred in Dublin since the early 1990s illustrates the importance of critical mass. Dublin's success has been assisted by its population size and structure, the levels of education, the availability of educational resources, the mix and clustering of different types of labour pools in niche sectors, transport links to other regions and countries, and informal networks of people and enterprise that provide the scale or critical mass to enable rapid economic progress to take place.

Critical mass can be achieved in different ways. It will normally require a concerted effort to develop a single town or city to play a larger role and deliver benefits to its wider hinterland. Alternatively, in some areas it might involve providing a package of supports to link a number of neighbouring towns in a polycentric network in order to collectively achieve a critical level of supporting infrastructures, facilities and services.

The same level of critical mass cannot be achieved everywhere. Concentration of critical mass to achieve stronger centres and thereby the development of related areas is a crucial dynamic in bringing about more balanced regional development. This will necessarily involve difficult choices of deciding how and where to concentrate efforts. However, concentrating on developing critical mass in particular places will achieve more benefits for their wider hinterlands and for the country as a whole in terms of enhancing the range of competitive locations for development, than would an approach that attempts to spread efforts too widely.

Maintaining an on-going dynamic of development is crucially dependent on the capacity to promote and sustain a high level of innovation within regions. The extensive literature on regional innovation systems points to the importance of supportive institutional structures to nurture an innovative milieu (Morgan and Nauwelaers 1999). There is a very strong emphasis on communication structures to facilitate both formal and informal knowledge exchanges, and also on maximising the potential of local resources. Much of the international experience also suggests that local labour markets need to be large enough to cope with relatively high levels of staff turnover. These requirements support the emphasis placed in the approach to BRD on developing local potential and achieving critical mass.

The foregoing analysis has implications for the choice of an appropriate spatial structure to fully realise the potential of the people and other resources throughout all parts of the country in a manner that will be sustainable, maintain overall competitiveness of the national economy and achieve balanced regional development. A number of alternative scenarios were considered including:

- continuing with present trends;

- adjusting present trends by restricting growth of Dublin and expanding significantly the other four cities;

- same as the first option with the addition of a new city in the regions where the urban structure is weakest; and

- restricting Dublin, no additional efforts targeted to other cities, and dispersal of supports to all towns with more than 1500 persons.

Each of these was considered and found to be deficient in relation to the goals that the NSS is seeking to achieve. The research undertaken for the NSS suggested that spatial trends and patterns of activity and development in Ireland could be seen in terms of functional areas containing cities or towns and their hinterlands that are loosely defined in terms of boundaries. According to the DOELG (2001) these are areas that typically tend to share common characteristics and issues, where people live their working, schooling, shopping and leisure lives and with which many can identify. This sense of identification spans the urban-rural divide and frequently extends across county boundaries.

Some of these areas, where there is a strongly dominant centre, such as the commuting catchment of a major city, are easier to identify than others. Another noteworthy feature is the merging of the various areas at their edges. Each of the areas contains an urban centre or a number of centres, which are central to the economic functioning of that area. There is also a recognised interdependence between the urban centre or centres and other parts of the overall area. The outputs from the research programme suggest that the whole of Ireland can be regarded as consisting of twelve functional areas (see DOELG 2001 for map of the functional areas).

Taking account of the concepts noted above strategic roles were identified for different parts of Ireland. For the greater Dublin area the primary role of the NSS is to consolidate its physical size and the public transport system in order to maintain the international competitiveness of the region and thereby contribute to the overall development of Ireland. Beyond the greater Dublin area it is proposed that the potential of the larger urban centres in the south, southeast, west and northwest should be strengthened through the implementation of planning, landuse and transportation strategies that will, over the medium to longer term, lead to the emergence of new polycentric networks with significant levels of critical mass. The urban system in the much of the midlands and southeast will need to be reinforced through inter alia new forms of cooperation, in order to achieve sufficient critical mass that will ensure the area maintains its own vitality and avoids becoming dominated by the greater Dublin area or the stronger urban centres to the south and west. The western areas furthest from Dublin will require sustained efforts to revitalise their economies principally through diversification into service related activities that capitalise on the existing urban centres and the richness and diversity of the natural resource base. Finally, in an all Ireland context it is proposed that opportunities for enhancing local potentials could be developed through greater emphasis on initiatives supported by more cross border cooperation.

Components of the National Spatial Strategy

A number of specific actions are proposed in order to achieve the NSS objectives. These include a settlement strategy, a transport framework and proposals in relation to other forms of major infrastructure (e.g. energy and information communication technologies).

The settlement strategy recognises the vital national role of Dublin as an international gateway in the future and it also recognises the possibilities for increased cooperation between Dublin and Belfast. The NDP in 1999 had already identified Cork, Limerick-Shannon, Galway and Waterford as additional gateways. The NSS envisages closer links being developed between these centres through improvement of transport infrastructure and measures to foster cooperation that will lead to a much greater level of critical mass in the context of a polycentric network. The achievement of this objective will be a major challenge, for which there are few international precedents (McCafferty 2002). As none of the gateways identified in the NDP (with the exception of Galway) are located in the Objective One region the NSS proposes four additional gateways: Dundalk in the northeast and centrally located between Dublin and Belfast, Sligo as the principal town between Galway and the new gateway for the North West based on Letterkenny linked with Derry in Northern Ireland. In the Midlands the current structure of the urban system suggests the need for a polycentric gateway based on the towns of Athlone, Mullingar and Tullamore. The system of gateways will be supported by another tier of Hubs that are each linked to a gateway. While in most cases the hubs are strategically chosen single centres there are two instances where towns will be twinned to create duo-centric hubs, Tralee-Killarney in the southwest and Castlebar-Ballina in the west (Figure 6.1). The principal characteristics of gateways and hubs are summarised in Table 6.1.

The gateways and hubs will be complemented by specific roles for smaller urban centres and also by general guidelines in relation to housing in the countryside. In order to promote balanced regional development the settlement strategy will be supported by a national transport framework that will include (a) strategic radial corridors linking each of the gateways to Dublin, (b) strategic linking corridors to improve interaction between the major centres and (c) international sea and air access points (Figure 6.2). The linking corridors are vitally important to altering the current pattern of movements between centres. The proposals include a western corridor from Derry to Limerick and Cork; a southern corridor linking the seaports and airports in the southeast, southwest and Midwest; and a central spine linking the proposed Midland Gateway to Dundalk, Waterford and Rosslare.

As the National Spatial Strategy provides a framework for achieving the government's regional policy objectives it will need to be supported by all government departments and public sector agencies. The Minister for the Environment and Local Government and his department will be responsible for leading the implementation of the NSS. All relevant government departments and agencies are required to put structures and mechanisms in place to support the strategy and to ensure it is embedded in their programmes and policies. A cabinet subcommittee representative of all relevant departments will monitor implementation of the strategy at the national level. regional plans will be prepared to assist implementation at the meso level and all local plans will need to comply with the NSS objectives.

Issues Arising from the Process

At this stage of the process it is useful to reflect on some of the more general issues that have arisen. Each will be treated very briefly.

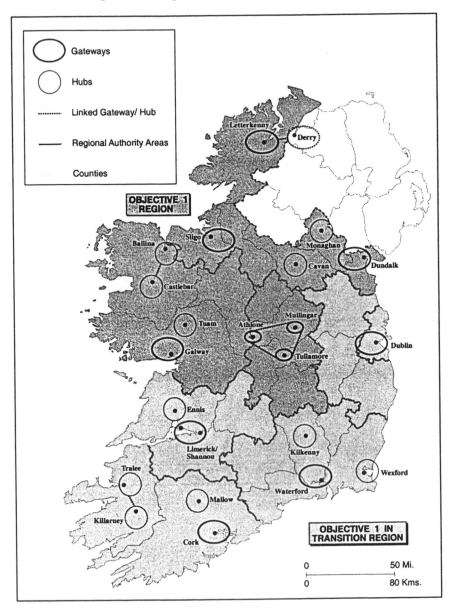

Figure 6.1   Gateways and hubs

Source: Based on map 2, *National Spatial Strategy* 2002

Table 6.1 Characteristics of gateways and hubs

A large urban population (100,000 or more) set in a large urban and rural hinterland	A significant urban population in the range of 20,000 to 40,000 with an associated rural hinterland
Wide range of primary and secondary education Facilities and national or regional third level centres of learning	Primary and secondary education facilities with the option of third level or outreach facilities
Large clusters-of national/international scale enterprises, including those involved in advanced sectors	A mix of local, medium sized and larger Businesses serving local, regional and national/ international markets
A focal point in transportation and communications terms: (a) on the national roads and rail networks (b) within 1 hour of an airport either with international access or linking to one such access (c) adequate, reliable, cost effective and efficient access to port facilities (d) effective, competitive broadband access.	An important local node in transportation and communications terms: (a) on the national road rail or bus networks, (b) with access to a national or regional airport, (c) having adequate, reliable cost effective and efficient access to port facilities, (d) effective and competitive broadband access.
Integrated public transport with facilities for pedestrians and cyclists	Effective local transport system with facilities for pedestrians and cyclists
Regional hospital/ specialised care	Local and/or regional hospital
City level range of theatres, arts and sports centres and public spaces/parks. Cultural and entertainment quarters	Wide range of amenity, sporting and cultural facilities including public spaces and parks
City-scale water and waste management services	Effective water services and waste management arrangements
Integrated land-use and transport planning frameworks	Strategies for physical, social and economic development
Phased zoning and servicing of land banks in anticipation of needs associated with growth	Phased zoning and servicing of land banks in anticipation of needs associated with growth
Strategic Development Zones	Industrial and local business parks

Source: National Spatial Strategy 2002: 40

Scope of the Strategy

Throughout the process it has been important to remain focused on the each of the three key words in the title, National Spatial Strategy. The exercise is about creating a national framework that will be supported by more detailed plans at regional and local levels. It is not appropriate for a national strategy to become overly prescriptive about local development plans. Rather the strategy should be flexible enough to cope with unanticipated external shocks to the economic system and also to facilitate repositioning within a rapidly changing global context. The National Spatial Strategy is just one level in a hierarchy of spatial plans that also includes county and regional strategies.

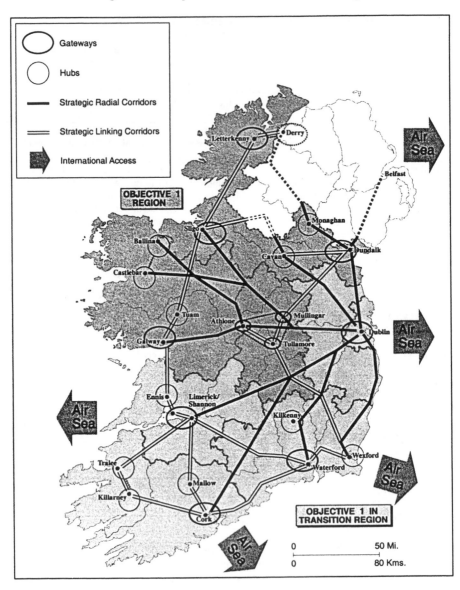

Figure 6.2   National transport framework

Source: Based on map 3, *National Spatial Strategy* 2002

As a spatial strategy the primary orientation has to be on addressing spatial issues. There are many other public strategies to address issues that do not have explicit spatial dimensions. It is very important that the spatial strategy remains focused on providing a framework for solutions that are achievable through other strategies. As a strategy it is important to avoid becoming immersed in too much detail. Rather it should aim to provide a framework for addressing the bigger issues that are likely to impact on regional development over the longer term.

Achieving Consensus

The previous attempt in the 1960s to devise a framework for regional development failed due in part to the inability to secure consensus around the main proposals. During the course of preparing this strategy considerable efforts have been made to secure the support of all of the main stakeholders. This has been time consuming and has at times required difficult negotiations and compromises. The achievement of widespread support in the political arena was perhaps the most difficult challenge as the strategy required making choices, some of which may not appear to be very attractive to politicians in some parts of the country.

Quality of Data

The background research for the strategy was hampered by the paucity of good data especially for sub-national level analyses. The strategy will need to be supported by on-going research that will explore the underlying dynamics of adjustment in different areas. In addition to the need for sound theoretical foundations the research will require the development of integrated databases that can be linked within the framework of geographical information systems. The strategy includes proposals to establish a National Spatial Data Infrastructure.

Conclusions

This chapter commenced with a reminder of the enormous changes that have occurred in Ireland over the past decade which have transformed the country from being a marginal region of Europe to a position where in 2002 it has a per capita level of income that is well above the EU average. Nevertheless, there are still wide disparities between and within regions which may become even greater if a comprehensive strategy for regional development is not adopted. The National Spatial Strategy will seek to address the needs of every part of the country through a framework that will seek to optimise local potential and also by striving to achieve sufficient critical mass at strategically chosen locations. Through this approach it will seek to provide opportunities for investments leading to additional enterprise formation, and employment and population growth that will lead to more balanced regional development.

The preparation of the strategy has raised a number of issues that have been discussed in the final section. Ireland has been to the forefront in pioneering models for local development that have involved the establishment of local partnerships and the provision of support for a wide range of "soft" interventions (OECD 1996, Walsh 1996, 1997, 1999). However, small scale local development programmes have not been able to alter the balance in the regional distribution of development opportunities. The challenge for the years ahead is to implement a comprehensive strategy for spatial development that will lead to an improvement in the relative position of the marginal regions and simultaneously contribute to achieving a more sustainable model of development in all dimensions – economic, social, cultural and environmental.

References

Albrechts, L. 2001, How to proceed form image and dicscourse to action – as applied to the Flemish diamond. *Urban Studies*, 38, 4: 733-745.

Barry, F. 1999. *Understanding Ireland's Economic Growth.* London: Macmillan.

Boyle, G., T. McCarthy and J. A. Walsh. 1998-99. Regional income differentials and the issue of regional income inequalities in Ireland. *Journal Statistical & Social Inquiry Society of Ireland*, 28, 1: 155-211.

Bradley, J., J. FitzGerald, P. Honahan and I. Kearney. 1997. Interpreting the recent Irish growth experience. In D. Duffy, J. FitzGerald, I. Kearney and F. Shortall, *Medium Term Review 1997-2003.* Dublin: The Economic and Social Research Institute.

Breathnach, P. 1998. Exploring the 'Celtic Tiger' phenomenon: causes and consequences of Ireland's economic miracle. *European Urban and Regional Studies*, 5, 4: 305-316.

Buchanan, C. and Partners. 1968. *Regional Studies in Ireland.* Dublin: An Foras Forbartha.

CEMAT (European Conference of Ministers Responsible for Regional Planning). 2000. *Guiding Principles for Sustainable Spatial Development of the European Continent.* Strasbourg: Council of Europe.

Central Statistics Office. 2001. *Regional Population Projections 2001-2031.* Dublin: Stationery Office.

Central Statistics Office. 2002. *Census 2002 Preliminary Report.* Dublin: The Stationery Office.

Commins, P. and P. McDonagh. 2000. Macroeconomic growth and rural development in Ireland. Paper presented to conference on European Rural Economy at the Crossroads, University of Aberdeen, Scotland.

Commission of the European Communities. 1999. *European Spatial Development Perspective, Final Draft.* Potsdam: European Commission.

Copus, A. K. 2001. From core-periphery to polycentric development: concepts of spatial and spatial peripherality. *European Planning Studies* 9, 4: 539-552.

Department of Environment and Local Government. 2000. *The National Spatial Strategy: Scope and Delivery.* Dublin: Stationery Office.

Department of Environment and Local Government. 2001a. *The National Spatial Strategy: Indications for the Way Ahead.* Dublin: Stationery Office.

Department of Environment and Local Government. 2001b. *The Irish Urban System and its Dynamics.* Report prepared for National Spatial Strategy by Brady Shipman Martin Consultants in association with NUI Maynooth and Fitzpatrick Associates. Dublin: Stationery Office.

Department of Transport, Local Government and the Regions. 2001. *Planning: Delivering a Fundamental Change.* London: Her Majesty's Stationery Office.

Department for Regional Development. 2001. *Shaping our Future: Regional Development Strategy for Northern Ireland 2025.* Belfast: Corporate Document Services.

Duffy, D., J. FitzGerald, I. Kearney and D. Smyth. 1999. *Medium Term Review 1999-2005.* Dublin: Economic and Social Research Institute.

Eser, T. and D. Konstadakopulos. 2000. Power shifts in the European Union? The case of spatial planning. *European Planning Studies* 8, 6: 783-798.

Faludi, A. 2001. The application of the European spatial development perspective: Evidence from the northwest metropolitan area. *European Planning Studies* 9, 5: 663-676.

Faludi, A. and B. Waterhout. 2002. *The Making of the European Spatial Development Perspective: No Masterplan.* London: Routledge.

FitzGerald, J., I. Kearney, E. Morgenroth and D. Smyth (eds.). 1999. *National Investment Priorities for the Period 2000-2006.* Dublin: ESRI.

Fitzpatrick Associates. 1999a. *Southern and Eastern Region Development Strategy 2000-2006.* Dublin.

Fitzpatrick Associates. 1999b. *Border Midland and Western Region Development Strategy 2000-2006.* Dublin.

Fitzpatrick Associates. 2000. *National Spatial Strategy study on Irish Rural Structure and Gaeltacht Areas.* Dublin.

Forfas. 2000. *Enterprise 2010: A New Strategy for the promotion of Enterprise in Ireland in the 21st Century.* Dublin.

Goodbody Economic Consultants. 2000. *The Role of Dublin in Europe.* Dublin.

Government of Ireland. 1997. *Sustainable Development: A Strategy for Ireland.* Dublin: Stationery Office.

Government of Ireland. 1999. *Ireland National Development Plan 2000-2006.* Dublin: Stationery Office.

Government of Ireland. 1999. *White Paper on Rural Development: Ensuring the Future.* Dublin: Stationery Office.

Government of Ireland. 2000. *Planning and Development Act 2000.i* Dublin: Stationery Office.

Government of Ireland. 2002. *The National Spatial Strategy 2002-2020: People, Places and Potential.* Dublin: Stationery Office.

Horner, A. A. 2002. Anticipating the shape of the future Dublin city-region: What development land sales signal about the urban footprint in coming decades. In F. Convery and J. Feehan (eds.), *Irish Environmental Issues at Rio +10*. Dublin: The Environmental Institute, University College Dublin.

Jensen, O. B. and I. Jorgensen. 2000. Danish planning: The long shadow of Europe. *Built Environment*, 26, 1: 31-40.

Kunzmann, K. R. 1998. Planning for spatial equity in Europe. *International Planning Studies*, 31, 1: 101-120.

McCafferty, D. and J. A. Walsh. 1997. *Competitiveness, Innovation and Regional Development in Ireland*. Dublin: Regional Studies Association (Irish Branch).

McCafferty, D. 2002. Balanced regional development, polycentrism and the urban system in the west of Ireland. In J. McDonagh (ed.), *Economy, Society and Peripherality: Experiences from the west of Ireland*. Galway: Arlen House Press.

McHugh, C. and J. A. Walsh. 2000. Developing an Irish rural typology. In Fitzpatrick Associates, *Irish Rural Structure and The Gaeltacht Areas*. Dublin.

Morgan, K. and C. Nauwelaers. 1999. *Regional Innovation Strategies: The Challenges for Less Favoured Regions*. London: HMSO.

National Economic and Social Council. 1989. *Ireland in the European Community: Performance, Prospects and Strategy*. Dublin. Report No. 88.

National Economic and Social Council. 1991. *The Economic and Social Implications of Emigration*. Dublin. Report No. 90.

National Economic and Social Council. 1999. *Opportunities, Challenges and Capacities for Choice*. Dublin. Report No. 104.

Nolan, B., P. J. O'Connell and C. T. Whelan. 2000. *Bust to Boom? The Irish Experience of Growth and Inequality*. Dublin: ESRI.

Nordregio. 2000. *Study Programme on European Spatial Planning: Final Report*. Stockholm.

OECD. 1996. *Local Partnerships and Social Innovation in Ireland*. Paris.

OECD. 1999. *OECD Economic Surveys: Ireland.* Paris.

O'Leary, E. 2001. Convergence of living standards among Irish regions: The roles of productivity, profit outflows and demography, 1960-1996. *Regional Studies*, 35, 3: 197-205.

Richardson, T. 2000. Discourses of rurality in EU spatial policy: The European spatial development perspective. *Sociologia Ruralis*, 40, 1: 53-71.

Richardson, T. and O. B. Jensen. 2000. Discourses of mobility and polycentric development: A contested view of European spatial planning. *European Planning Studies*, 8, 4: 503-520.

Walsh, J. A. 1989. Regional development strategies. In R. W. G. Carter and A. J. Parker (eds.), *Ireland: Contemporary Perspectives on a Land and Its People.* London: Routledge.

Walsh, J. A. 1992. Economic restructuring and labour migration in the European Union: The case of the Republic of Ireland. In M. O'Cinneide and S. Grimes (eds.), *Planning and Development of Marginal Areas.* Galway: Centre for Development Studies.

Walsh, J. A. 1993. Demographic and labour force adjustments in the context of economic restructuring: Ireland in the 1980s. In T. Flognfeldt (ed.), *Conditions for Development in Marginal Regions.* Lillehammer: Oppland College.

Walsh, J. A. 1993. Modernisation and marginalisation under the Common Agricultural Policy: Irish agriculture in transition. In T. Flognfeldt, (ed.), *Conditions for Development in Marginal Regions.* Lillehammer: Oppland College.

Walsh, J. A. 1996. Local development theory and practice: Recent experience in Ireland. In J. Alden and P. Boland (eds.), *Regional Development Strategies: A European Perspective.* London: Jessica Kingsley Publishers.

Walsh, J. A. 1997. Development from below: An assessment of recent experience in rural Ireland. In R. Byron, J. Walsh and P. Breathnach (eds.), *Sustainabale Development on the North Atlantic Margin.* Aldershot: Ashgate.

Walsh, J. A. 1998. Facing up to the challenges of regional development. Paper presented to Conference of Irish Association of Regional Authorities on Effective Regional Policy for Ireland, Cork.

Walsh, J. A. 1998. Ireland 2000+: Towards a strategy for sustainable regional development. Paper presented to Conference of Regional Studies Association (Irish Branch) on Ireland 2000+: Developing the Regions, Dublin.

Walsh, J. A. 1999. A strategy for sustainable local development. In R. Byron and J. Hutson (eds.), *Local Enterprise on the North Atlantic Margin.* Aldershot: Ashgate.

Walsh, J. A. 1999. The path to a spatial development strategy. *Geonews*, 45: 24-33.

Walsh, J. A. 2000. Dynamic regional development in the EU periphery: Ireland in the 1990s. In D. Shaw, P. Roberts and J. Walsh (eds.), *Regional Planning and Development in Europe.* Aldershot: Ashgate.

Walsh, J. A., C. McHugh and H. Craigie. 2000. The National Spatial Strategy: rationale and context. Paper presented to Conference on Building the Framework for Development: the National Spatial Strategy. Regional Studies Association (Irish Branch), Tullamore.

Western Development Commission. 1999. *Blueprint for Success: A Development Plan for the West 2000-2006.* Ballaghaderreen, Roscommon: Dillon House.

Chapter 7

Constraints and Incentives in the Regional Development of Northwestern Norway: Three Futures

JØRGEN AMDAM AND FINN BÅTEVIK

Introduction: Challenges to Development

In the course of our work on the regional analysis of western Norway (Amdam et al. 2000) as part of the regional Green Paper, we identified joint challenges facing the whole area and which generally also apply to the northern part of the region, called *northwestern* Norway. Western Norway and the coastal area in particular are full of potential for the years ahead and in many fields. In spite of the fact that the oil reserves in the southern part of the North Sea are beginning to be depleted, possibly resulting in less activity in exploration and development, a fund of know-how has been established that ought to be able to adapt to other forms of activity or to activity in other countries. There are tremendous challenges linked to the national processing of oil and gas. Prospects are bright for the fish farming industry, and western Norway has the know-how in research and economic activity that is necessary to exploit such opportunities, as long as investment is made with a definite aim in R and D and entrepreneurial skills to cultivate new species, improve technology for the transport of these products, marketing, and so on. The marine and maritime environments are strong in western Norway and have great potential for further development especially in relation to petroleum and fish farming activities. In addition there are other locally active environments in tourism, the metallurgical industry, furniture, etc.

A disadvantage for the economic and business environment in northwestern Norway compared to the southern part, and especially the Oslo area, is that in particular private services to industry based on specialised know-how are underdeveloped, along with research and educational activities. Northwestern Norway produces and exports goods, Oslo has the services associated with these activities and creams off the profit and advantages – this is an accurate description of the actual situation. This will be one of the greatest challenges facing the region in the years ahead: not to reduce the manufacturing activity, but to increase the research, development and service activities in order to establish the best possible learning and development environment, which in turn will make it possible to recruit well-educated youth of both sexes.

Culturally and historically, northwestern Norway (with the possible exception of Nordmøre) has a single identity on the basis of common features such as spoken language, an egalitarian small fisherman and farmer culture, a region facing the sea and dependent on the ocean, sea and fjords from the point of view of both its economy and infrastructure. This complex structure with good access to the sea that was vital to establishment of human settlement is today an obstacle to further development. The coastal regions and the most densely populated regions are enjoying growth in northwestern Norway. However, regions with small residential and labour markets, especially in the fjords and on the islands, face great problems in recruiting and keeping young people even though there is an increase in the number of jobs.

As a region, northwestern Norway has many features that are associated internationally with "learning regions" (Asheim 1996, Asheim and Isaksen 1997, Hansen and Selstad 1999) or "dynamic regions" (R. Amdam 1997a, 1997b, Nilsson 1998), except for the fact that research and know-how-developing activities aimed at business and industry have been poorly developed. What is typical for such areas is that industrial environments have grown up from below and on the basis of the so-called French model (Wicken 1997), in which there is a close interaction between customers' demands and production characterised by craftsmanship. The key industries in the area are marine and maritime enterprises (processing, shipyards, tools and equipment, design, etc.) related to the fishing and oil supply activities and the furniture industry; all have witnessed a steady growth in employment in the 1990s and have assumed a dominant role also in a national context. But due to communication problems, small labour markets, very few young people taking education for work in industries and/or returning back, and a national economy that is dependent and focused on oil income, it is our hypothesis that this region will have growing problems regarding both "self development" and "regional dynamics". A change from local to international ownership is another challenge, which could easily reduce initiatives and entrepreneurship and create a dependence on other regions and a need for restructuring of the economy of the kind that is seen all over Europe in regions dependent on traditional industries (Stöhr 1990).

The distance as the crows flies between Ålesund and Ørsta/Volda is about 60 km, but the actual travelling distance is about 120 km. Investment in the coastal highway with the shortest possible distances between the larger centres in northwestern Norway could result in an "urban area" encompassing

Ørsta/Volda, Ulstein, Ålesund, Molde and Kristiansund within about 2.5 hours' driving of one another (as opposed to about 4 hours today (depending on ferry times) and with a population of almost 200,000 which could function in interconnected residential and labour markets (Amdam et al. 2000). With increasing demands for urbanisation and variety of opportunity, many regions – in fact the whole of northwestern Norway – will face huge developmental challenges, if it is not possible to establish larger and more varied labour markets.

The southern part of western Norway is today dominated by three urban concentrations: Stavanger, Haugesund and Bergen. Almost 90 percent of the population lives within commuting distance; communications changes in the next 10 years will make it possible to integrate these regions (the travel time by car will be a little more then two hours from Bergen to Stavanger). The challenge for northwestern Norway is – currently – a rural structure with a lack of towns, low population density and the high cost of crossing fjords and mountains if one is trying to achieve bigger labour markets. Three scenarios at the end of this chapter illustrate the difference between the south and the north under different developmental assumptions.

Regional Structure and Developmental Features

The term *northwestern* Norway as a region is usually used to refer to the counties of Møre og Romsdal (MandR) and Sogn og Fjordane (SandF). The core industrial area may perhaps be defined as the regions of Florø, Nordfjord, Ørsta/Volda, Ulstein, Ålesund and Molde.

The area is extremely good at producing and exporting. As in many other regions with "flexible industrial production" (Nilsson 1998), it is the traditional industries that dominate (see Figure 7.1, which shows jobs in industry in Møre og Romsdal in 1998 and Sogn og Fjordane in 1997). A high-cost country like Norway requires the ability to adapt and renew, so that businesses can survive. Theories of "dynamic" or "learning" development point to the need for interactive learning and close networks and relationships, many meeting-places and so on, if the necessary dynamics are to be created (R. Amdam 1997a, Storper 1997).

Business, Trade, and Industry

Table 7.1 shows the structure of business, trade and industry in 1998. Compared with western Norway and Norway as a whole, the share of secondary industries is particularly high, but then so is that of primary industries. Just one of the regions of northwestern Norway (Førde with its

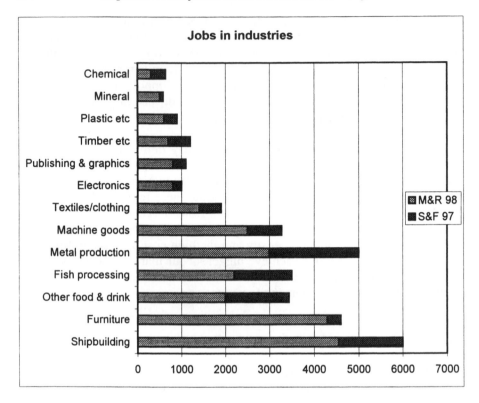

Figure 7.1   Jobs in industry in northwestern Norway

Source: County authorities' website

regional hospital and trade) has a lower percentage of jobs in secondary industries than the national average.   On the other hand, the level of employment in private service industries is lower than the national average in all the regions.   Northwestern Norway is without doubt a manufacturing region and with exports that totalled NOK 26.5 billion in 1999. In 1999 Møre og Romsdal had just five percent of the country's population, but boasted 12 percent of the exports (NOK 19.3 billion) from mainland Norway (Amdam et al. 2000).

A look at the industrial changes in the 1990s (Table 7.2) shows that it is especially the regions of Ålesund and Ulstein that appear as the winners with a growth in employment from 1992 to 1998 of 17 percent. This is higher than the average for western Norway and for the country as a whole.   The growth

Table 7.1   The structure of business, trade and industry in northwestern Norway in 1998

Share of employment/jobs 1998

Region	Primary	Secondary	Priv.services to individuals	Priv.services to industry	Public services
Høyanger	13 %	31 %	16 %	5 %	35 %
Sogndal/Årda	8 %	32 %	22 %	7 %	31 %
Førde	11 %	21 %	28 %	9 %	32 %
Florø	10 %	35 %	22 %	10 %	23 %
Nordfjord	14 %	31 %	24 %	6 %	25 %
Ålesund	6 %	33 %	28 %	11 %	23 %
Ulsteinvik	12 %	40 %	20 %	8 %	20 %
Ørsta/Volda	9 %	26 %	26 %	8 %	30 %
Molde	8 %	29 %	26 %	7 %	30 %
Kristiansund	8 %	26 %	29 %	9 %	28 %
Sunndalsøra	8 %	42 %	18 %	5 %	26 %
Surnadal	18 %	30 %	22 %	5 %	26 %
Vestlandet	6 %	29 %	28 %	11 %	27 %
Norge	4 %	23 %	30 %	14 %	28 %

Source: Amdam et al. 2000

Table 7.2   Employment in 1998 compared with 1992, percentages

Region	Employment 1998 Number	Changes 92 - 98 Total	Primary	Secondary	Priv.services to individuals	Priv.services to industry	Public services
Surnadal	4302	108	83	117	115	131	111
Sunndalsøra	4371	101	80	98	94	129	119
Kristiansund	13452	105	82	111	106	97	110
Molde	27278	109	79	111	122	121	106
Ålesund	38350	117	83	123	115	129	117
Ulsteinvik	11485	117	77	131	123	141	110
Ørsta/Volda	7637	109	69	106	128	157	109
Nordfjord	13091	105	76	113	115	114	109
Florø	6686	105	87	98	117	137	105
Førde	12189	108	69	121	121	122	110
Høyanger	4482	105	81	109	102	115	112
Sogndal/Årdal	12251	100	71	104	94	111	109
Vestlandet	534062	113	84	115	119	129	107
Norge	**2064244**	**114**	**86**	**110**	**119**	**139**	**108**

Source: Amdam et al. 2000

has been particularly large in secondary industries, but also in private service industries. On the other hand, the whole of western Norway is greatly affected by the decline of the primary industries, especially agriculture. In spite of the fact that northwestern Norway has higher employment in both primary and secondary industries than the rest of the country and fairly strong industrial growth, the share of (and growth in) private services to industry is lower in most of the regions than in the country at large. While, for example, Ålesund has an 11 percent share of employment here, the figure is as high as 26 percent in Oslo. Also in the field of private services to individuals, a town like Ålesund, along with most of the other regions, have a lower share of employment and lower growth than the national average. All in all, northwestern Norway is "underdeveloped" in the service sector.

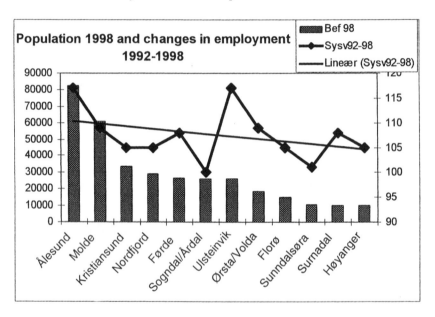

Figure 7.2   Regional population (*bef*) size 1998 and changes in employment from 1992 to 1998

Source: Amdam et al. 2000

Figure 7.2 illustrates the relationship between regional size and growth in employment in the 1990s. What is typical is that the growth in general is greatest in the largest regions in northwestern Norway, but at the same time modified such that regions in the core area enjoy larger growth than the others and that regions in Nordmøre and in Sogn show lesser growth than their size would seem to indicate. There are also distinct differences between coastal and inner fjord areas, with the growth being generally stronger on the coast, while municipalities and regions in inner fjord areas revealing stagnation or decline in employment, especially during the 1990s.

Strategic Assets

Energy: oil and gas Western Norway has traditionally been a large net producer of energy, with considerable exports in the form of electricity to eastern Norway and the energy-intensive processing of raw materials. In recent decades the huge finds of oil and gas have resulted in enormously valuable exports and also in great economic ripple effects, especially in Rogaland and gradually in Hordaland – and also in the rest of western Norway. A greater emphasis on renewable energy sources such as wind and wave energy offers enormous potential for western Norway and for northwestern Norway in particular.

Smelting plants and the production of energy for these have been important in western Norway and still are in regions like Sogndal/Årdal, Høyanger, Sunndalsøra and municipalities like Bremanger. The total number of jobs in metal production is about 5,000. Further development in Sogn and in Nordmøre will to a large extent be dependent on increased supplies of energy and increased production in order to maintain the level of employment.

In 1998, petroleum-based activities employed a total of about 92,500 (Leknes and Steineke 2000). Of this total, just under half were employed in the building of permanent and floating constructions. About 70 percent of these are employed in Rogaland and Hordaland, but only five percent in northwestern Norway. On the other hand, this part of Norway is important for the supply industry, in Herøy alone there is a fleet of over 40 supply boats. It is likely that the oil and gas-related activities reached an historic peak in 1998 and that the number of jobs will be reduced by 50,000 to 70,000 the next 10 to 20 years, at the same time as activities will gradually be moved northwards. One cannot, however, count on any particular increase in northwestern Norway (Amdam et al. 2000, Leknes and Steineke 2000).

Sea farming and fishing The fishing industry is huge in Norway; in fact it is the second-largest export industry after crude oil and on a par with natural gas in terms of value. In 1998, 1.95 million tonnes of seafood were exported at a value of NOK 28.2 billion. The farming of salmon and trout accounted for about a third of this figure. The fisheries represented roughly 8.5 percent of Norwegian exports.[1] Møre og Romsdal has established a strong position. In 1980 about 20 percent of all fish measured by value was landed in this county;

this increased to 28 percent in 1990 and 32 percent in 1997 (Central Bureau of Statistics [SSB] 1999). The fishing industry in northwestern Norway (MandR and SandF) accounted for 42 percent of the total value of fish landed in Norway and 39 percent of the quantity, in addition to also having decisive control over much of the industry and exports from northern Norway. The future development of regions like Ålesund, Ulsteinvik, Nordfjord (Måløy) and Florø will be strongly influenced by developments in the fishing industry.

Table 7.3 shows that Western Norway's four counties account for about half of the value of fish landed and for 53 percent of the value of farmed fish. In the fisheries, Møre og Romsdal has a dominant position, while in fish farming Hordaland is slightly more important than Møre og Romsdal.

Table 7.3   Firsthand value of fish landed and farmed 1998, NOK 1000

County	Value of catch	Value of farmed fish	Total
Rogaland	794716	556166	1350882
Hordaland	296891	1774130	2071021
Sogn og Fjordane	931888	781250	1713138
Møre og Romsdal	3184356	1389406	4573762
The West Coast	5207851	4500952	9708803
Norway	10409428	8513332	18922760

Source: Statistical Central Office internet site

Within the traditional fisheries, the increase in the amounts caught is very limited and species like cod are probably over-fished. On the other hand, the value of other whitefish in particular has increased considerably in recent years, which has raised interest in farming these varieties. With quantities of fish caught held constant in the long term, the challenge will be to increase the value by improved management of the raw materials and making better use of the products. This also applies to the secondary catch and to the by-products from waste, such as from feed and bio-chemical manufacture. Improving quality, processing, by-products and new markets would seem to be the main challenges in the field of traditional fishing activities.

The fishing chain in Møre og Romsdal has roughly 2,300 jobs in processing and conserving fish and fish products. By comparison there were about 1,300 industrial workers in fish and fish products in Sogn og Fjordane in 1997, and together with other activities connected with these in Møre og Romsdal it must be assumed that the fishing chain there employs about 2,600.

This means that the total number of jobs in the fishing chain in northwestern Norway is over 7,000.

There are great expectations of growth in the fish farming industry, anticipated on the basis of figures showing that the quantity of farmed salmon sold increased by over 100 percent from 1993 to 1998, from about 160,000 tonnes to about 360,000 tonnes. The value has increased somewhat less, by about 80 percent. In the report, *Norway's opportunities for the formation of values in fish farming* (DKNVS 1999) it is suggested potential for a tremendous growth in value in fishing, fish farming, and associated activities from about NOK 40 billion in the year 2000 to about NOK 240 billion in 2030. A great deal of this growth will eventually come from the cultivation of species that previously have simply been caught – but also from a five-fold increase in the quantity of farmed salmon. Such a change will, however, demand dramatic escalation of research and development efforts. It is reasonable to suppose that northwestern Norway will get its share of such growth. At the same time, the effects of fish farming on employment have so far been small due to the low degree of processing in Norway. Just 4,284 persons were directly employed in this industry in 1997, of these 389 in SandF and 678 in MandR (SSB Internet). In addition there are anticipated jobs in associated activities such as export companies, transport, etc., which for example were calculated by the Directorate of Fisheries to be about 9,700 in 1994 (Leknes and Steineke 2000) – all told, a job effect of about 14,000, of which at least 25 percent are in northwestern Norway.

Maritime industries Historically fishing activities and shipping have been very decisive for the development of the marine industry in northwestern Norway. The development has followed the "French" model (Wicken 1997) where craftsmen have developed the industry in close co-operation with users in the face of new stimuli, challenges and technical possibilities. From wooden boatbuilding, the technology of steel boats and modern shipbuilding was developed. The copying of simple engines and other equipment led to the production of the advanced equipment necessary in modern vessels. In principle the industry has developed products that fishermen and ship-owners required as needs were defined and technology made it possible to meet these requirements.

After the discovery of oil in the 1970s, these environments have been basically divided into two. In southwestern Norway an "oil cluster" was formed where the maritime industry to a large degree transformed itself to establish the capacity to meet the demands of searching for and extracting oil. The centres of these efforts are Rogaland and Hordaland. In northwestern Norway the construction of vessels and equipment has continued, but with new types of vessels such as supply boats for the oil industry along with boats for fishing and various specialised vessels. The latest addition to this category is vessels for laying optical cables on the seabed. The centre of activities here is Møre og Romsdal with a base in the Ulstein and Ålesund region, and also Sogn og Fjordane.

These two partly integrated maritime clusters are of vital importance to northwestern Norway. To indicate the dimensions and degree of integration we offer the figures in Table 7.4. Of the roughly 13,700 jobs in 1999, as many as 3,700 were in the Ulstein region; 3,600 in the Ålesund region excluding Haram; 2,800 in Haram, Sandøy, Midsund and Vestnes; 1,500 in the remainder of Møre og Romsdal; and 1,900 in Nordmøre (Hervik et al. 2000). Similar figures can be presented from Nordfjord and the Florø region. In Sogn og Fjordane in 1997 about 1,700 were employed in "other means of transport", which means to all intents and purposes shipbuilding. In that county the other parts of the cluster are far less developed (just 500 were employed in SSB's groups 29-33, which are machines and electrical equipment). The same cluster in northwestern Norway probably represents somewhere between 15,000 and 18,000 jobs.

Table 7.4   The maritime cluster in Møre og Romsdal in 1997/98

Trade	No. of firms	Turnover 1997, NOK mill.	Jobs	Operating margin
Shipyards	23	5700	3000	1.2 %
Suppliers & Ship consultants	190	6000	4900	6 % 15 %
Shipping firms (shipping/ seafishing)	13 trad. Shipping 130 boats fishing	2700 2900	5300	29 % 15 %
Total		15700 (1)	13000	

(1) – Corrected for internal supplies

Source: Hervik et al. 1998

In reality the shipyards that are the most visibly active represent just one-third of the total of a set of closely related activities. Hervik's survey shows that while these ship constructors have the whole world as their market, many of their vessels are constructed in Norway and in particular Norwegian equipment is used. They have a key role in the development of the synergy effect in the cluster. In the period 1994 through 1997 the ship constructors in the county were responsible for the total planning of 198 vessels, of which 101 were for overseas owners. Forty-three percent of the vessels were built in the county, 31 percent abroad. Regional ship owners also tend to use regional shipyards and equipment manufacturers.

Furniture manufacture Møre og Romsdal is Norway's leading county in the production of furniture (Møre og Romsdal County Authorities 2000). The county boasts half of the Norwegian furniture industry, both in terms of jobs and gross production value, as well as over half of the total exports of furniture. The trade, with its almost 4,300 employees (furniture, fitting out and wood products), is second only to shipbuilding in the industrial sector in Møre og Romsdal. It therefore is of vital importance for employment and income in northwestern Norway, even though Norway as a whole is regarded as a small nation in the furniture trade. The furniture industry is in general struggling to be profitable, especially the small companies and in the production of pine furniture. Actual production is mainly concentrated in the Ålesund region with the centres of activity being Sykkylven, Stranda and Stordal. But there are active environments in Skodje, Haram, Ålesund and Ørsta within the core area and other smaller environments in other places like Surnadal and in Nordfjord (about 300 employees in Sogn and Fjordane in 1997).

Knowledge industries and IT In their analysis the maritime cluster (see above), Hervik et al. (1998) point out the key role of the ship constructors, in respect of their ability to attract orders from all over the world, which leads to ships being built in Norway and equipment from Norwegian manufacturers being used. During the 1980s and 1990s, private services to industry expanded strongly, especially the part of these activities that demand a high degree of technical expertise. Employment in services aimed at manufacturing and demanding know-how, such as business services and research, grew by as much as 71 percent in the 1980s (Selstad 1998). In fact, most of the national growth of 14 percent in these trades came in this field.

Table 7.1 (above) shows that while Norway has about 14 percent of its job total in the field of private services to industry, western Norway has only 11 percent. The major towns Stavanger-Sandnes and Bergen are in fact barely on a par with the national average or just above; Ålesund with its 11 percent is on the average for western Norway. Counties like Møre og Romsdal and especially Sogn og Fjordane are way below the national average. Figure 7.3 shows that there is a relatively clear connection between the size of the region and the level of private services to industry in western Norway, as might be expected. The capital Oslo and Asker-Bærum have as many as 26 percent and 25 percent of their jobs in this field. What is clear is that in this line of business, the Oslo area dominates completely with many activities that serve a national market.

In the field of research and IT, there is roughly the same centralised pattern as above (see Leknes and Steineke 2000). In 1997 R and D costs per inhabitant varied greatly in the four counties of western Norway. While

Hordaland lay just above the national average in costs per inhabitant, Rogaland was below 50 percent, Møre og Romsdal about 25 percent and Sogn og Fjordane just 10 percent of the national average. In Hordland almost half of the R and D activity was carried out in the university and college sector, while business and industry were responsible for most of the R and D work in both Rogaland and Møre og Romsdal. In Sogn og Fjordane the university sector contributed about half of the R and D effort in the county. Seen in relation to the high level of industrial activity in western Norway, this is a clear indication of a lack of public sector R and D involvement in areas close to business and industry – a factor that makes it difficult to establish interactive learning between research environments and business and industry (Isaksen and Spilling 1996, Isaksen 1997).

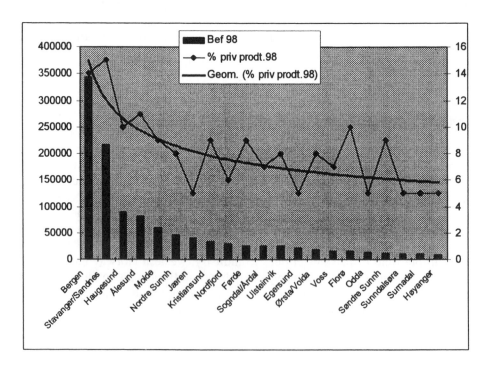

Figure 7.3   Regional shares of jobs in private services to industry in western Norway 1998, seen in relation to the population (*bef*) size of the region

Bergen and Stavanger-Sandnes are the dominant regions in the IT business in western Norway – both absolutely and relatively. In Bergen there are 8.5 IT jobs per 1,000 inhabitants, making a total of almost 3,000 persons. In Stavanger-Sandnes these figures are 7.65 and 1,650 respectively. Of the other economic regions in western Norway, only Ålesund, Molde and Haugesund had more than 1,000 persons employed in IT businesses at the end of 1998. Northwestern Norway is lagging behind both compared to the rest of western Norway and especially the Oslo area.

Regional Population Dynamics

Population and Employment

In western Norway there is a relatively clear connection between the sizes of the regions and the growth in population and in employment during the last 10 to 20 years (Amdam et al. 2000). The larger regions of Bergen, Stavanger-Sandnes, Haugesund and Ålesund show growth, while the small (isolated) regions reveal decline. As indicated in Figure 7.4, the connection is not as obvious in northwestern Norway; a large number of the regions have greater or smaller population growth than expected on the basis of their size. On the positive side, there are regions like Førde (public sector development and services), Florø (maritime activities), Ulsteinvik (fishing and manufacturing) and Ørsta/Volda (public sector development). On the negative side, we find especially Kristiansund, Nordfjord, Surnadal and the "hydro-electric power regions" of Sogndal-Årdal, Høyanger and Sunndalsøra. The most typical feature is that there has been growth in the "core area" of northwestern Norway – with a slight exception for Nordfjord – and decline in Nordmøre and in Sogn.

If one looks at the connection between population change and changes in employment in the 1990s, a situation appears as is shown in Figure 7.5. Most of the regions have enjoyed considerably greater growth in employment than in population, and the difference is particularly noticeable in the very small regions and in Ulstein and Ørsta/Volda. The Ulstein region has had a 17 percent growth in the number of jobs compared to a population growth of just 2.7 percent. This can partly be explained by large unemployment at the start of the period (the crisis in the shipbuilding industry), but during the 1990s there has been a fairly large out-migration of young women and in some degree in-migration of men. This has meant that the ratio of young women to men has deteriorated during the period and is as low as 0.85 for the age group 30-39 in the Ulstein region.

A striking feature of the development in the region as a whole is that population growth is relatively weak in relation to the strong growth in the number of jobs. There is no single region in which the growth in the population has been stronger than in employment. This is the opposite of eastern Norway, where many regions have experienced just such a situation (Selstad 1999: 49). Not even in the larger urban regions in western Norway has the population grown faster than the number of jobs. There is a clear deficit of women in the strategic age groups with regard to establishing a home in northwestern Norway. This has no doubt to a large extent to do with the low share of employment in the service industries. Certain regions that are relatively dominated by manufacturing show for example growth both in the number of jobs and in the age group 30-39. Even so, what is remarkable is the

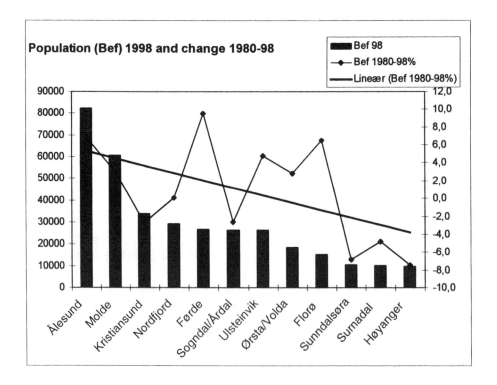

Figure 7.4   **Regional population size 1998 and demographic changes from 1980 to 1998**

fact that such growth can lead to an even greater imbalance between the sexes in the same age groups. Thus certain regions show a larger surplus of men at the end of the nineties than they had in 1980, which is an indication that the recruitment of newly established young adults has declined in relation to the previous decade.

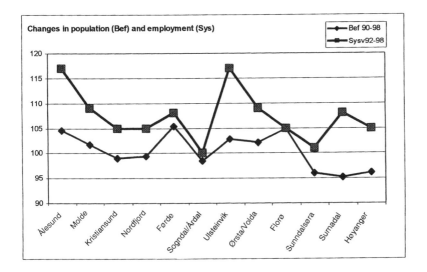

Figure 7.5 Changes in population and employment in the 1990s

Source: Amdam et al. 2000

There might be several reasons why the population growth does not correspond to the growth in the number of jobs. It may be due to the fact that it is difficult to get people to take the jobs that are created, which to a large extent means that these vacancies must be filled in other ways. In industry such situations are usually solved by, for example, employing hired labour either from other parts of Norway or from abroad. The correspondence between demand for and the supply of labour also depends on what skills are being demanded and supplied. Youth in rural areas, in the same way as young people in general, are most interested in gaining an education, often involving a long course of study. Such choices of an education are often motivated more by what one wants to become than by the demand for labour in the region in which one grew up (see also Hansen, this volume). In such a situation, a mismatch between supply and demand in the labour market can often be the result. This will in particular affect regions that have difficulties in recruiting a workforce through migration. Finally, difficulty in finding two jobs for two persons from the same household in one and the same place is also a well-documented problem. When a family is looking to establish a home it will often be a prerequisite that both individuals can find suitable jobs.

Labour Migration

The two largest cities in western Norway are Bergen and Stavanger. These two cities represent the biggest growth areas in western Norway. Bergen has a population of approximately 200,000 and Stavanger approximately 150,000. The largest urban settlements in northwestern Norway, Ålesund, Molde, and Kristiansund are much smaller and have a much weaker population growth than the cities in southwestern Norway. Ålesund, the largest of the three urban settlements, has a population of 35,000 inhabitants. In fact, the population growth of the urban settlements in northwestern Norway hardly can be characterised as outstanding. If one considers the net in-migration among young people that settle down in the region of Ålesund, Molde, or Kristiansund, these regions by no means represent strong growth regions. Is this an indication of the lack of attractiveness of these urban settlements?

This might be illustrated by the migration of the cohorts born in 1960-64.[2] These cohorts went trough their most active period of migration from the late 1970s to the late 1990s. We have studied this period, or more exactly the period from the year each birth cohort was fifteen until they were thirty-five years old. Every boy and girl born in 1960-64, who was living for an example in Molde when he or she was fifteen years old, was registered. Together these boys and girls represent those who have grown up in Molde. In the following figures these boys or girls account for 100 percent. Through migration the population of the cohorts is changed. Some of the boys or girls do not move or just move within the area. These are called non-migrants. Some moved away, but came back. These are the return migrants. All the rest have moved away and live elsewhere. Newcomers, in-migrants who have settled in Molde, might replace these. If the non-migrants, the return migrants and the newcomers outnumber the boys or girls who lived there as fifteen-year-olds, there is net in-migration in the area regarding the actual birth cohorts. If not, the area loses people as a result of the migration process.

If we look at the actual situation for the largest urban settlements of northwestern Norway, they are experiencing net out-migration. There is only one case where the newcomers outnumber those who have left their hometowns. This is in Molde, where the number of thirty-five year old women is larger than the number of fifteen-year-old women twenty years earlier. This illustrates the lack of large centres of net in-migration as well as the large regions of net out-migration in northwestern Norway. As shown in Figures 7.6 and 7.7, it is not only the urban settlements that are short of in-migrants. This is also true for the commuter hinterlands surrounding these

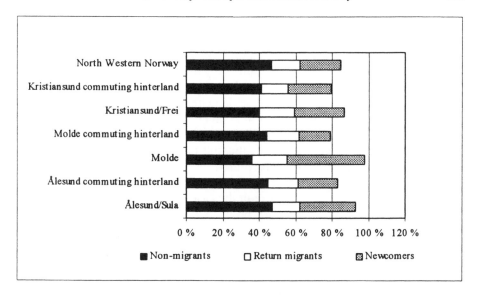

Figure 7.6 Balance of migration among men born from 1960 to 1964

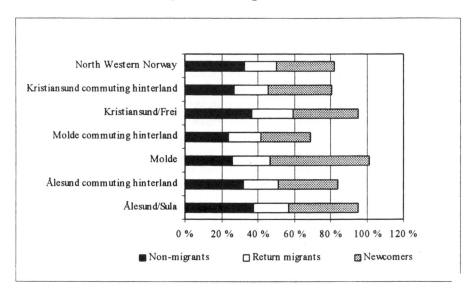

Figure 7.7 Balance of migration among women born from 1960 to 1964

urban settlements. The loss of people through the migration process is larger in the commuting hinterlands than in the centres.

What does this suggest about the attractiveness of the urban settlements in northwestern Norway? We can measured this in two different ways. First it is a question of the attractiveness of the urban settlements to their own youth, i.e. people who have grown up in these settlements. For men there is very little variation from one urban settlement to another. Approximately 60 percent of all who grew up in Molde, Kristiansund, or Ålesund settled down in the same area as grown-ups. This is also the situation in the commuter hinterlands as well as for northwestern Norway altogether.

Women, more than than men, settle down in areas other than those in which they grew up. This is not true in the case of Kristiansund and Ålesund, however. In these two cases the proportion of non-migrants and return migrants is almost as large among women as men. The proportions of newcomers also give a picture of the attractiveness of the urban settlements. It is in this way the large urban settlements differ from many other places in northwestern Norway. The proportion of newcomers is larger in the urban settlements than in most other parts of the area. The problem is, however, that newcomers are usually too few to replace all the out-migrants who settle down somewhere else. These urban settlements are more attractive than many other areas in northwestern Norway, but could hardly be described as very attractive to large proportions of newcomers.

The paradox is that the largest urban settlements represent some of the regions were the population is growing fastest in northwestern Norway. One reason is the large birth cohorts of the 1950s and the 1960s. The combination of moderate net out-migration and large birth cohorts has been the foundation for the growth of population. There are more 35-year-old men and women settling down in these urban settlements today than some decades ago. This also leads to relatively high numbers of children in the same areas, at least compared to the peripheral areas in northwestern Norway. However, when Ålesund, Molde or Kristiansund is compared to the largest cities in western Norway, Bergen and Stavanger, the growth of population is moderate. One important reason for this is that they do not, the same extent as the larger cities, attract adults when they are settling down.

Such structural features will also influence future development. Because business and industry in northwestern Norway are so dependent on international trends and on the number of jobs available in the primary and secondary industries, coupled with the younger generation's preferences for work and residence, societal development in northwestern Norway is particularly uncertain. It is especially frightening that surveys of young people and young adults in various municipalities reveal a high degree of dissatisfaction and that many plan to move away (Amdam et al. 2000b).

Northwestern Norway 2020: Three Futures

As we have shown above, the future of northwestern Norway will be dependent on changes in north-south communications and development in manufacturing industries and population changes. In 2000 we developed three scenarios for western Norway as a whole (Amdam et al. 2000a), where we also tried to forecast the possible differences in development between the north and the south and the various regions.

Future 1: Western Norway (Vestland-Vestland)

The basis of the first scenario is the establishment of a north-south transport system with good links direct to Europe. In 2020, we envisage that it is possible to travel without ferries between Stavanger and Trondheim after the opening of a tubular steel bridge across the Sognefjord. This transport corridor is linked to the Continent and the UK with high-speed vessels. This huge investment has been made possible through a public-private partnership and the establishment of a special development and operating company for the National Coastal Highway. Over-capacity in the offshore industry has been mobilised for the mass production of tubular steel bridge elements – which have also become an export commodity. The National Coastal Highway was a joint project for the huge County of Western Norway, the project designed to unite western Norway as one single unit. In reality two conurbations with enormous growth potential have been created, the axis of Stavanger-Haugesund-Leirvik-Bergen with a population of over 800,000 within commuting distance to one or more of these centres and the axis of Stryn-Ørsta/Volda-Ulstein-Ålesund-Molde-Kristiansund with about 220,000 inhabitants within commuting distance from one or more of these centres.

Halfway between these two we find Florø-Førde with some degree of growth. Within these urban areas created by the Coastal Highway, there are partly overlapping labour markets. On the other hand, the coastal areas in between and the inner fjord districts are characterised by stagnation and thinning out – in particular because agriculture has been dramatically reduced, with the exception of those areas that have managed to readapt successfully to social care activities and which have invested in becoming good environments for housing the elderly who "are seeking refuge" from the towns. There is considerable rivalry between in particular Bergen, Stavanger and Ålesund.

This scenario is a "political scenario" where western Norway is established as a strong political unit financed in part by oil incomes and which invests in infrastructure to unite the area. It is also an "urban scenario" with strong growth in population and employment in the four major urban regions, among them Ålesund in the northwest. It is assumed that northwestern Norway maintains a strong presence in the fisheries, fish farming and in the maritime cluster – a positive trend as in the 1990s, but the reduction in employment and population in rural areas is almost as high as the growth in the urban areas.

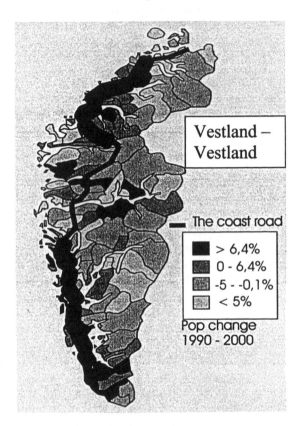

Figure 7.8   Regional structure scenario Vestland-Vestland

Future 2: North and South, Fjord and Sea

The basis for this scenario is that the value of the production of fishing and fish farming has quadrupled from 2000 to 2020. Even though the level of employment has not increased appreciably in the primary and secondary industries, there has been a resounding increase in know-how based activities related especially to sea farming. This is due to the fact that in the last twenty years R and D activity and pioneers in this field have been stimulated so that a large number of small and medium-sized companies has been established that specialise in the development and cultivation of new species, enzyme discovery and production, quality-control activities, market development, etc. Western Norway has assumed the role of sea farming's Silicon Valley. Simultaneously many new finds of petroleum have been made, resulting in a fairly high level of activity in the North Sea, in spite of low prices. This is the result of the introduction of tax and duty reductions on the development of marginal fields and tail-end production from existing fields. Even so there has been a decrease in the number of jobs in the petroleum industry in South western Norway.

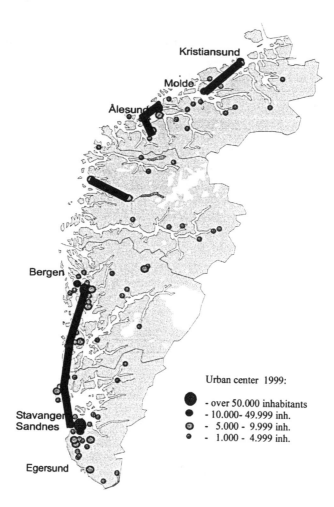

Figure 7.9   Regional structure scenario 2

In communications, the National Coastal Highway has been built between Stavanger and Bergen so that it is possible to drive the distance in 2 hours 15 minutes and the area has the look and feel of a conurbation. Further north, most of the fjords can be crossed on high-speed ferries. The labour markets of Florø-Førde, Ålesund-Ulstein-Ørsta/Volda and Molde-Kristiansund have been amalgamated. Western Norway appears to be ever more divided between the "real western Norway" south of the Sognefjord (which has been designated as a nature reserve) and the more fragmented northwestern Norway with its links with eastern Norway. There is also a considerable antagonism between the strongly growing coastal strip and the more stagnating fjord districts.

The lack of infrastructural investments and major problems in the maritime cluster and other manufacturing industries means that northwestern Norway is lagging behind. Most of major industries are bought and controlled from outside the area. Only the Ålesund region has real growth in population and employment.

Future 3: The Regional Division of Western Norway

The third scenario describes what might happen if western Norway were divided into 11 regional municipalities (Surnadal, Molde-Kristiansund, Ålesund, Nordfjord, Førde-Florø, Sogndal, Bergen, Hardanger, Leirvik-Haugesund, Stavanger and Egersund) after the abolition of the county authority level of administration. Since the challenges and development potential vary enormously, some of which are characterised by co-operation, while others result in "quarrels between neighbours", it is really necessary to write 11 scenarios here. There are still nine ferry crossings along the Coastal Highway, but some of these have high-speed ferries. Road investments have mainly been spent on improving the existing road system in and around the urban centres, where the toll road income has guaranteed government funding.

The regions north of the Sognefjord gave priority to improved road links with eastern Norway, while the other regional municipalities put their money into the National Coastal Highway. The petroleum industry is enjoying a relatively high level of activity with many finds in the Norwegian Sea and high prices. The development of fields where time is critical has helped to maintain activities in southwestern Norway, whilst in mid-Norway there is an increase in the number of jobs in operations and maintenance. The sea farming industry is characterised by large growth, but has been bought and is controlled by international food companies who do their R and D and processing overseas, but with Ålesund as the centre of their mercantile activities.

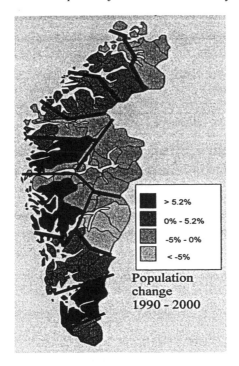

Figure 7.10   Regional structure scenario 3

There is a strong polarisation culturally and in other respects between the regions and the state authorities exploit this situation through a "divide and rule" approach to negotiations on compensation for public welfare production. Employment in the public sector, especially linked to control and administration, is increasing considerably, but is fairly evenly shared between the regions combined with strong growth in Oslo. Compared to the other scenarios this gives a more balanced growth between urban and rural areas and the north and the south, especially because of high public spending in each regional centre.   The rural areas in each region will have a reduction in population, especially in the fjord areas in the northwest.

Conclusions

In this chapter we have tried to show the challenges to northwestern Norway as compared with the rest of western Norway and the capital area around Oslo.

Three things are especially important: communications and urban structure, employment, and population changes and attitudes.

Northwestern Norway is fragmented into small labour markets because of the fjords and mountains and since the population density is very low, each region is greatly dependent on primary and manufacturing industries and public spending, since there are few possibilities to develop advanced service industries. Reduction in employment in manufacturing industries and/or less recruitment of young well-educated people will hit this area very hard.

Heavy investment in infrastructure could improve the situation. A new Coastal Highway would benefit most urban areas. High investment to increase labour markets could lead to more balanced development, but still leave problems in rural areas inside regions and differences between regions where people are "working together" to meet challenges and regions with internal conflicts (Nilsson 1998).

Notes

[1]   Source: www.fiskeoppdrett.no (Eksportutvalget for Fisk).

[2]   Based on Statistic Norway's database that contains information on every registered migration. Kjetil Sørlie has made this material available.

References

Amdam, J., F. O. Båtevik, E. Leknes and J. M. Steineke. 2000. *Framtid for Vestlandet? Scenario for Vestlandet 2000-2020.* Forskingsrapport nr. 43. Volda: Møreforsking og Høgskulen i Volda.

Amdam, J., K. Beite, F. O. Båtevik, G. M. Olsen, T. Hanken and G. Tangen. 2000. *Vurdering av funksjonalitet og attraktivitet til sentra Brattvåg, Fiskåbygd og Ulsteinvik.* Arbeidsrapport. Volda: Møreforsking og Høgskulen i Volda.

Amdam, R. 1997a. *Den forankra planen: Drøfting av kriterium for alternativ næringsplanlegging.* Forskingsrapport nr. 25. Volda: Møreforsking og Høgskulen i Volda.

Amdam, R. 1997b. *Den forsømde regionen: Vurdering av næringsplanlegginga i Ålesund-regionen.* Volda: Forskingsrapport nr. 26. Møreforsking og Høgskulen i Volda.

Asheim, B. T. 1996. Industrial listricts as "learning regions": A condition for prosperity. *European Planning Studies* 4 (4): 379-400.

Asheim, B. T. and A. Isaksen. 1997. Location, agglomeration and innovation: Towards regional innovation systems in Norway? *European Planning Studies* 5 (3): 299-330.

DKNVS. 1999. *Norges muligheter for verdiskaping innen havbruk.* www.ntnu.no/ntva/rapport.

Hansen, J. C. and T. Selstad. 1999. *Regional Omstilling – Strukturbestemt eller Styrbar?* Oslo: Universitetsforlaget.

Hervik, A., E. Nesset and Ø. Opdal. 1998. *Utviklingen i maritime næringer i Møre og Romsdal.* Rapport nr. 9805. Molde: Møreforsking Molde.

Hervik, A., E. Nesset and Ø. Opdal. 2000. *Utviklingen i maritime næringer i Møre og Romsdal: Status år 2000.* Rapport nr. 0004. Molde: Møreforsking Molde.

Isaksen, A. and O. R. Spilling. 1996. *Regional utvikling og små bedrifter.* Kristiansand: Høgskoleforlaget.

Isaksen, A. (ed.). 1997. *Innovasjoner, næringsutvikling og regionalpolitikk.* Kristiansand: Høyskoleforlaget.

Leknes, E. and J. M. Steineke. 2000. *Landsdelsstudie Vestlandet 1980-2020.* Arbeidsnotater RF-2000/175. Stavanger: Rogalandsforskning.

Møre og Romsdal Fylkeskommune. 2000. *Omstilling og nyskaping i næringslivet.* Molde: Arbeidsgrupperapport.

Nilsson, J.-E. 1998. *Blomstrande näringsliv: Krafter och motkrafter bakom förändringar i europeiska och amerikanska regioner.* Stockholm: IVA.

Nås, S. O. 2000. *Innovasjon i Møre og Romsdal.* STEP rapport R-02. Oslo.

Selstad, T. 1998. *Distriktsregioner i vekst og nedgang, 1980-1995: Innspill til områderettede studier i det nye regionalforskingsprogrammet.* Lillehammer: HiL.

Selstad, T. 1999. *Østlandets framtid – oslodominert eller polysentrisk? Scenarier 1996-2015*. ØF-rapport nr. 08/1999. Lillehammer: Østlandsforskning.

Stöhr, W. (ed.). 1990. *Global Challenge and Local Response: Initiatives for Economic Regeneration in Contemporary Europe*. London and New York: Mansell.

Wicken, O. 1997. Regionenes industrialisering: Et historisk perspektiv. In A. Isaksen (ed.), *Innovasjoner, næringsutvikling og regionalpolitikk*. Kristiansand: Høyskoleforlaget.

Chapter 8

Regional Development in Norway: The Role of the State

PAUL OLAV BERG

The International Context

A recent book, *The Fragmented State* (Tranøy and Østerud 2001), refers to the changes that are currently taking place within the Norwegian state administration, taking it in the direction of structural devolution, a market orientation and the outsourcing of public administration. This change is in accordance with international trends known as New Public Management (NPM). The result of this is a fragmentation which gradually reduces the state's power to influence the structural changes, among them the process of centralisation, that characterises present development trends. Over the last few years increasing attention has been directed towards the reduced influence and position of the nation state, as national economies are increasingly exposed to stronger international competition through economic liberalisation and deregulation. Because of her externally oriented economy, Norway has to respond to increasing competition that follows from internationalisation and economic liberalisation, or "globalisation".

Norway is also observing that national policies for defining the economic framework of particular sectors or regions have increasingly been on collision course with agreements entered into through the World Trade Organization (WTO) and with EU competition laws, with which Norway is obliged to comply under the EES Agreement. In addition, the extensive adaptations to various EU regulations that take place under the EES Agreement have weakened the national influence in a number of other fields. The internationalisation process has resulted in reduced tax incomes from trade and industry, as a consequence of the emigration of production and jobs to countries with lower wage and capital costs. Many national companies become increasingly transnational, transferring capital and taxable income to countries with lower cost levels, better prospects for investment, and more favourable taxation regimes. It may be concluded that the internationalisation process and the economic liberalisation, with corresponding international commitments, have placed restrictions on the scope for the national state to pursue policies that seek to correct the market, protect trade and industry from international competition, and makes it possible to support activities that should survive for national reasons.

The National Context

Although the national scope for political direction has been reduced, it should not be forgotten that the state still plays an important role within the Norwegian mixed economy. The state still exerts strong influence in the capacity of legislator, as budget authority and increasingly also as the owners or majority shareholder of autonomous companies. A considerable part of the gross national product passes through government budgets. State activities influence in various ways the framework for economic development and living conditions at regional and local levels, within shorter as well as longer time perspectives.

The new international framework does not prevent the state from investing in immaterial and material infrastructure, nor for the provision of social and welfare facilities for the population. It should be remembered that high incomes from the oil and gas industry have enabled Norway to keep up welfare service facilities that other Western European countries, such as Germany and Sweden, have had to reduce for state financial reasons over the last few years. Important parts of what could be called the economic foundation of the welfare state are thus still under full national direction and control. This applies to social security benefits and public service and welfare facilities that secure minimum standards of living and basic social services for the population. Most important are social security benefits from the National Insurance System based on rights that individuals gain or qualify for. Next come state grants which in principle make it possible for municipalities to offer basic service facilities according to national standards, when such have been defined through legislation. The state has a direct responsibility for investing in, and for the operation of both immaterial and material infrastructure, communications, health services, education, research and public administration. In these fields the state is, with a few exceptions, free to set national priorities largely unaffected by international limitations.

Effects of Sectoral Policies on Regional Development

A request for coordination between regional development goals and sectoral policies has been repeatedly emphasised in white papers on regional development policies presented to the Parliament (Storting) every four years since the beginning of the 1970s. If sectoral policies do not support regional policies, the efficiency of regional development policy programmes will inevitably be low. In practice, sectoral authorities have been able to pursue internal goals rooted in internal historical and sector-based power structures. There has been a lack of political determination to influence sector-based priorities from an overall point of view, however.

In recent years, the scope for political guidance of sector-based priorities has been weakened. This is partly a result of the extensive conversion of public services into autonomous state corporations since the beginning of the 1990s. By endorsing such reorganisations, the Storting has inevitably reduced the scope for political guidance that was formerly possible. Such guidance may, however, be necessary to ensure that the new and more autonomous state owned bodies attend to societal considerations, regional considerations included, that they initially are supposed to pay regard to.

When state owned corporations, originally established to account for societal infrastructure are given a more autonomous status and become market orientated, there arises a need to ensure that regions and market segments that may be less interesting from a commercial point of view, are also served properly. In recent years a number of control institutions have been set up to oversee that legal provisions and conditions for concessions stated to ensure that current societal considerations are met, are lived up to in practice. Serious doubts, however, have been expressed as to whether this new "control industry" works well enough under its present organisational framework (Statskonsult 2000, Berg 2002).

An explicit goal of this reorganisation, market orientation and other NPM-inspired reforms has been to make the political guidance and control of subordinate bodies more efficient. The political authorities should, according to these principles, not have the responsibility for running operations, but should concentrate on long-range and strategic aspects of the activities in question. A recently published report states, however, that this strategy works only to a limited extent. In practice, the NPM-inspired reforms have resulted in a weakening of political guidance and democratic influence, whereas the public administration and state-owned corporations have increased their power (Christensen and Lægreid 2002). This fragmentation within the public administration has also given more power to sectoral authorities, making horizontal coordination between sectors more difficult. This implies that coordination of priorities of the various sectors, which is a condition for the implementation of a comprehensive regional policy, has been further weakened in recent years.

Regional Policies – Rhetoric or Realities?

In his annual address in February 2002, the director of the Bank of Norway stated that increased domestic use of Norway's oil revenues would result in a strengthening of the Norwegian Krone, higher wages and consequently further employment reduction in export oriented trades and industries. At the same time his statement was an illustration of a situation conceived as being run by market forces, that are susceptible to political influence only to a minor extent. But in reality they still can be controlled, provided there is sufficient political determination. His observations have been increasingly relevant throughout 2002. This example shows that there is a risk in exaggerating the limitations that follow from the new international commitments, and also in ignoring the possibilities for national political guidance that still remain. In the present ambiguous situation, where strong forces try to reduce the political influence on societal trends, there are many reasons to take a critical look at the different roles performed by the state as a regional developer. In this context, the focus would be on narrow measures and programmes explicitly defined as "regional development policy", such as firm-related incentives for the stimulation of regional economic development, known as the "small" or "narrow" regional development policy.

A better alternative would be to focus on the comprehensive, or "wide" regional policy, i.e., how the state through sectoral policies in various ways influences the framework for economic activity, welfare and living conditions within local communities and regions of various sizes. Such influence is taking place, whatever it is intentional or not. The topical issue is whether regional development happens as a result of political guidance, or as a result of market forces and the never-ending ubiquitous fight for political influence over the use of state money.

Let us for a moment concentrate on what may seem to be an illusion in the present situation. Let us assume there exists a political determination to prevent or counteract negative regional effects of the structural changes that the society goes through. This implies resource allocations aiming at an efficient stimulation of various regions' contributions to national economic development, but at the same time ensures that national standards for basic public and local government services are met. The terms "local" and "regional" are used in this context to signal that these dimensions are important, not least in a country with Norway's geographical characteristics.

It may be convenient to distinguish between policy measures aiming at stimulating economic activity and employment directly, and political measures that influence conditions for economic activity and, indirectly, living conditions. The living conditions of the population, which depend to a large extent on the quality standards of public services and welfare facilities locally and regionally, constitute at the same time an important framework for economic activity at local and regional levels. The conditions of living are also goals in themselves, having a bearing upon which national quality standards are to be applied in the Norwegian welfare society and how they are to be achieved. It may also be useful to distinguish between policy measures that are meant to ensure regional growth, and policy measures that are supposed to ensure a just resource distribution between regions. A division along such lines has been brought forward in the latest Swedish report to parliament on regional policy, submitted in 2000 (SOU 2000: 87). This inquiry distinguishes between the three regional policy fields and measures:

- regional growth policy;

- regional sector policies; and

- regional welfare policies.

In the following discussion this distinction will be referred to in a comment on how these three concepts are related, based on examples from corresponding policy fields in Norway.

Regional Growth Policy

Regional development policies in Norway are mainly associated with measures and programmes within the category of regional growth policy. Specific focus has been directed towards the "small" regional development policy that has been aiming to

promote activities that will contribute to increased, lasting and profitable employment in regions with specific employment problems or a weakly developed economic base,

borrowing a wording from the object clause of the Regional Development Fund Act of 1965. The most important measures have been risk loans, investment grants, guarantees and various branch and regionally based development programmes, together with a regionally differentiated labour poll tax. The ambitious goal has been "to preserve the main geographic settlement pattern", a heroic, but also vague formulation repeatedly used in government white papers on regional development since the beginning of the 1970s. Many have expressed doubts about the effects of the policy measures used, particularly within the "small" regional development policy. This policy has not been given high priority in recent state budgets. A look at previous white papers on regional policy reveals that the lower priority given to this field of policy is not of recent date; with few exceptions the funding has been reduced over the last 10 or 15 years. Looking back, it is almost pathetic to reread the repeated incantations of ambitious goals related to coordination of sectoral policies that only to a very modest extent have been implemented. The term "politics of symbols" is not a very friendly one, but the distance between rhetoric and deeds in this context justifies the use of the term.

There is no doubt that the present regional growth policy is confronted with serious challenges, whether they are acknowledged by the political authorities or not. The major challenge is a persistent centralisation of economic activitites and of population. In topical political jargon one might say that the challenge we are facing today is to stimulate the opportunities for the formation of values that are embedded in each region, aiming at maximizing every region's contribution to the nation's total growth and development. To attain this goal, an active policy for trade and industry combined with a regional growth and development policy is needed. Such a policy also has to include policies for agriculture, forestry and fisheries.

An evaluation of the Norwegian regional development fund (SND) undertaken in 1997 – still valid – emphasises that it may be highly profitable for government to offer risk capital to firms who are confronted with market failure. There is a need for seed money to small companies who invest in projects promoting innovative ideas, but have difficulties in obtaining credit in the private financial markets because of the high risks attached to such investments. The private financial market is also reluctant to give credit to enterprises located in small communities on the periphery, where the second-hand value of non-removable mortgages often will be low. In such situations, state investment grants in the form of risk or venture capital may actually be a condition for the implementation of profitable investment projects. This form of compensation for market failures does not necessarily mean subsidising. On the contrary, such investments may yield high returns both for the firm and for the society. At present there is a trend to shift from targeted to general growth incentives, such as tax incentives and state engagement in investment companies. Better conditions for entrepreneurship and endogenous growth can be obtained through increased investment in education and R&D. This investment should also be used to reduce disadvantages of peripheral regions.

Regional Sectoral Policies

These policies cover a wide range of sectors. This section singles out two sectors where the need for a better coordination between sectoral policies and regional policy goals is evident: communications, notably national roads and air transport; and higher education and research.

National Road Policies

A National Transport Plan for 2002-2011 (St. meld. nr. 46, 1999-2000) passed the Storting in February 2001. It gives a very positive view of transport policy as a regional policy measure, and on its importance for regional development. These policy declarations are, however, mainly concentrated in a separate chapter where they have a somewhat lonely existence. When it comes to priorities, there are few traces of this rhetoric elsewhere in the plan document.

When reading the plan closely, it is possible to identify a tendency to withhold important priorities from the political process by defining them as objective, politically neutral calculations. Within the communication sector this applies when cost-benefit analyses are used in ranking investment priorities in the national road system. Even if one assumes that such analyses in principle can include all kinds of benefit and cost elements, there are good reasons to ask which elements or criteria are actually included in the calculations.

A study carried out at the Nordland Research Institute analysed how commercial transportation was treated in cost-benefit analyses used to rank investment projects in national road system (Pedersen and Solvoll 1997). It appeared that current cost-benefit analyses did not pay much attention to the importance of road connections in a long-term regional development perspective. Neither was the importance of the removal of, or widening of bottlenecks in the road system paid much attention to. When cost-benefit analyses are linked to traffic censuses and criteria for environment and safety, it seems inevitable that investments in roads in centrally located and densely populated areas are given a high priority. A recent study found that the share of national road investments allocated to the centrally located counties of Oslo, Akershus and Vestfold doubled from 1989 to 1998 (from 15.2 percent to 32.7 percent), whereas the share of the more peripheral county Nordland in Northern Norway was reduced by a half during the same period – from 13.4 percent to 6.7 percent (Lea 2000). This example illustrates effects of the new cost-benefit model introduced during that period, contributing to the change of the regional profile of investments in national roads.

Air Transport Policy: Regional Effects

Air transport also calls for a closer analysis of consequences in a regional policy context. More than any other form of transport, air transport ties Norway with its long internal distances and scattered population together.

Without a well-developed air transport system, it is hard to see how viable trades and industries could still be scattered all over the country.

A demand for equal treatment of air transport with other forms of public transport such as railways, roads and coastwise traffic is now emerging. As is the case with the other forms of transport, the state should, at least partly, take on responsibility for investments in the infrastructure of air transport. The current situation is that the annual cost of this infrastructure of 3000 million kroner (1 Euro = 7.50 kroner), of which 800 million kroner is investment in new infrastructure, is paid by the travellers themselves. In contrast to this, the annual investment of 4400 million kroner in railway infrastructure is in its entirety paid for by the state, according to the National Transport Plan 2002-2011 (St. meld. nr. 46, 1999-2000).

Not only is the state paying for investments in the railway network and infrastructure, it is also subsidising part of its costs of operation. This subsidy amounted to 1300 million kroner in 2002. Of this, 820 million kroner (63 percent) is allocated to the part of the railway network that serves Central South-Eastern Norway. Subsidies to local traffic within the Oslo region alone amounts to 500 million kroner. This last amount could be compared to the annual amount spent by the state to keep up the countrywide air traffic on the regional airports. This subsidy amounted to 412 millioner kroner in 2002. It is hard to find a political justification for a practice like this, when investment in the form of air transport that ties the country together, is entirely paid for by the users whereas investment in railways, which mainly serve the central parts of the country, in its entirety is being covered over the government's budget.

The fact that both the operation and investment costs of air transport is to be paid for through the air tickets contributes to the generally high costs of air transport in Norway, which could also be attributed to a lack of competition in the domestic air market. The main cause of the high tax level is that geographical and topographical conditions necessitate a relatively dense network of airports, which again results in relatively high costs of operating and investing in the infrastructure of air transport. The costs of safety demands currently introduced are also to be paid for by travellers over the air ticket. The willingness to pay for expensive air tickets can be explained by the fact that there are fewer alternatives to air transport in Norway than in the other Nordic countries, for reasons mentioned above. Dependence on air transport results in high demand, which together with lack of price competition in the domestic market gives room for, and willingness to pay for, the high prices of air transport.

There are reasons to question the fairness of the inequalities between the different forms of transport, especially between railways and air transport, till now supported by the state. As long as the state does not contribute to investment costs of air transport there is a risk that the parts of the country and especially the peripheral regions with initially high transportation costs, will suffer increasing disadvantages of competition. The Air Transport Board even envisages the closure of several small airports with a low number of passengers, because of their high costs that in addition will have to cover necessary upgradings.

The fact that air transport is the underprivileged member of the communication family was recently illustrated through the introduction of a notorious air passenger tax fee on top of already existing taxes. In a country that has been so plentifully allotted with distances, this punishes even more those who have chosen to live in peripheral parts of Norway. Sector policy and regional development policy are on a collision course. The additional distance tax was abolished after one year, an implicit acknowledgement of the need for fresh political thinking on the role of the state in the financing of air transport.

Higher Education and Research

When the first regional colleges were established in the late 1960s, an important step was taken in the direction of decentralisation of higher education in Norway. That resources for research were allocated to these new colleges right from the start, since staff members were paid not only to teach but also to do research, was a very important move. The regional research institutes that were later established associated with the regional colleges have played an important role contributing to further development of research activities at the colleges. It is worth noting that many of these research institutes were the result of initiatives taken by county politicians and administrative staff. Their growth has to a considerable extent been financed through national and international research programmes and projects, where the regional research institutes had to compete with national research institutions. The regional research institutes represent an important supplement to the regional colleges, founded and operated by the state.

The fact that more young people can find higher education institutions within easy reach means that a greater part of the national reserve of talents thus has had an opportunity to qualify for jobs that require higher education. As an incentive for regional development, this decentralisation of higher education has perhaps been the most important regional policy measure of all which have been applied over the last decades. But this has not happened without struggle. At times there have been good reasons to remind one of the doubts that reigned in Bologna, Italy, in the 14th century, where prospects to establish new universities north of the Alps were considered highly doubtful! Centrally located universities and national colleges have known how to defend their interests, not least in the competition for resources for research. After the professional and regional colleges were amalgamated in 1994 and established as new state colleges, it has been a challenge to ensure and to further develop the research-based teaching that was developed at the first generation of regional colleges. In the continued competition between national and regional institutions, political authorities will have to contribute to make it possible for regional institutions to compete for resources for research on equal terms with others.

Regional Welfare Policies

This section looks into the third regional policy field, and asks if there is a particular regional welfare policy. If there is, what does it look like from a regional development point of view?

The very bedrock of the Norwegian welfare society is the National Insurance System, which ensures standard benefits all over the country based on individual rights. In addition, the state has taken over the responsibility for the hospital sector, recently reorganised as autonomous state-owned health institutions. How this reform will work from a regional development point of view remains to be seen. The situation contains both opportunities and threats.

Municipalities as Agents of State Welfare Policy: A Brief History

Welfare policies on regional and local levels are implemented by county councils and municipalities. As already pointed out, the state welfare policy is mainly implemented through the National Security System, where benefits are based on individual rights. The municipal sector has over the last 50-60 years been given the responsibility for the most important collective services and welfare benefits. Examples are primary schools (municipalities), the secondary schools (counties), primary health services, care of old people, social services and local psychiatric services. To some of the collective services, the primary school, are attached individual rights, whereas to most others, such as health and social services, few such rights are attached.

The costs of investments in infrastructure and operation of services were partly financed by municipal taxes, but also through a system of redistribution from richer to poorer municipalities. In addition, state money was earmarked for specific services. Throughout the 1970s it became evident that state transfers to municipalities, based on earmarked grants and on tax equalisation (which in the meantime had to be strengthened also through substantial state grants), were not satisfactorily adjusted to the individual requirements of municipalities. In addition, the system impeded the state's efforts to control the total sum of transfers to municipalities, which was important in a trade cycle policy context.

In order to remedy these shortcomings a new transfer system was introduced in 1986. The tax equalisation scheme was replaced by an income equalisation grant, ensuring each municipality a minimum tax income per inhabitant, related to the national average. Around 50 different earmarked grants were converted to one cost-compensating grant. This grant is distributed among the municipalities according to a distribution key that is supposed to reflect the cost structure of each municipality. At the outset, this key or index reflected the geographical distribution pattern of state grants between municipalities, developed under the previous system of state financial transfers to the municipalities. This index, based upon weighted demographic and social criteria, was assumed to give an objective transfer system.

Since the new transfer system was introduced in 1986, the criteria and mutual weights that used to construct the index have been adjusted several times. More weight has been given to social problems, which occur on a larger scale in centrally located and larger municipalities. At the same time criteria reflecting costs related to geographical characteristics like internal distances, scattered settlement and small-scale operations have been given less weight, thus reducing the cost compensation given to smaller and less central municipalities. A similar tendency towards centralisation is also embedded in other changes in the transfer system carried out in recent years. These changes to the index are not officially regarded as part of the current regional development policy. Nevertheless, the changes have a regional dimension, because the effect is a reduction of transfers to peripheral municipalities.

Map and Terrain

The examples given above illustrate a trend in regional policy which increases the difference between map and terrain. There is a widening gap between explicit regional development policy goals and the more implicit tendency towards centralisation and polarisation between centre and periphery which can be observed. Recent development trends in regional policy give the periphery good reasons to worry. If regional development policy is to play a role beyond the production of symbolic statements, the consequences of political priorities affecting the framework for regional development will have to be made more visible than is currently the case. The political agenda is at any time set by responsible political authorities. The examples referred to in this section show there are competing agendas. Priorities set in transport policies and in the state transfers to municipalities have negative consequences for the current regional development policy. To avoid the impression of inconsistent policies, lacking in substance and full of symbolic rhetorics, it is necessary to be more open about regional consequences of sectoral policies.

Regional Development Policy in Sweden

The discussion of strength and weaknesses of Norwegian regional policy could be enriched through a sidelong glance to Norway's easterly neighbour. Seen from Norway, Sweden's regional policy has been developed from above, and therefore not particularly successful. But in Sweden, recent political initiatives to ensure regional coordination of sectoral policies deserve attention in Norway. Extending the existing regional growth agreements between county partnerships and the state, 27 state sector authorities have been invited to coordinate their activities with those of the county authorities, with the aim of releasing and stimulating each region's growth potential and each region's contribution to national growth. These new regional development programmes will replace the existing regional growth agreements. The overall aim is to stimulate the growth of well-functioning labour market regions in all parts of the country. A targeted coordination process will ensure that the nation as a whole will gain from stimulating each region's potential for development, with active participation from the various state sector authorities.

These efforts are politically anchored in the new Swedish regional policy, recently renamed regional *development* policy, a change that may be seen to signal an stronger emphasis on a nationwide regional growth policy, based on the assumption that the national growth is constituted by the sum of growth generated locally and regionally. As a rhetorical move, to maximise each region's contribution to national growth, it has positive appeal.

The redistribution aspect of regional policy is still supposed to be included. One of the main goals for the new regional development policy is to stimulate "well functioning and lasting local labour market regions in all parts of the country". The new regional development policy thus consists of regional growth policy which will also mobilise regional sector policy and regional welfare policy. This is why as many as 27 state sector authorities take part in this coordination effort, which will be presented in the new regional development programmes in late 2003 (NUTEK 2002).

From Local to National Regional Growth Policy in Norway?

An emphasis on growth in the outlining of regional policy goals has also taken place in Norway lately. A white paper presented by the Labour government in April 2001 stated that:

regional policy represents an extra effort in favour of regions that need separate attention in relation to the general economic growth and development of welfare. (St. meld. nr. 34, 2000-2001)

Signals from the coalition centre-right government which took over in October 2001 can be summarised in the words "growth – over the whole nation". It remains to be seen if this reorientation implies a weakening of the traditional regional growth policy. However, some indications of change in this direction was given in the 2003 budget.

A conspicuous difference between the two countries is, however, that Norway does not explicitly promote coordination through a regional sector and welfare policy, as is at present the case in Sweden. In 1997, Norway made an attempt in a similar direction through the introduction of county-based development programmes. However, state sector authorities seem only to a minor extent to have been motivated to cooperate. It is difficult to see what has been achieved so far through this effort.

Is National Solidarity Possible?

At present, structural devolution and the market orientation of state activities has many supporters. Many politicians see them as universal remedies for achieving higher efficiency and a leaner and more result-oriented state sector. At the same time, however, there is a risk that NPM-inspired and market-oriented reorganisation of state activities will have not only positive, but also negative effects. Centrally located and densely populated regions will be of greatest interest to the new "disconnected" and autonomous public corporations, whereas peripheral regions with long internal distances and a scattered population may be neglected by the market forces (Berg 2000, 2001).

This is illustrated through the important question of the nationwide development of broadband data lines. Investment in societal infrastructure has traditionally been seen as the responsibility of public agencies, most often the state. At present, the development of broadband data lines is supposed to follow markets and demands. State authorities are important users of such data lines, and can influence the development in the capacity as regular customers. In parts of the country where the accumulated demand is too small to attract private investors, municipal authorities are supposed to give economic support to necessary investment.

This represents a break with the basic principle of national cross-subsidising which up to now has been the foundation for financing the development of societal infrastructure. This structural devolution of public corporations is accompanied by a new model for political action, where the state as owner is expected to maximise the value added and profits. Societal or sector-oriented political considerations are supposed to be taken care of by the state in its capacity of public authority. Nationwide coverage of service facilities can be obtained through the setting of conditions for giving concessions, the setting of maximum prices or through subsidising operations.

There are indications that the institutions of this new state "control industry" are not well enough developed and equipped to do their job efficiently, i.e. to compensate for the abolition of the previous system of cross-subsidising. This weakening of political control may have the effect that regions with less purchasing power in the future will become the losers, as the broadband example illustrates, in the competition for investments in infrastructure and public service facilities (Berg 2001).

Other characteristics of current regional development trends may also give reason for disquiet. The centre-periphery dimension of the Norwegian political landscape also divides the political parties, and does not have the highest priority. In current political debates the impression is often created that "everything" that the state does in peripheral regions is related to transfers and regional policies, whereas it is just about "ordinary" policy when the same things are done in more central parts of the country. In debates often dominated by media based in the capital region there is often a hidden reference to the notion that peripheral regions live on welfare.

Dominant trends in the political landscape in recent years indicate that competition for state resources and for the state's favour will be markedly accentuated in the years to come. National unity and national solidarity may be put on a severe test. In a letter to the editor in a newspaper, the writer put a question that strikes a tune and demonstrated a temperature which may be more and more common in political debates in the future: "Why will investments in national roads in the county of Nordland accentuate inflation, when the same is not supposed to be the case when the new opera house is to be built in Oslo?"

Summing Up

- Even if changes in the international framework reduces the scope for national policies, considerable national possibilities for direction remain, especially within the regional sector and welfare policy.

- A regional policy for growth and innovation will depend on the deployment of public risk capital.

- Close scrutiny is needed when quantitative models of priorities replace political judgment. This applies for example to cost-benefit models used when setting up priorities for investing in national roads, and the use of quantitative models to estimate the distribution of state transfers between municipalities.

- Regional and local consequences of policy changes should be clarified in advance. This applies both in the structural devolution of state activities and when earmarked grants are integrated in the general per capita grants to municipalities.

- Air transport should be treated as what it is: an important part of the national system of public transport. An equal treatment compared to other forms of public transport is a question of fairness.

- The total consequences of imminent reduction of various forms of state grants to smaller and peripheral municipalities should be elucidated. Is it acceptable to reduce the quality of municipal services, with the implicit intention to enforce amalgamations of municipalities?

- Rules regulating the transfer system for state grants to municipalities should contain qualitative elements, correcting the rigidity of quantitative indexes.

- Although the "small" regional policy is needed, regional equity can best be supported through upholding minimum national quality standards implemented all over the country, whether they apply to employment, infrastructure, public service or welfare facilities.

- Knowledge and competence are important competitive advantages. Investing in R&D institutions outside university cities is a relevant policy both for growth and development and for regional development. It is a challenge to ensure that these institutions are ensured equal terms in the national competition for funds for research.

References

Berg, P. O. 2000. Uforutsette regionale konsekvenser av statlig "fristilling". In H. Teigen (ed.), *Bygdeutvikling: Historiske spor og framtidige vegval.* Oslo: Norges Forskningsrød og Tapir Akademisk Forlag.

Berg, P. O. 2001. New public management and peripheral regions. In R. Byron and J. Hutson (eds.), *Community Development on the North Atlantic Margin*. Aldershot: Ashgate.

Berg, P. O. 2002. Statlige selskaper og samfunnshensyn. *Tidsskriftet Plan*, 4-5.

Christensen, T. and P. Lægreid. 2002. *Reformer og lederskap: Omstilling av den utøvende makt*. Oslo: Universitetsforlaget.

Lea, R. 2000. *Geografisk kartlegging: Statens investeringer i fylker og regioner 1989-1998*. Asplan Analyse.

Pedersen, P. A. and G. Solvoll. 1997. *Samferdsel og verdiskapping: Hvilken nytte har næringstransportene av samferdselsinvesteringene og hvordan tas denne nytten hensyn til i nytte-kostnadsanalysene?* NF-arbeidsnotat 1001/97.

SOU. 2000. *Slutbetänkande från den regionalpolitiska utredningen*. Stockholm.

St. meld. nr. 46. 1999-2000. *Nasjonal transportplan 2002-2011*. Oslo.

St. meld. nr. 34. 2000-2001. *Om distrikts- og regionalpolitikken*. Oslo.

Statskonsult. 2000. *Statlige tilsyn: Problemer med dagens organisering og forslag til ny struktur for tilsynsorganer*. Oslo.

Tranøy, B. S. and Ø. Østerud. 2002. *Den fragmenterte staten: Reformer, makt og styring*. Oslo: Gyldendal Akademisk.

Verket för näringsutveckling (NUTEK). 2002. *Nationell samordning för regional utveckling*. Stockholm.

Chapter 9

Regional Development in the Faroes: What is the Right Size for Effective Local Government?

DENNIS HOLM AND BJARNI MORTENSEN

Introduction

This chapter examines the existing municipal system in the Faroes and presents arguments for and against amalgamation of municipalities. The present system is heterogeneous with many small municipalities. For many years the right size for Faroese municipalities has been debated. Most of the participants in the debate have put forward arguments against the present municipal structure, because the large number of small municipalities is seen as dysfunctional when it comes to the local management and governance. Amalgamation has also been seen as a prerequisite for a decentralisation of important government functions.

The questions taken up in this chapter are: Why are there so many municipalities in the Faroes? What are the problems with the present Faroese municipal structure? Who wants the municipalities to amalgamate and what is the background to the resistance? To what extent is the municipal structure able to meet the challenges that the Faroese society faces today?

The Faroes in Brief[1]

The Faroe Islands are an archipelago consisting of 18 islands located in the North Atlantic (62'00" N, 7'00" W; see Figure 9.1 below). The total population of the Faroes was around 47,000 at the end of 2002. The distance to the closest neighbours is 300 km to Shetland, 450 km to Iceland and 675 km to Norway. There are flight and ferry connections to most of the neighbouring countries. The connection to Denmark is the most comprehensive with at least two flight departures each day to Copenhagen and a weekly ferry link to Hanstholm. The flight time to Copenhagen is 2 hours and 15 minutes, while the trip with the ferry takes 36 hours.

The Faroes are an industrialised country with a standard of living that is comparable to the Nordic countries (in 2000 the GNI was around 200,000 DKr per capita). The Faroes are an extreme case of a resource-based economy as it is very dependent on the fishing industry, which accounts for more than 95 percent of export value. Further, more than a quarter of the GDP comes from fishing and the fish processing industries. The economy is very open as exports are around 50 percent GDP.

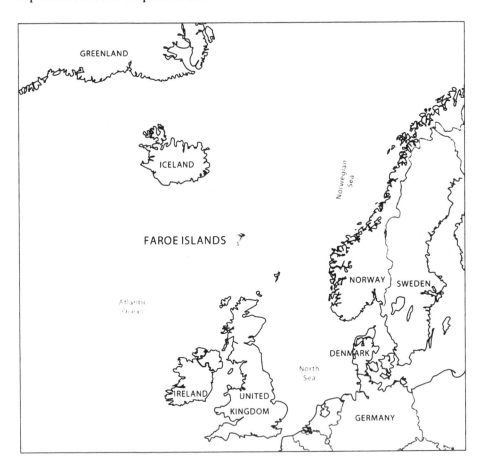

Figure 9.1   The Faroe Islands in a European context

The European Union is by far the most important export market, taking 80 percent of exports. Nevertheless, the Faroes are not a member of EU. Besides the fishing industry, a considerable subsidy from the Danish Government is one of the cornerstones of the economy. Most of the Danish subsidy is a general block grant. For the last couple of years the block gran t has been on around 1 billion DKr. In 2002 the grant was reduced by 356 million DKr, as a part of the Faroese effort to gain more economic and administrative independence. In addition to the block grant, the Danish Government spends 280 million DKr directly in the Faroe Islands – mainly to cover public order and administration of justice.

The Faroese Municipalities: The First Hundred Years

When discussing the organisation of the Faroes in general, three organisational levels can be identified: the Danish State, the Faroese government and the Faroese municipalities. The Faroes are a self-governing part of Denmark. The provisions in the Home Rule Act of 1948 regulate the political, administrative, and financial responsibility of Faroese matters, and the relations between Denmark and the Faroes. The Danish state is responsible for foreign affairs, defence, monetary policy and the judicial system, while the Faroese government (Landsstýrið) is responsible for most other activities related to people's everyday lives, such as industrial policy, educational matters, health care, social security, postal services, and public transport services. Though some of these activities administratively are Faroese responsibilities, they are paid for by Denmark. This is for example the case regarding parts of the health and social services.

The Faroese government is responsible for the organisation of the municipalities, but the Danish State has in some cases tried to set the premises for the organisation, as for example during the economic crisis of the Faroes in the early 1990s. Originally the Faroese municipal system was based on Danish laws. Following two Danish laws on Faroese municipalities in 1872[2] and 1908,[3] there were originally eight municipalities in the Faroes. The geographical division of these municipalities was based on the existing system of parishes (Prestagjald), and did not take into account the fact that the Faroese had close ties to the village in which they lived. However, since the municipalities had very few responsibilities, there was no real demand for local taxation, and this system was workable.

When the Faroes developed from a (feudal) agrarian society into a more capitalistic fishing society in the early twentieth century, the demands for more active municipal boards emerged. The need for local taxation also became evident as investments in harbours and roads became necessary for further economic development. These societal changes influenced the view of the public about the appropriate size of the municipalities. People from one village were reluctant to pay taxes to a municipality that also, or primarily, made investments in other villages. This was the main reason for the creation of many new municipalities, which in most cases geographically cover just one village. In this way, the number of municipalities increased from eight at the beginning of the twentieth century to more than 50 municipalities in 1967. The latest division of a municipality took place in 1967, when one village broke from its municipality in order to develop a local fish processing plant (Wang 1974). This case indicates the importance that the municipalities have had as a formal institution when it comes to local economic development.

Thirty Years of Inertia (1970-2000)

Since the late 1960s, the municipal structure in the Faroes has been on the political agenda. Numerous committees, boards, and commissions have been set up to propose a foundation for a new municipal law and a new municipal structure for the Faroes (see Table 9.1).

Table 9.1   Committees come, committees go

1966	A government committee was set up to evaluate the municipal structure in the Faroes. Its proposal for new legislation was presented in 1971.
1972	A new municipal law was passed in Parliament (Løgtingið).
1992	A committee was set up to analyse the division of labour between the central administration and the municipalities.
1993	The Danish government presented demands for a simplification of the Faroese municipal structure.
1994	In October 1994, a new committee was established by Landsstýrið to come up with a mandate for an investigatory committee that would, in turn, recommend a new municipal structure.
1995	Parliament accepted the investigatory mandate with minor changes.
1996	The government set up a new investigatory committee, Kommununevndin[5], to carry out the work.
1997	Kommununevndin published its first report.
1998	Kommununevndin finished its work, and published two more reports.
2000	A new municipal law was passed in Parliament, based on the recommendations made by the Kommununevndin.
2001	The Municipal Department at the Prime Minister's Office finishes and publish a report on a new division of labour between the government and the municipalities.

Source: Kommuneunevndin 1997, 1998a, 1998b; Løgmansskrivsovan 2001

The committees, boards and commissions all share the view that there should be a clear division of labour between central government and the municipalities, and that amalgamation of municipalities is necessary if an administrative decentralisation of central government functions is to take place.

Following the 1971 report of the first commission (set up in 1966), a new municipal law was put into force in 1972. This law was changed and updated in 2000, after the Kommununevndin finished its report in 1998. Both laws assume that an amalgamation of the municipalities will occur. The 1972 law regulated activities of municipalities with more than 1,000 inhabitants. At that time, this was the case for only seven municipalities, which meant that exceptions from the law could be made for 44 municipalities (Høgenni 1992: 57). The 2000 law included municipalities with at least 500 inhabitants, which means that exceptions from the law can be made for 29 of the 48 municipalities.

In the early 1990s, the government acknowledged that the existing municipal system was not well defined, and that the existing system was one of the reasons for the financial crisis, which affected many municipalities in the early 1990s. An economic crisis had devastated the Faroese economy by 1992, and as a consequence the Faroese government was put under administration by the Danish state, which became the primary creditor for the Faroese government when the Faroese foreign debt was refinanced by the Danish state. In conjunction with loan agreements made between the Faroes and Denmark between 1992 and 1995, the Danish government put forward several demands about the way a number of issues in the Faroes should be managed. Among other things, there were requests to restructure the fish harvesting and processing industries, legislation regarding trade and industry as a whole, the banking system, and other major matters. In addition, the Danish government also had some comments on the need for change in the municipal structure.

A series of meeting took place between the Faroese government and the Danish government in 1993, 1994 and 1995. The following statements regarding municipal matters from these meetings are relevant:

- "The Faroese government takes initiative to stabilise the municipal debt without putting strain on the Faroese treasury and to simplify the municipal structure." (1993)

- "The Faroese government will continue the work on completing the simplification of the municipal structure." (1994)

- "The Danish government has furthermore noted that the Faroese government has started the preparation of a new report on the future municipal structure in the Faroes." (1995)

(Rigsombudsmanden på Færøerne 1998)

Why were the Danes so interested in a reform of the Faroese municipal system? Probably they assumed that a municipal reform would result in economies of scale, and that a reform would improve the foundation for the better governance of Faroese society.

Even though the municipal structure in the Faroes has been unchanged since 1967, the question of structural changes has been part of the municipal debate during this whole period. The municipal legislation has for example since 1972 been based on notions of municipal amalgamation, but there have not really been any amalgamations, and most municipalities remain about the same size as in 1972. There have only been a few municipal amalgamations since 1972. All of them were amalgamations of suburban municipalities to Tórshavn with the municipality of Tórshavn. The latest such merger occurred in January 2001, when the municipality of Kollafjørður amalgamated with the municipality of Tórshavn. Also, the municipalities of Runavík and Skála decided to amalgamate after a local referendum in October 2001 showed considerable support with around 80 percent favouring the proposed amalgamation (Dimmalætting, October 9, 2001). These municipalities are located respectively on the east and the west side of the Skálafjord, which is the most dynamic and prosperous area outside the capital area. The amalgamation of these two municipalities will come into effect at the next municipal election, which is scheduled in December 2004, and at this election, citizens in the two municipalities will elect one municipal board, and not the two they did at the last election in December 2000.

Furthermore the municipalities in the northern part of Streymoy and Eysturoy have decided to have a local referendum regarding municipal amalgamation in May 2003. These municipalities have since the mid 1980s participated in the most comprehensive formal inter-municipal cooperation scheme in the Faroes: Kommunufelagsskapurin í Sundalagnum,[5] which has its own administration. Several municipalities have transferred the administration of certain matters to this cooperative scheme.

At present, there are 48 municipalities in the Faroes, and by 2004 there will be 47 municipalities (and 43 if the municipalities mentioned above amalgamate). The smallest, Mykines, had at the end of 2002 a population of 20; the largest, Tórshavn had 18.000 (Hagstova Føroya 2001): see Figure 9.2 and Table 9.2.

As mentioned, the municipal law of 1972 was based on a municipal size of 1,000 inhabitants, while the law of 2000 was based on a municipal size of 500 inhabitants. In both cases exceptions from the law have to be made for a large proportion of the municipalities, as shown in Table 9.3 below. The small size of a large part of the Faroese municipalities means that the municipalities have very limited capacities, both administratively and financially.

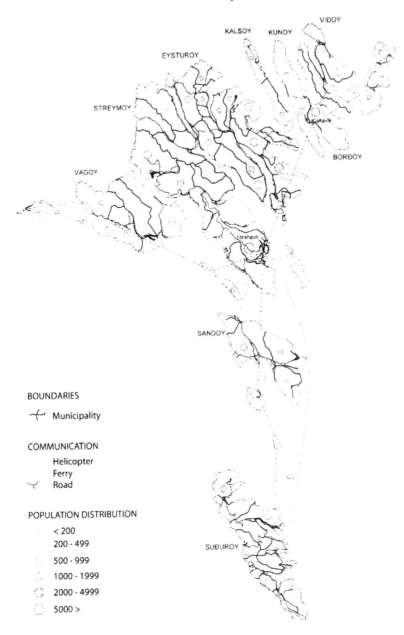

BOUNDARIES

  ⊣ Municipality

COMMUNICATION

    Helicopter
    Ferry
    Road

POPULATION DISTRIBUTION

    < 200
    200 - 499
    500 - 999
    1000 - 1999
    2000 - 4999
    5000 >

Figure 9.2   The Faroe Islands

Table 9.2 Population by size groups

Population	20 – 199	200 – 499	500 – 999	1.000 – 1.999	2.000 – 4.999	> 5.000
Number of municipalities	18	10	11	6	2	1

Source: Hagstova Føroya 2001

Seen in a Nordic context the Faroese municipalities are also very small.

Table 9.3 Size of municipalities in the Nordic countries

	Denmark	Finland	Norway	Sweden	Iceland	Faroe Islands
Number of inhabitants	5.3 mill	5.2 mill	4.5 mill	8.9 mill	280.000	46.000
Number of municipalities	275	452	435	288	124	48
Mean population in the municipalities (Approximations to the nearest 000)	19.000*	11.000*	10.000*	31.000*	2.300*	1000

* All figures are from 1999, except the Faroese figures, which are from 2000.

Source: Hagstova Føroya 2001, Aalbu 2000

Municipal Autonomy

The "local" Faroese constitutional law, Stýriskipanarlógin, states that: "The municipality's autonomy to organize its own affairs under the supervision of the Faroese government is recognized by national law regarding, for example, the right to incur municipal and inter-municipal debt, guarantees and other matters." (Stýrisskipanarlógin para. 56; our translation). In other words, Parliament decides which tasks should be placed under municipal rule, and how extensive municipal autonomy should be.

According to Faroese law, the municipalities in principle are responsible for a wide range of functions. The most important services are:

* protection services: fire fighting service, consumer and food safety;

* environmental services: environmental control, local roads, planning;

* personal services: education, health and social services, child- and day-care, housing planning;

- recreational services: sports facilities, museums, libraries and other cultural facilities;

- commercial and promotional services: physical infrastructure, local economic affairs.

To finance these activities, the municipality has the right to collect taxes. It can also raise loans to finance the above-mentioned activities if the municipal debt is lower than the annual income of the municipality. The 1972 law stated that municipalities with fewer than 1,000 inhabitants might get permission not to fulfil the responsibilities enumerated in the law. This implied that only seven of 51 municipalities were obligated to have all the functions mentioned in the law. The 2000 law lowered the threshold to 500 inhabitants, which implied that 29 of the 48 municipalities might be permitted not to fulfil all the municipal functions enumerated in the law.

The legislation thus accepts that only a limited number of municipalities are capable of administering the full range of functions. This means that in many municipalities there are functions which are not dealt with at all by the municipality. In some cases the central administration does have the responsibility. In some cases, larger municipalities administer some functions for small, neighbouring municipalities. In other cases, tasks are carried out in the form of regional co-operation between several municipalities. To take an example, education is by law a municipal matter. There was a primary school in all but two Faroese municipalities in 1999. But in most places, the schools only provides seven grades, and only nine of the 48 municipalities offer all 10 grades. Other examples are environmental control and food control, which are both municipal matters (Matvørulógin 1985, Umhvørvislógin 1988). In 1997, 22 of the 48 municipalities claimed to have their own environmental control, seven municipalities cooperated with the national Food and Environmental Agency (Heilsufrøðuliga Starvsstovan), while 19 had no control at all. Only five municipalities had their own food control, nine municipalities cooperated with the Food and Environmental Agency, while the remaining 34 municipalities had no control (Kommununevndin 1998a: 494-496).

When other functions are examined, the picture is largely the same. The two largest municipalities, Tórshavn and Klaksvík, administer almost all of the tasks specified by law as municipal responsibilities. The medium-sized municipalities provide many of the designated services. The general trend is that the smaller the municipality, the fewer tasks it administers. This means that most municipalities do not have any real administrative capacity to deal with the implementation and enforcement of all the responsibilities they have according to the laws. In other words, assignments that should formally be administered by the local municipality are in most cases run by the central administration in Tórshavn.   Following this, one could argue that the municipalities can be seen as a hindrance to the implementation of laws passed by Parliament. This also has some consequences for the local democracy, as discussed below.

Evaluation of the Present System

In 1996, the government decided to set up a committee, Kommununevndin, which was intended evaluate the existing municipal system and make proposals for a new municipal system in the Faroes. This decision was made in conformity with the agreements made with the Danish government in 1993. The committee consisted of six members, all of whom were public servants, three from the central administration, and three from the municipalities. The Committee had a full-time secretary, conducted extensive hearings and held no less than 55 meetings. The chairperson and the secretary visited all municipalities and all the institutions which were involved in municipal matters. The committee also visited Iceland, Greenland and Denmark.

The report from Kommununevndin enumerates some advantages of a municipal structure with many small municipalities. One advantage is that the municipal administration is inexpensive and very flexible. In many cases, it is also possible for the citizen, on short notice, to get in contact with the municipal council. Another advantage of the system is that it gives citizens good possibilities to influence the decision-making process. Since small municipalities did not have the economic basis for large investments, most of them have never created a heavy debt burden (Kommununevndin 1998b: 25).

The present municipal structure was also found to have its disadvantages. One major disadvantage is that the economic and administrative capacity was too limited. For example, 14 municipalities did not have a secretary, and in several other municipalities, the office was open only for a limited number of hours each week (Kommununevndin 1998b: 25). An effect of their limited capacity was that many municipalities were not able to offer the services that citizens in a modern society expect or demand. As a result many functions, which formally are municipal matters had to be taken on by the central administration, which might not have sufficient knowledge of local matters.

Many of the inhabitants of the small municipalities who were not able to offer the services needed made use of services offered in neighbouring municipalities. This could be a problem for the bigger municipalities, because outsiders typically did not pay the full cost of the services, especially regarding overhead costs (Kommununevndin 1998b: 26). In many cases council members in the small municipalities were disqualified because of partiality from participating in council decisions.

The report also criticises the widespread "refund" system from the central administration to the municipalities. The system was organised in such a way that municipalities could obtain a transfer of up to 85 percent of the cost of investments such as harbours, provided that the central administration approved the investment. The refund system had several shortcomings. The central administration could control and eventually overrule municipal decisions. On the other hand, this control generated much administrative work, since there are so many municipalities to collect information from. The refund system in some cases made it difficult to see who really had the responsibility for different tasks. Finally, the system was so complicated that it was difficult to know the real cost of municipal activities (Kommununevndin 1998b: 86-87). Today the refund system has been to some extent abandoned, mainly because of the economic crises in the 1990s. But there still is an unclear division of labour between the central administration and the municipalities, as operational costs in different areas are split between the central administration and the municipalities. Thus it is still difficult to identify the real cost of municipal activities.

Proposal for a New Municipal System

The root meanings of the Greek word *demokratia* are *demos* (people) and *kratos* (rule); that is, rule by the people. The Kommununevndin argues that in order to have real local democracy, there must be some allocation of responsibility, and there has to be something that can be ruled (Kommununevndin 1998b: 25-28). The Faroese municipalities are in principle responsible for many functions, regulated by legislation. But due to limited economic and administrative capacity, many of the municipalities have delegated most of their tasks to the central administration.

After a discussion of strengths and weaknesses in the present municipal structure, Kommununevndin concludes that [our translation]:

> the existing municipal structure does not give the municipalities any real self-government. The reason for this is that many of the municipalities have no opportunities to choose priorities because of limited economic and administrative capacity. This means that more self-government for the municipalities requires the establishment of bigger entities – i.e., amalgamation. (Kommununevndin 1998b: 28)

In order to solve these problems the Kommununevndin proposed that the number of municipalities should be reduced from around 50 municipalities to seven or nine. The amalgamations should take into consideration:

geographical conditions, physical infrastructure, population structure, and existing cooperative arrangements. According to the report the new municipalities should be defined as shown in Figure 9.3 below.

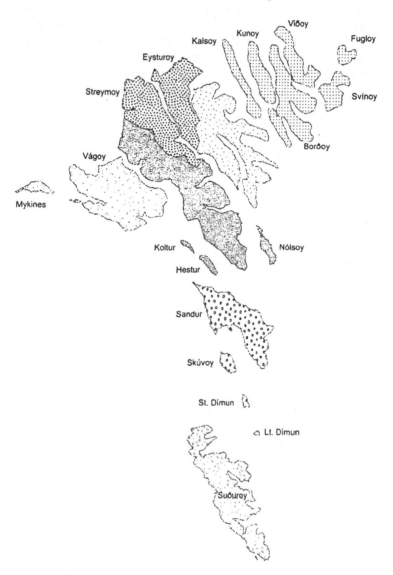

Figure 9.3 The municipal structure proposed by the Kommununevndin

In addition to the proposed seven municipalities, as shown in Figure 9.3, Kommununevndin proposed that Eysturoy also perhaps could be split into two municipalities: East Eysturoy and West Eysturoy. Furthermore, instead of one municipality on Suðuroy there could be two municipalities: North Suðuroy and South Suðuroy.

The Kommununevndin argued that although local administration of tasks regulated by legislation and delegated from central authorities still will be an important part of the work performed in the new municipalities, larger municipalities will also have human and economic resources to set up lists of priorities given to tasks they want to take on. A condition for success is that

> the division of tasks and responsibility go together, and this makes the citizens better capable to estimate what the municipal functions, in reality, cost. This also makes citizens capable of putting forward demands regarding the use of their tax money. The other requirement for decentralisation is that a municipality has the financial and administrative capability to make decisions, so that the resources are used as optimally as possible. (Kommununevndin, 1998b: 16)

Regarding the division of labour between the central administration and the municipalities, the committee emphasised the importance of two aspects:

- Proximity: the tasks have to be as close to the citizens as possible.

- Sustainability: the region has to have a sustainable size in order for the assignments to be carried out in an efficient way.

(Kommununevndin, 1998b: 16)

In order to realise the latter, the Kommununevndin proposed that municipalities should be allowed to amalgamate voluntarily (along the lines shown in Figure 9.3), but if they had not amalgamated voluntarily by 2002, the Kommununevndin proposed that they should be forced to amalgamate by law.

Reaction to the Report

The Government

In a statement in Parliament in April 1999, the Prime Minister, who at that time also was the Minister for Municipal Affairs, defined the government's tasks regarding the municipalities and made his view on the main arguments of the Kommununevndin report clear (www.logting.fo). The main goals of the government were:

- to solve the financial difficulties of the most indebted municipalities;

- to modernise the municipal law; and

- to strengthen municipal independence and responsibility.

The new municipal law would to a large extent be based upon the report. It would strengthen the municipal decision-making powers, and ensure more independent responsibility for municipalities within the legal frameworks. The Prime Minister acknowledged the importance of and need for a clear division of labour and responsibility between the central administration and the municipalities, and the government would continue the process of making the division of responsibilities clearer.

As mentioned above, the Kommununevndin proposed that the municipalities should have the opportunity to amalgamate voluntarily before 2002, and if they had not amalgamated before that time, they should be forced to amalgamate by law. The Prime Minister as well as the government did not agree on this issue, and stated that amalgamation should still be voluntary. In this respect the government has chosen a principle which in the other Nordic countries have led to very few amalgamations.

The Political Parties [6]

The People's Party The People's Party is the Prime Minister's party, and the Prime Minister's view is thus seen as the People's Party's response to the report.

The Republican Party The Republican Party supported the main arguments put forward in the Kommununevndin report, and agreed on the necessity to update the division of labour between the central administration and the municipalities, which according to the Republican Party, should also be seen as a main part of regional development in the Faroes. But the Republican Party did not support the idea of enforced amalgamation. A preferred alternative was to decentralise more functions to the municipalities, which would then lead to more cooperation among municipalities. This would also make municipalities aware of the advantages of working with larger municipal entities. In this way, some municipalities would perhaps amalgamate voluntarily, but this should only be allowed within the geographic areas mentioned in the report.

According to the republicans a new division of labour between the central administration and the municipalities makes it necessary to modify the present national and municipal tax system. Acknowledging the municipal right to administer and finance its own activities, the Republican Party also agreed with the proposal in the report to remove the refund system. The role of the municipalities in industrial development should be restricted to providing infrastructure. Direct government and municipal involvement in businesses, common in the 1980s, should not be pursued. The Party's view is that a municipality should not be able to accumulate debts larger than one year's income.

The Social Democrats The Social Democrats supported the proposals to update the existing municipal law, and to strengthen municipal independence and responsibilities, but were against municipal amalgamation enforced by law and did not expect that many municipalities would amalgamate voluntarily in the near future.

As opposed to the Republican Party and the Unionists (see below), the Social Democrats do not want to change the present transfer of tax income from the national to the municipal level, fearing that it will limit the national government's ability to determine tax policies. This is a principal matter for the Social Democrats, who do not want to reduce the national government's opportunity for income redistribution through the tax system. In addition, national government control of tax policy remains important because the national tax system is progressive, while the municipal ones are not.

In addition to debating the report, the Social Democrats also presented a new proposal. Their proposal takes traditional social democratic arguments as a point of departure. The main goal of social development in the Faroes should be to create a solidary society. All citizens should have equal opportunities in a welfare society, no matter were they choose to live.

Whereas Kommununevndin proposed that the municipalities should be forced to amalgamate, the Social Democrats proposed the introduction of a new institutional entity: the region. The argument is that nobody is better able to decide how the village or town should be organised than the people living there, but some tasks are better solved in bigger regional entities. The tasks of the three different institutional levels proposed by the Social Democrats are shown in Table 9.4.

This three level system circumvents the resistance to amalgamation, and therefore this plan may be easier to implement. On the other hand, one might question the wisdom of having three administrative levels in a country with less than 50,000 inhabitants.

Table 9.4   The three-level system proposed by the Social Democrats

The Municipality	The Region	The Central Administration
The technical organization of the municipality (Roads, sewage, town planning, water) *Well-being* (Cultural activity, housing policy, playgrounds, sports activity, village hall etc.) *Other* (Local industrial development initiatives, smaller harbours)	*Education and culture* (Primary school, recreational classes, other school activities) *Harbours* (Building and operation of bigger harbours) *Health and social security* (Child care, child protection, children's dental care, health visitor system, home help, municipal medical system, old people's home, primary health service, recreational opportunities for children, youngsters, and senior citizens, etc.) *Labour market and environment* (Analysis of labour and business opportunities in the area, health and environmental protection, fire-fighting service, coordination of a contingency plan)	*Control of the municipalities* (This institution shall exercise control of both the municipalities and the regions) *Customs and tax authorities* (The customs and tax authorities shall collect all taxes, customs, and VAT for both national and municipal taxes. The customs and tax authorities will have branches around the country) *Education* (General teaching systems, hiring of teachers and directors, wages) *Health* (Hospitals and transport of patients) *Social issues* (Counselling, projects and payments according to the law on social benefits, in order to have the service as close to the citizens as possible, the Social Service Department (Almannastovan) will establish branches in the regions, social pensions)

Source: Javnaðarflokkurin 1999

The Unionists The Unionists support a clearer division between the central administration and the municipalities, and a larger degree of self-governance to the municipalities. The Unionists agree that the municipal structure has to be changed, and that it would be desirable to have bigger municipal entities. The party does not support the Social Democrats' three level system. The Unionists argue that larger municipalities could be given more functional and economic responsibilities than smaller municipalities. The party shares the Republicans' view on municipal involvement in industrial life.

The Local Politicians

A review of the articles in the newspapers on municipal matters in the period after the publication of the report shows that there were very different opinions among local politicians regarding the question of municipal amalgamation. Generally there was an opposition towards amalgamation, but some politicians were positive.

One of the reasons for the general opposition towards amalgamation was that many municipal members were afraid of losing influence. Another reason is the dissimilar financial situation among the municipalities, and (as one mayor expressed it) it is quite understandable that municipalities that have no debt are reluctant to amalgamate with municipalities that are heavily indebted (Dimmalætting, January 17, 1999).

The municipalities that were positive towards amalgamation can be split into two categories. First there were municipalities that wanted to become larger in order to gain power from the central administration. One mayor stressed, "if we amalgamate, then we can administer matters, which today are decided by the central administration in Tórshavn on our behalf" (Sosialurin, January 25, 1999). Besides the municipality of Tórshavn, this category consists of a few medium-sized municipalities, which favour the amalgamation process proposed by the Kommununevndin. One mayor also emphasised that a large municipality is "necessary if you are to compete with the large municipality of Tórshavn" (Dimmalætting, January 17, 1999). Secondly there are a few medium-sized municipalities that favour amalgamation, but these municipalities prefer smaller amalgamations where there is no competition between urban centres. For example the mayor of the second largest town on Suðuroy (Vágur) explained, "that if the municipalities on Suðuroy were amalgamated into one municipality, then the island as a whole would be paralysed because of competition between the two natural centres on the islands (Tvøroyri and Vágur). In his opinion an amalgamation on Suðuroy would only be positive if there were two municipalities where the natural centres would be the largest towns" (Sosialurin, September 8, 1998).

Although no general trend can be identified among smaller municipalities, some are not interested in amalgamation with larger partners as proposed by the Kommununevndin. A few say that they prefer voluntary cooperation, which in turn eventually could lead to an amalgamation, while others prefer to keep things the way they are.

Public Opinion

In an opinion poll, which was conducted in March 1999, people were asked: "How do you think the country should be organized in municipalities?"[7] The answers to the question were as shown in the Table 9.5 below.

The poll showed that two-thirds of the sample was in favour of some kind of change. Around one-third preferred Regional Councils, and around one-third preferred seven or nine municipalities as proposed in the Kommununevndin report. About one-third of the population favours the existing system. This means that around two-thirds of the population want some kind of change, but there is no majority for any of the three options.

Table 9.5   Opinion poll on Faroese municipal structures

Choice	Number of Respondents	Percentage
Existing system	542	31,7
Regional Councils	480	28,0
7 – 9 Municipalities	521	30,4
1 Municipality	73	4,3
Do not know	96	5,6
Total	*1712*	*100,0*

There are regional variations, and a centre-periphery dimension seems to emerge. Support for the existing system is lowest in the capital region (one sixth of the respondents), while in all other regions more than a third favour the existing system, with the highest support on the island of Eysturoy (almost one half of the respondents).

Table 9.6   Opinion poll on Faroese municipal structures, by size of municipality

Size of municipality	Existing system	Regional Councils	7 – 9 Municipalities	1 Municipality	Do not know	*Number of Respondents*
< 200	41,2	26,5	24,5	3,9	3,9	*102*
200 – 499	40,2	29,9	19,7	3,6	6,6	*137*
500 – 999	42,3	29,3	21.9	3,5	3,0	*369*
1000 – 1999	40,7	25,2	26,3	3,7	4,1	*270*
2000 - 4999	24,8	34,6	33,6	2,3	4,7	*214*
> 5000	18,7	26,7	40,8	6,1	7,7	*561*
Total	*31,5*	*28,3*	*30,6*	*4,3*	*5,3*	*1653*

Table 9.6 shows that the resistance to change, or support for the existing system, is biggest in the smaller municipalities (under 2,000 inhabitants). On the other hand, support for the committee's recommendation of seven to nine municipalities is strongest in the larger municipalities.

Result: Status Quo?

The debate on the Kommununevndin report in Parliament, as well as the public debate, showed that the majority of both the political parties, the municipalities and the public would not accept an amalgamation process enforced by law. This general resistance has confirmed the status quo concerning the question of the (right) size of the municipalities. Why should it have done so?

In the Scandinavian countries, central governments have implemented enforced municipal amalgamations, in defiance of resistance towards amalgamation by some municipalities. The Faroese political system – local (the municipalities) as well as national (Parliament) – opposed a top-down, enforced amalgamation process. How can we explain this?

Faroese politics can be analysed by the traditional left-right characterisation of politics. In addition, Faroese politics also encompasses two other central dimensions. First there is the international[8] dimension, which concerns political conflicts about the nature of the relation the Faroes should have with Denmark. Second, there is an intranational dimension, which concerns the traditional internal centre-periphery orientation of Faroese politics. The latter refers to the fact that national politics in the Faroes is locally rooted, not only within a regional centre-periphery context, but also within an even more small-scale, localistic orientation where municipalities, towns and villages have always played an important role in political life.

The Faroese electoral system consists of seven constituencies. This system is established to guarantee that the interests of the different areas will be taken into account in Parliament, which also indicates that Faroese politics is locally rooted. Furthermore, several members of Parliament are present or former, members of municipal boards, which indicates their local bonds. When the behaviour of the voters is explored, it is apparent that the voters are extremely locally oriented and that voters to a large extent prefer candidates from their own town or village. The general picture is that many of the elected members of Parliament get a major share of their votes in one single town.[9] An extreme example was in the constituency of Sandoy at the 2002 parliamentary election. Two members of Parliament are elected in the constituency of Sandoy, which has two major towns, Sandur with 578 inhabitants and Skopun with 496 inhabitants (at the end of 2002). At the election the mayors of the two towns were elected. The mayor of Sandur got 82 percent of his votes in Sandur, while the mayor of Skopun got 80 percent of his votes in Skopun. Furthermore the mayor of Skopun got almost 50 percent of the total number of votes given in Skopun. Though this is an extreme case, all elected members at the 2002 parliamentary election, with just few exceptions, got more than 50 percent of their votes in one town. A majority of the members got more than 65 percent of their votes in one town, while some members got more than 80 percent of their votes in one town. In many cases the elected members did not only get most of their votes in one town, but the votes they got also counted for a large proportion of total votes given in the town. The behaviour of the voters indicates that a large proportion of the electorate considers it very important that their town or village be represented in Parliament.

The local dimension of Faroese politics has been characterized as clientelistic[10] (Justinussen 1999), where personal relations and local support are of great importance. It is quite common – and expected – that a member of Parliament or a minister will act so that his or her constituency benefits. Not only should the constituency benefit, but also the town or village from which the politician originates. This is also illustrated in the dialogue between voters and members of Parliament or ministers, where voters continuously remind the politicians of their local identity and that they should work for their constituency and above all their home place. These strategies were much used in relation to the industrial development policies in the Faroes during the 1970s and 1980s, which was highly connected to what is normally characterized as a policy of "village development" (bygdamenning). This policy was above all focused on geographically spread industrial development, and "never did obtain concrete political substance, but became in fact a philosophy or symbol enabling territorial interests to claim their share of industrial modernisation" (Hovgaard 2002: 15).

When a large number of the members of Parliament find their base of support in individual towns or villages, they have to take the local opinion into consideration when expressing their opinion or voting on a matter in Parliament. In cases where local preferences do not correspond with national or public preferences, politicians can either behave as office-seeker or policy-seeker (maker); either to take local opinion into consideration or not. When the Kommununevndin report and the proposed law-enforced municipal amalgamation was proposed, the negative attitude in the municipalities as well as in the towns and villages towards enforced amalgamation was reflected in a general opposition to enforced amalgamation in Parliament.

What Next?

The widespread resistance towards enforced amalgamation, however, did not bring the debate on the municipal structure to an end. This debate seems to be an ongoing process in the Faroes. The process is also reflected in changes both in the central administration and in the legislation on municipalities. The latest notable change within the central administration is the establishment, in 2001, of a new separate department, the Department of Municipal Affairs (Kommunudeildin), within the Prime Minister's office.[11] It is also worth noting that the head of this department is the former chairman of the Kommununevndin.

Regarding legislation, a new, updated law on the municipal structure was put into force on January 1, 2001. This law was passed by the Parliament in May 2000 by 20 votes. Seven members voted against (the Social Democrats), three cast blank ballots, and two members of Parliament did not vote. Compared to the old law there are several changes introduced in the new law. The most notable change was that the mayor should have more responsibilities. Furthermore it was stated that the mayor should be a full-time job in the larger municipalities (with more than 500 inhabitants) and a part-time job in the smaller municipalities (Kommunustýrislógin 2000). This increases the administrative capacity of the small municipalities significantly. Also, the law prevents municipalities raising debts larger than their annual income.

Law on Voluntary Amalgamation

Additional changes in legislation were made in March 2001, when the government presented a proposal on voluntary amalgamation among municipalities. The proposal was passed by Parliament in May 2001. The proposal confirms the Parliamentiary vote of 1999 that amalgamations should be voluntary, but certain conditions had to be met. An amalgamation would have to take place within specific areas – natural geographic areas – as defined in the law. An amalgamated municipality should preferably have at least 2,000 inhabitants. Before an amalgamation can be made, the municipalities involved have to agree on some specific arrangements such as a plan for the new administrative structure, an agreement on the location of the administration and the name of the new municipality. The municipalities involved would also have to agree on a timetable for the completion of the amalgamation process (Lóg um sjálvbodna kommunusamanlegging 2001).

The draft proposal was circulated among the municipalities for consideration. Three-fourths of the municipalities did not respond at all. Shortage of time could be one reason. Another reason could have been that they chose to ignore the proposal because they were not prepared to accept it. Only two of the 48 municipalities responded positively to the proposal. One of them was Tórshavn. Three municipalities raised questions regarding procedural problems. Two responded that they did not have the enough time to reply before deadline. Five municipalities were against changes.

Plans for Decentralization

The extensive political and public opposition towards an amalgamation process enforced by law proposed by the Kommununevndin was also one of the reasons for the establishment of a new government committee in October 2000. The objective for this committee was to demonstrate how a clearer division of labour could be created between the central administration and the municipalities. The committee presented its report in December 2001. The report includes a list of areas where there is a need for clearer division between the central administration and the municipalities. The report also states that the administration of a wide number of areas should be decentralised to the municipalities. The committee also created a schedule for decentralisation. In its report the committee emphasises:

• the importance of assignments or functions being administrated as close to the citizen as possible; and

• that the municipality must be capable of handling tasks that are decentralized to the municipalities, either individually or through inter-municipal cooperation with other municipalities in the nearby area.

(Lógmansskrivsstovan, 2001)

These core principles are very similar to the recommendations of the Kommununevndin. But compared with earlier reports on municipal matters, this report introduced a new possibility, which had not been given great concern in previous reports: that of inter-municipal cooperation when administrating functions.

The ongoing governmental work on clarification of the division of labour between the central administration and the municipalities includes a plan for decentralising functions from the central administration to the municipalities. The existing municipal structure with a large number of small municipalities will, however, probably cause problems when decentralising occurs, as only a small number of municipalities will be capable of administering these new functions. In such cases, the picture will be much the same as that pertaining to the existing administration of social services, where central agencies administer social services for most of the municipalities, while the largest ones (Tórshavn and Klaksvík) partially administer their own social services.

Earlier reports on municipal matters considered municipal amalgamation as a precondition for the decentralisation of functions to the municipalities, but the latest report as well as the government has replaced the one-sided plan of enforced amalgamation with a two-sided option which allows the municipalities to choose between the alternatives of voluntary amalgamation or establishing inter-municipal cooperation with neighbouring municipalities.

Future Challenges

In this chapter on municipal change in the Faroes, we have seen that there has been an ongoing discussion about "the right size" for Faroese municipalities. Several proposals have been put forward which presume that Faroese municipalities should be amalgamated into bigger entities. On the other hand, these propositions for reorganisation have not had any general support in society, and therefore these propositions have never been carried through Parliament.

The municipality as an institution can be seen in two different perspectives. On the one hand the municipalities are administering functions on the behalf of the state, primarily in the provision of the welfare services. On the other hand, the municipalities are also local political institutions with a constitutionally-secure right to a substantial amount of local autonomy.

In the last couple of years a continuous process has been going on to make the demarcation of responsibilities between the municipalities and the central administration more clear. It is also the trend that more functions will be decentralized to the municipalities in the future. The reason for this is the principle that the function should be carried out as close to the citizens as possible. Decentralisation can in some cases result in more dynamic decisions that are more in harmony with local needs. Examples of this are local solutions regarding the care of children and the elderly. But some of the new functions will require a larger population base then many of the Faroese municipalities have today. If the municipalities are not able to handle these assignments by themselves they can either amalgamate with other municipalities or try to establish some inter-municipal cooperation. All municipalities in the Faroes are already involved in some inter-municipal cooperation such as education, fire-fighting services and care of the elderly. Furthermore municipalities are cooperating on the provision of electricity and the collection and incineration of refuse. But even in cases where the administration of assignments is handled through an inter-municipal cooperation scheme, the financial decisions and responsibility still rest with the individual municipal boards. This also means that inter-municipal cooperation has its shortcomings in areas that are very dynamic.

The Faroes are today struggling to meet a number of different challenges. Some of the challenges are among other things related to changes in the modern nuclear families and modern lifestyles. The families are smaller then before and thus the need for elderly care is significant. An increasing number of the women in the Faroes are seeking employment outside the homes, which has resulted in a considerable and increasing demand for childcare. New educational principles and a new law for the primary school have resulted in demands for improvements and changes to schools and the educational system.

It is an enormous challenge for the municipalities to supply their inhabitants with the services that modern citizens require in today's society, for example care of the elderly, childcare, and education. It is a fact that the great majority of the municipal income comes from personal taxation. Some municipalities have also stated that the provision of quality services is part of their development strategy; this means that municipalities try to attract inhabitants by offering quality services.

Municipalities and Economic Development

In order to provide its inhabitants with modern welfare services, it is a considerable advantage for a municipality to have a high level of economic activity. Furthermore, it is expected that the municipalities try to foster local economic development. It is not possible to discuss the municipalities' opportunities in this regard without having the general industrial and commercial policy in the Faroes in mind. After the economic crises of the 1990s the paradigm for the Faroese industrial policy has changed significantly. Under the old system the Faroese authorities were very active in the economic life. There existed a very comprehensive system of different types of subsidies and state guaranties. Some of the municipalities were also heavily directly involved in the economic life. Direct municipal involvement was a way for municipalities to play a very clear role in the local development that gave significant and concrete results. Nevertheless, in the long term the consequences were that the some of these municipalities became extremely indebted because of failed business ventures, and are still struggling to pay off their debts.

After the big economic crisis in the 1990s, the focus of the industrial policy has been to establish a clear division between the public and private economy, and to establish institutional structures that secure high levels of competition and incentives for increased productivity and innovation. The question is, how the municipalities can foster local economic development? How can the municipalities help local companies to prosper in an atmosphere of global competition? The municipalities have a much more difficult task today in this respect – and a much more indirect role – and there is no doubt that the Faroese municipalities still have to find their role in the learning economy.

Some Faroese municipalities have tried to use new tools for industrial development. One municipality took (in a Faroese context) a new and innovative step in 1997 when they employed a local development officer. The task of the development officer is to initiate cooperation among the companies in the municipality and to establish networks on concrete projects. The development officer makes contacts of his own initiative to the companies and the companies have the opportunity to contact the development officer in order to give him ideas or to ask for advice. It is also the responsibility of the development officer to assist the local trades and industries to use national institutions for development and subsidies of different kinds, and to monitor what other municipalities are doing regarding local development. The development officer is also working with the marketing of the municipality and local businesses and has been coordinating participation in both Faroese and international fish fairs and other exhibitions. Other municipalities have either alone, or in cooperation with others, established information offices that are mainly doing work relating to tourism, but also other in other spheres, that will make the area more known. A few municipalities have tried to establish local investment funds, but the central authorities have prohibited this. Two neighbouring municipalities on Streymoy have challenged this decision, but the outcome of this case is not final at this stage.

Today, the unemployment rates in the Faroes are very low, and business as a whole is in a sound financial state. In these circumstances the pressure to find new initiatives in local development is limited. Nevertheless, it is highly likely that if the economic situation in the Faroes changed for the worse the situation will be different. If the situation becomes a matter of life and death for local communities, the pressure for local action probably will be immense. In such a case there are two main options for municipalities. One is to seek to return to the old system of direct financial support and participation in industry. The other option is that the municipalities take a more proactive role regarding encouraging entrepreneurship, innovation, networking, and human resource development. In this latter case, a certain critical mass is probably needed, partly because the financial means that have to be used for this role, and partly because a small community normally also means that the number of local actors will be too small to create an really dynamic and innovative environment.

Notes

[1]   This description draws heavily on Information Memorandum 2002 from the Governmental Bank (Landsbanki Føroya 2001).

[2]   Lov nr. 30 of 28 February 1872 "om de færøske landkommuners styrelse" (law on the organization of the Faroese municipalities).

[3]   Lov nr. 126 of 27 May 1908 "om byen Thorshavns kommunalbestyrelse" (law on the organization of the municipality of Tórshavn).

[4]   "Kommununevndin" is the Faroese word for municipal committee. When the word Kommununevndin is used in this chapter, we refer to the municipal committee established 1996.

⁵ For a more detailed description of the inter-municipal cooperation in the Kommunufelagsskapurin í Sundalagnum, see Holm and Mortensen 2002.

⁶ This section is based on the statements that the spokespersons from the political parties made in the parliamentary debate on the Kommununevndin report in April 1999.

⁷ The opinion poll was based on a survey sample of 1,755 people, randomly chosen among all persons in the Faroes older than 18 years. The survey was a questionnaire, which, in cooperation with classes from the upper secondary schools around the islands, was delivered to the chosen persons and collected a few days later (Fynd 1999).

⁸ The portrayal of Faroese politics having both "international" and "intranational" dimensions is presented in Hovgaard and Johansen 1994.

⁹ In some electoral areas (e.g. the northern islands) an outcome of the differences in size between towns and villages is that a large proportion of voters in the area are situated in one town, with the natural result that all of the elected members of Parliament get greatest support in this town. This is also the case in the electoral area Suður-Streymoy, which includes Tórshavn.

¹⁰ Clientelistic politics reflect a choice of a political strategy that focuses on the delivery of particularistic benefits rather than public policies. The prevalence of clientelistic politics depends on factors such as the politicians' ability to claim credit for their actions, the opportunities to provide such benefits, and the relative cost of alternative political strategies (Indriðason 2001).

¹¹ Later, in May 2002, the department of municipal matters became a part of the new Ministry of Justice, which was established by the new coalition formed in Parliament in May 2002.

References

Aalbu, Hallgeir. 2000. Do we need regions?" *North*, 4: 5-9.

Fynd. 1999. *Opinion poll: Tórshavn.* Søgu- og Samfelagsdeildin: Fróðskaparsetur Føroya.

Hagstova Fóroya. 2001. *Hagtíðindi*, Nr. C2. Tórshavn: Hagstova Føroya.

Heimastýrislógin. 1948. *Færø Amts Kundgørelse nr. 11 af 31.3.1948 af Lov om Færøernes Hjemmestyre.*

Holm, Dennis and Bjarni Mortensen. 2002. *Kommunalt samstarv: Ein onnur loysn enn kommunusamanlegging?* Klaksvík: Granskingardepilin fyri Økismenning.

Hovgaard, Gestur. 2002. *Coping Strategies and Regional Policies: Social Capital in the Nordic Peripheries. Country Report Faroe Islands.* Nordregio.

Hovgaard, Gestur, and Rógvi F. Johansen. 1994. *Samfundskonflikter eller sygehuskonflikter? Om konflikt og magt i den færøske selvforvaltning.* Studie-serien. Roskilde Universitetscenter.

Høgenni, Hilmar. 1992. *En færøsk kommunalreform?* Unpublished dissertation. Økonomisk Institut, Københavns Universitet.

Indriðason, Indriði H. 2001. *A Theory of Coalitions and Clientelism: Coalition Politics in Iceland 1945-2000.* Unpublished dissertation. Department of Political Science, Michigan State University.

Javnaðarflokkurin. 1999. *Nýtt býti millum land og kommunur.* Tórshavn: Javnaðarflokkurin.

Justinussen, Jens Christian S. 1999. *How the Faroe Islands became an unplannable society.* Paper presented at the International Conference on Microstates, Tórshavn.

Kommununevndin. 1998b. *Nýggj kommunuskipan.* Niðurstøða og tilmæli. Táttur II. Tórshavn: Føroya Landsstýri.

Kommununevndin. 1998a. *Frágreiðin um kommunurnar í Føroyum.* Nýggj kommunal skipan. Táttur I, Partur II. Tórshavn: Føroya Landsstýri.

Kommununevndin. 1997. *Uppgávu- og ábyrgdarbýtið.* Nýggj kommunal skipan. Táttur I, Partur I. Tórshavn: Føroya Landsstýri.

Kommunustýrislógin. 2000. *Løgtingslóg nr. 87 frá 17.05.2000 um kommunustýri.* Tórshavn.

Landsbanki Føroya. 2001. *Information Memorandum 2002.* Tórshavn: Landsbanki Føroya.

Lov om byen Thorshavns kommunalbestyrelse. 1908. *Lov nr. 126 fra 27.5.1908, "om byen Thorshavns kommunalbestyrelse".*

Lov om de færøske landkommuners styrelse. 1872. *Lov nr. 30 fra 28.2.1872, "om de færøske landkommuners styrelse."*

Lóg um sjálvbodna kommunusamanlegging. 2001. *Løgtingslóg nr. 77 frá 08.05.2001 um sjálvbodnar kommunusamanleggingar.*

Løgmansskrivstovan. 2001. *Staðfesting og raðfesting av uppgávu- og ábyrgdarbýti millum land og kommunur.* Tórshavn: Løgmansskrivstovan.

Matvørulógin. 1985. *Løgtingslóg nr. 46 frá 21.6.1985 um matvørur v.m.*

Rigsombudsmanden på Færøerne. 1998. *Beretning 1998.* København: Statens Informationstjeneste.

Stýriskipanarlógin. 1994. *Løgtingslóg nr. 103 frá 26.07.1994 um stýriskipan Føroya.*

Umhvørvislógin. 1988. *Løgtingslóg nr. 134 frá 29.10.1988 um umhvørvisvernd / miljøbeskyttelse.*

Wang, Zakarias. 1974. Preface in Ottar Brox, *Hvat hendir á bygd?* Hoyvík: Forlagið Futura.

CONCLUSION

Chapter 10

Concepts and Tools, New and Old, and the Future of Marginal Regions

REGINALD BYRON AND TIM JENKINS

The chapters in this book have considered marginal regions and communities in terms of theoretical developments, of practical considerations, and of policy. Most have been based on the lessons to be drawn from studies of specific marginal regions. While all these concerns are clearly important and necessary to any consideration of the future prospects for marginal communities, this brief final chapter seeks to go beyond a conventional editorial summary and drawing-together of the chapters. Our intention here is to give a personal overview of three issues, which we regard as being of great significance for the future: the migration of young people, problemmatic representations of heritage and culture, and the troubled moral economy of regional development. All three have been suggested in one way or another in the preceding chapters, but have not necessarily been the main focus of any of them.

The Young People Who Leave

In Chapter One, Jens Christian Hansen demonstrates that it is not primarily a lack of employment, or housing, that provokes young people to move out of small places in Norway, but social and cultural claustrophobia. Even where employment and housing are available, most of those who leave never return, and many of these non-returners – especially women – say they would not do so under any circumstances. This is, perhaps, the greatest single problem of these regions; it is one of long standing and one that seems, on the evidence of current trends, likely to worsen steadily as young people become better educated and more informed about life-prospects elsewhere. Yet it is a problem that has received remarkably little attention in the regional development literature, although it is recognised in other branches of scholarship.

Why are the conventional approaches to regional policy seemingly so blind to something so obvious? Is it because the theoreticians, promoters, and practitioners of these approaches are not comfortable in dealing with anything other than the hard, quantifiable facts of economic and spatial quantities and dispositions of employment and housing, and assume – unwarrantedly – that all else will somehow follow? Is it because the testimony of out-migrants is an unwelcome challenge to cherished, romanticised, and mostly metropolitan beliefs about the nature of rurality and "community" that, typically, inform these approaches? Does it have anything to do with the possibility that most regional policy specialists are either urban-based or, even where local, have been trained to see things from a metropolitan perspective and have, in consequence, distanced themselves from their own experience and that of their friends and relatives who have grown up in isolated rural places and moved out of them? Does it have anything to do with the possibility that parochial political interests are, often, not far beneath the surface of regional policy: give us our share of the national cake, provide the means for us to keep our bright young people at home (irrespective of whether or not they actually want to stay), stop "our" countryside from being colonised by urban refugees, weekenders, retired people and other "white settlers"?

The out-migration of young people because of social and cultural claustrophobia is a pressing and fundamental issue that demands to be confronted head-on in future regional development efforts. If young people find life in small places claustrophobic, it is because they regard their social and cultural prospects and latitude for self-realisation to be too limited. They rarely, or less often than they would wish, meet anyone new. It is impossible for them to remain anonymous or maintain much privacy when everything they do within the locality is under the watchful gaze of someone whom they know, or whom they know knows their parents or siblings, aunts, uncles, or cousins. Everyone places them socially as someone's son, daughter, brother, or sister at a time in their lives when they want to establish themselves as individuals, to create and negotiate their own identities, to make new friends and acquaintances of their own choosing. They do not want to be confined to the roles and relationships that have already been defined for them by virtue of their parentage and their status within a largely fixed social order. This is a matter of social scale, and there is very little that a young person, or indeed anyone, can do to change this. The choice confronting a young person is clear: either to accept these constraints upon their individuality, or leave.

Those who do return are typically older and at a different stage of their life-trajectories. For these older returners, social relations are less claustrophobic than they are for teenagers and younger adults. If they have reached a stage in their lives that involves parenthood and young children, the local family network becomes an asset rather than a liability; it is also an asset that housing is cheap, there is ample building-space, schools are small and intimate, and that the local environment is uncrowded and safe for children. On the other hand, returners frequently do not return to their actual point of origin but to a more-or-less nearby regional centre where better jobs and more public and private services are available. In choosing to live nearby, but not actually to live in their home place, they can exercise more discretion in the ways that they engage with the social milieu of the place which they chose to leave at an earlier stage in their lives, and this may be an important consideration to them.

The evidence from Norway tells us that about half of youngsters will choose to leave whether or not there are jobs and housing for them in their locality, and that not all returners return to the particular place that they left but rather, through choice, to another place in the region. Were such studies to be carried out elsewhere on the European side of the North Atlantic, the indications would probably be much the same (in Newfoundland, the evidence is similar to that of Norway: see Davis 2003 and Sinclair 2003). A realistic approach to development policy must not assume that, given the right fix or balance of fixes, young people will stay at home. About half will probably leave anyway, in whatever region they live, and whatever policies are put in place. A realistic approach should simply accept this fact, take it as a starting point, and build upon it.

Two obvious consequences follow. The first is that local young people need skills that will equip them to succeed and prosper not just within the regional economy and its social order, but also to compete on favourable terms with other well-educated young people in the wider metropolitan world beyond. Policies that deny young people access to a higher education of the kind, and in the language, that they will need to succeed outside their regions will not stop the young leaving; such policies will merely have the effect of guaranteeing that a substantial proportion of the leavers will probably suffer lifetimes of very limited choices or low-wage employment, or both, and will close the door on the possibility that some might return with higher-order skills and income-generating capacities of value to the locality.

The second consequence is that new settlers are vitally needed to replace the young people who leave and do not return. Local and regional development policy ought to campaign actively and effectively to recruit new settlers with no previous connection with the locality, especially those with wealth and higher-order skills, and not just the entrepreneurs who promise to provide local jobs who, typically, are currently pursued by the regional development agencies. Such people will not be attracted to places which seem, to them, turned in on themselves and suspicious of, or positively unwelcoming to "middle-class" people, or retirees, or those of a different cultural background. This is likely, in some places, to involve working to change local attitudes and to temper public utterances by regional spokespeople, politicians and political parties, where these appear to be acting as deterrents to new settlement by people from other parts of the country. It may also require changing entrenched regional attitudes towards the primacy of local culture and language, attitudes which are fundamentally rejected in urban areas where cultural openness and the dynamism that cultural mixing creates are often regarded as valuable public goods and economic stimulants.

In practical terms, these two consequences may mean giving young people greater choice in school and college curricula and, where relevant, an unfettered freedom to choose the language of instruction, if the local language differs from that of the metropole. Computer-based learning and electronic schools, colleges, and universities can extend educational provision within the region and should be built into local school and college programmes of instruction, rather than being treated as add-ons. It may also mean making positive provision in physical planning for residential development of a kind that will be attractive to new settlers, and aimed specifically at them. Predictably, they will want space and views, and will not want to be ghettoised in segregated, cramped estates of "executive" McMansions; they can buy houses like this on the outskirts of almost any city. They will want what they cannot find in more heavily populated parts of the country, and the one thing that characterises marginal regions is that they have a lot of land in relation to the population, land which – if deployed imaginatively – has the potential to attract the new settlement and investment that these localities so vitally need. In Britain, this would mean reversing the usual planning priority: what is the maximum number of houses can be got on an acre? to its opposite: what is the minimum number of acres that should surround a house?

Regional development thinking has, since its earliest days, been dominated by economic theory, as Peter Sjøholt's chapter demonstrates. One school of thought after another has eventually been found deficient and has been replaced by a successor. Partly, of course, this is a consequence of the intellectual shifts and fashions over time that characterise most academic disciplines, but – more significantly – it may also alert us to the possibility that an exclusive reliance upon economic theory has had a limited capacity to explain satisfactorily the fundamental problems of marginal regions: among the main ones being, on the North Atlantic periphery, the out-migration of young people. Since the recent evidence from Norway and Newfoundland shows that half or more leave for reasons that are not mainly attributable to a lack of jobs and housing – and there is nothing to suggest that this is an especially new phenomenon (young people were leaving rural Ireland and rural England for many of the same reasons in the nineteenth century) – narrowly economic approaches have left us ignorant of the full extent of this problem and its implications for regional policy. This is not to say that economic approaches are in themselves unsatisfactory, or do not provide important tools of analysis, only that they have not yet, and perhaps cannot, provide a full and nuanced understanding of what is, fundamentally, as much a social and cultural problem as an economic one. The issue runs much more deeply than merely being a problem of the North Atlantic margin: the world is full of young people on the move, whose motives, means, and ends are, quite probably, only partly and simplistically captured by economic theory.

The Representation and Commodification of Heritage and Culture

Part Two of this book, "Marketing Marginality and History" raises the question of whether there are practical limits to the niche and heritage industries, and what their wider and longer-term prospects and effects might be. These things are frequently said to be palliatives, if not solutions, to economic problems of marginality. Are they? The heritage industry has seen considerable growth in recent years, and it cannot be denied that it has generated jobs and visitor spending in peripheral regions. But at what price?

The down-side of the heritage industry is that there is a propensity to play to popular stereotype and to portray – and frequently to reify – the concepts of "history" and "culture" in sometimes rather distorting and unfortunate ways. The case of Ireland is instructive. When tourists from North America arrive at Shannon Airport, they expect their "Celtic Ireland" package tour to live up to their romanticised expectations; myths are superimposed on history, and may eventually come to displace it altogether. Most Americans believe, for example, that most, if not all, of the nineteenth-century Irish migrants to the United States were the Irish-speaking rural poor from the western counties who were uprooted from the land by avaricious landlords, the spectre of starvation, or banished by the British authorities for their political beliefs and forced to board the coffin ships from Galway, and so were consigned to an early death or to lives of poverty and exile in Hell's Kitchen in New York City. The heritage industry on both sides of the Atlantic has been quick to capitalise on this heart-wrenching myth – the stuff of folktale and folksong – and to reinforce it in the imaginations of those who follow the "Irish Heritage Trail". In fact, for anyone who cares to look at it, the historical evidence shows clearly that the greatest number of nineteenth-century Irish migrants were English-speakers from the better-off eastern and midlands counties, and were step-migrants who had first lived and worked in Britain before taking a trans-Atlantic steamer passage from Liverpool. Most never set foot in the Irish immigrant ghettos of New York or Boston, and many eventually ended their days on a half-section of rich farmland in Indiana, Illinois, or Iowa.

Myth is often more saleable than historical plausibility, however. Tourists and day-trippers vote with their feet and their purses. They are, it seems, mainly interested in novelty and in a catchy story (a tie-in to a Hollywood film, perhaps) or in having their preconceptions confirmed – and sometimes they are interested in things that are mildly educative – but not, on the whole, in things that are unsettling, uncomfortable, and challenging to their beliefs, as Douglas Caulkins and Alison McCleery point out. In nineteenth-century Ireland, there is plenty of evidence that heads of farming households were exporting their daughters to relatives in the USA or delivering them into religious servitude in Ireland to avoid paying a dowry or suffering the social embarrassment of a daughter's love-match with a young man of the wrong sort: that is, propertyless, of lower social standing, or a Protestant or a Catholic. The daughter who stayed at home did not count herself lucky if at the age of 17 or 18 she was obliged to accept a loveless arranged marriage with a 50-year-old farmer and consigned to a life of ceaseless childbearing, domestic drudgery, and farmyard muck. By the end of the nineteenth century, more frequently than anywhere else in Europe, young rural women regarded permanent celibacy as preferable to an arranged marriage if they had to stay in Ireland, and few of them were not eager to emigrate to America as soon as they had finished school (Guinnane 1997).

There is a serious risk in the heritage industry's selectivity, based on market demand, that produces partial, biased, or distorted views of events and ways of life in these places. Only that part of the story is told which people want to hear and are willing to pay for. So, predominantly urbanised tourists are left to wonder why anyone would leave the rural idyll of an artfully groomed and romanticised Irish farmstead set amidst tranquil, bucolic scenery unless they were forced to do so by oppression or persecution. Idealised pasts are contrived. Regret for lost never-lands is instilled through these highly selective and emotive representations of the place, the people, and the past. Even anger and blame for the purportedly wanton destruction of "our" language, culture, traditions, and way of life by the malign forces (or stereotyped representatives) of the outside world may be deliberately cultivated if it plays well on popular sentiment.

The ways in which "heritage" interrelates with regional development is not only as a marketplace commodity, but it may also involve more generalised concepts and sets of cultural beliefs and attitudes that have come about through selective representations of the past and of ways of life that the heritage industry reflects, exploits, and reinforces. In Britain, perhaps more so than in the other countries of the region, rurality and the rural landscape have increasingly come to be regarded in aesthetic and cultural rather than instrumental and practical terms. Britain is a heavily urbanised country; relatively few Britons any longer have any first-hand experience of living directly from the land or have parents or grandparents who were connected with farming or other rural ways of life. What most townspeople know of rurality is what they see through the windows of trains or cars as they pass through the landscape. In the metropolitan imagination, the preservation of the aesthetic qualities of the rural landscape overrides all other considerations. Time is fixed at some point in the past. Modernity and the rural landscape are viewed as incompatible. These views of the landscape, and of the past, are articulated not only by city people but also by rural people, local politicians, and cultural spokespersons when it is convenient for them to do so. These beliefs and attitudes deflect their attention away from things that are of far greater significance to the future of their localities and regions: as, for example, the reasons their brightest youngsters might give for leaving, if anyone were ever to ask them and were willing to listen to and learn from their answers. Too often, those people who ought to be the champions of the future of their regions are, instead, champions of the past and – frequently – an idealised, imagined past of perfect homogeneity and harmony that never actually existed. Change is resisted rather than welcomed: outsiders are to be kept out, because they make it too expensive for our youngsters to find a place to live, which is why – it is believed, or politically expedient to claim – they leave; and new residential and commercial developments are not wanted if they intrude upon the aesthetic qualities of our "traditional" landscapes.

If the marketing of heritage has reached saturation levels in some places, or is approaching these levels now, this raises the question of how sustainable it is. In Britain and Norway, many heritage enterprises have been established on weak economic foundations, and the number of visitors is falling; many of these attractions, evidently, depend upon a novelty value that does not remain effective indefinitely. Will a similar fate befall niche products and farmhouse branding? The question has to be asked. The growth in the "organic" sector of the British consumer market over the last 10 years has been phenomenal, and the supermarket and drugstore shelves are loaded with foodstuffs and other products purporting to be organic. When organics began to take off in the 1990s, it was a minority niche market involving mostly small-scale independent producers. Now that it has achieved widespread popularity, the large-scale food and toiletries manufacturers and the major supermarket and drugstore chains have moved into organics in a big way. Organic foodstuffs are defined in EU law, but other consumer items branded as organic – and there are many of them – are not, and the consumer has no way of knowing exactly what this description means, if it means anything at all. Farmhouse-labelled and niche-branded foods and other products, should their popularity take off to a point that it begins to make a real difference to local prosperity in these regions, will have demonstrated either a capacity to derive profit from new markets, or to make inroads into the market dominance of the established industry giants. The major manufacturers and retailers who have successfully adapted to the popular demand for organics (for example) will not be slow to react; they have learnt how to tune into minority trends and tastes in a fiercely competitive and ever-more-rapidly-changing marketplace. The "Made in

Ireland" legend on packages of shamrock-embroidered linen handkerchiefs sold to American tourists at Shannon Airport refers only to the provenance of the wrappings, and not to the contents, which are nowadays made in China. Appropriate and effective legal descriptions of method and origin similar to *appellation d'origine controllée* are essential to safeguard the interests of small-scale regional agricultural and crafts producers; without this, the benefits may be short-lived.

The Moral Economy of Regional Development

The driving forces behind regional development on the North Atlantic margin, and elsewhere in the world, are not merely economic but also moral: they involve concepts of a fair deal for the poor, or for people who live in isolated places where the kinds of public goods taken for granted by people in the more metropolitan parts of the country are not, or would not otherwise, be available. Is this charity or paternalism? Altruism or self-interest? What are governments' responsibilities? Are there better or worse ways of discharging them? Are there limits to what is legal, or achievable, or cost-effective, or sustainable?

The chapters in Part Three raise questions about the global and the local. At a time when decentralisation, deregulation, and local empowerment have become the political rhetoric of the day, as well as – variably – the practice of governments, the role of national states is still very important. National parliaments decide how much money is to be budgeted for regional affairs and are willing to allocate money for some kinds of development efforts, but not others. Thus the development agenda is still set at the highest levels of government, and while there have been trends toward the regionalisation of development policy, sectoral policies and international agreements and treaties made at the level of nation-states continue to have profound effects on the regions, imposing sets of constraints that limit their scope for action. The devolution of administrative powers to regional authorities complicates the picture. Jørgen Amdam's chapter shows that some local experts see this as a welcome change, offering the promise of an enhanced capacity to identify local solutions to local problems, and they are eager to press ahead to secure an accelerated regeneration of the economic foundations of their regions. Yet whether these aspirations are achievable is ultimately out of local hands, and will depend on international markets, trade agreements, and national sectoral policies over which regional administrations have little control or influence. The opposite view, expressed in Paul Olav Berg's chapter, is that deregulation, devolution, and the encouragement of New Public Management policies have – as far as development is concerned – left the regions considerably worse off:

the coordination between regional development priorities, national sectoral policies, and international markets and trading arrangements is most effectively done at the level of the nation state. While regional administrations have more power than formerly, one wonders just what this will mean if they do not have enough of the right kinds of resources, expertise, or channels of communication to allow them to manage development as effectively as central government. Small may be beautiful, but too-small (as in the case of some Norwegian and virtually all Faroese municipalities) is not. Will regional development suffer as a result?

Those European countries like Britain, Denmark, and Sweden which joined the EEC/EU long after its ground rules were laid down by France and Germany found the transition from national autonomy to Community conformity to be a difficult and painful experience as regards sectoral policies and regional development. What could now be done to support these nations' industries was limited by treaty obligations. Norway, even as merely an associate member of the European club, is bound by some of these rules. Norwegian shipyards are in deep trouble because they cannot compete on price, and there are legal constraints on what the state can do to ameliorate the problem and prevent orders by Norwegian buyers going to shipyards in other countries. In north Norway, the fishing industry is also in deep trouble, mainly because of excessive resource utilisation, but also because fish processing is too costly and cannot recruit the low-skill, seasonal labour that it needs. In fact, Norwegian salmon is sent to China for processing and from there to market on behalf of Norwegian exporters.

Regional development in all the countries mentioned in this book, no matter how well organised and forward-looking (as in the case of Ireland's National Spatial Strategy), exists within the context of a globalised economy. The EU countries have, to an extent, insulated themselves from the naked forces of the global market with their agreements to pool their assets and adopt common strategies and a system of transfers to promote the development of the Community's lagging regions. There is still the problem of the regions-within-regions in the current EU countries, however; and the continuity of the EU regional development programme cannot be regarded as secure, if the new member countries that are scheduled to join the Community make demands upon the system that are too great. Norway is enabled, for the moment, to remain semi-independent of the EU because of its oil income, but even here, in the one remaining major country in the region where we might expect an independent, national moral economy of regional development to be clearly articulated, the messages have become blurred by external pressures and new fashions in political economy that are sweeping the western world.

References

Davis, D. L.   2003.   In the Beginning: Region, Crisis, and Occupational Choice among Newfoundland's Youth.   In Reginald Byron (ed.), *Retrenchment and Regeneration in Rural Newfoundland*. Toronto: University of Toronto Press.

Guinnane, T. 1997. *The Vanishing Irish: Households, Migration, and the Rural Economy in Ireland, 1850-1914*. Princeton: Princeton University Press.

Sinclair, P.   2003.   Moving Back and Moving In: Migration and the Structuring of Bonavista.   In Reginald Byron (ed.), *Retrenchment and Regeneration in Rural Newfoundland*. Toronto: University of Toronto Press.